FIA

FAB

ACCA

F1

ACCOUNTANT IN BUSINESS

P R A C T I C E & R E V I S I O N K I T

BPP Learning Media is the **sole ACCA Platinum Approved Learning Partner – content** for the FIA suite of qualifications. In this, **the only FAB Practice and Revision Kit to be reviewed by the examiner:**

- We include **Do you know?** Checklists to test your knowledge and understanding of topics

- We provide you with **two** mock exams including the Pilot paper

- We provide the **ACCA examiner's answers** as well as our own to the Pilot paper as an additional revision aid

BPP's **i-Pass** product also supports this paper and is a vital tool if you are taking the computer based exam.

Note
From December 2011 FIA *FAB* and ACCA *Paper F1* will be examined under the same syllabus and study guide.

FOR EXAMS FROM DECEMBER 2011 TO DECEMBER 2012

LEARNING MEDIA

First edition May 2011

ISBN 9781 4453 7311 9

e-ISBN 9781 4453 7891 6

British Library Cataloguing-in-Publication Data
A catalogue record for this book
is available from the British Library

Published by

BPP Learning Media Ltd
BPP House, Aldine Place
London W12 8AA

www.bpp.com/learningmedia

Printed in the United Kingdom

Your learning materials, published by BPP
Learning Media Ltd, are printed on paper sourced
from sustainable, managed forests.

A note about copyright

Dear Customer

What does the little © mean and why does it matter?

Your market-leading BPP books, course materials and
elearning materials do not write and update themselves.
People write them: on their own behalf or as employees
of an organisation that invests in this activity. Copyright
law protects their livelihoods. It does so by creating
rights over the use of the content.

Breach of copyright is a form of theft – as well being a
criminal offence in some jurisdictions, it is potentially a
serious breach of professional ethics.

With current technology, things might seem a bit hazy
but, basically, without the express permission of BPP
Learning Media:

- Photocopying our materials is a breach of copyright

- Scanning, ripcasting or conversion of our digital
  materials into different file formats, uploading them
  to facebook or emailing them to your friends is a
  breach of copyright

You can, of course, sell your books, in the form in which
you have bought them – once you have finished with
them. (Is this fair to your fellow students? We update for
a reason.) But the e-products are sold on a single user
licence basis: we do not supply 'unlock' codes to people
who have bought them second hand.

And what about outside the UK? BPP Learning Media
strives to make our materials available at prices students
can afford by local printing arrangements, pricing
policies and partnerships which are clearly listed on our
website. A tiny minority ignore this and indulge in
criminal activity by illegally photocopying our material or
supporting organisations that do. If they act illegally and
unethically in one area, can you really trust them?

Contents

Question index

Helping you with your revision – the ONLY FAB Practice and Revision Kit to be reviewed by the examiner!

BPP Learning Media – the sole Platinum Approved Learning Partner - content

As ACCA's **sole Platinum Approved Learning Partner – content**, BPP Learning Media gives you the **unique opportunity** to use **examiner-reviewed** revision materials for exams from December 2011 to December 2012. By incorporating the examiner's comments and suggestions regarding syllabus coverage, the BPP Learning Media Practice and Revision Kit provides excellent, **ACCA-approved** support for your revision.

Selecting questions

We provide signposts to help you plan your revision.

* A full **question index**
* A **topic index** listing all the questions that cover key topics, so that you can locate the questions that provide practice on these topics, and see the different ways in which they might be tested

Attempting mock exams

There are two mock exams that provide practice at coping with the pressures of the exam day. We strongly recommend that you attempt them under exam conditions. **Mock exams 1** is the Pilot paper. **Mock exam 2** reflects the question styles and syllabus coverage of the exam.

Using your BPP Practice and Revision Kit

Aim of this Practice and Revision Kit

To provide the practice to help you succeed in both the paper based and computer based examinations for FAB *Accountant in Business.*

To pass the examination you need a thorough understanding in all areas covered by the syllabus and teaching guide.

Recommended approach

- Make sure you are able to answer questions on **everything** specified by the syllabus and teaching guide. You cannot make any assumptions about what questions may come up on your paper. The examiners aim to discourage 'question spotting'.

- Learning is an **active** process. Use the **DO YOU KNOW?** Checklists to test your knowledge and understanding of the topics covered in FAB *Accountant in Business* by filling in the blank spaces. Then check your answers against the **DID YOU KNOW?** Checklists. Do not attempt any questions if you are unable to fill in any of the blanks - go back to your **BPP Interactive Text** and revise first.

- When you are revising a topic, think about the mistakes that you know that you should avoid by writing down **POSSIBLE PITFALLS** at the end of each **DO YOU KNOW?** Checklist.

- Once you have completed the checklists successfully, you should attempt the questions on that topic. Each question is worth 2 marks and carries with it a time allocation of 2.4 minutes.

- Once you have completed all of the questions in the body of this Practice & Revision Kit, you should attempt the **MOCK EXAMS** under examination conditions. Check your answers against our answers to find out how well you did.

Passing the FAB exam

FAB introduces students (who may not have a business background) to the business entity made up of people and systems which interact with each other. There is a lot to learn, but none of it is particularly difficult and a good grasp of these topics will help you in higher-level business papers (ACCA papers P1 and P3).

For conversion arrangements from CAT to FIA and to access CAT and FIA syllabuses, visit the ACCA website.

http://www2.accaglobal.com

The exam

You can take this exam as a paper-based exam or by CBE. All questions in the exam are compulsory. This means you cannot avoid any topic, but also means that you do not need to waste time in the exam deciding which questions to attempt. There are fifty MCQs in the paper-based exam and a mixture of MCQs and other types of OTQ (number entry, multiple response and multiple response matching) in the CBE. This means that the examiner is able to test most of the syllabus at each sitting, and that is what he aims to do. So you need to have revised right across the syllabus for this exam.

Revision

This kit has been reviewed by the FAB examiner and contains the Pilot paper, so if you just worked through it to the end you would be very well prepared for the exam. It is important to tackle questions under exam conditions. Allow yourself just the number of minutes shown next to the questions in the index and don't look at the answers until you have finished. Then correct your answer and go back to the Interactive Text for any topic you are really having trouble with. Try the same question again a week later – you will be surprised how much better you are getting. Doing the questions like this will really show you what you know, and will make the exam experience less worrying.

Doing the exam

If you have honestly done your revision you can pass this exam. There are certain points which you must bear in mind:

- Read the question properly.

- Don't spend more than the allotted time on each question. If you are having trouble with a question leave it and carry on. You can come back to it at the end.

Approach to examining the syllabus

FAB is a two-hour paper. It can be taken as a paper based or a computer based examination.

The exam is structured as follows:

	No of marks
50 compulsory multiple choice questions of 2 marks each	100

The Computer Based Examination

Computer based examinations (CBEs) are available for the first seven FIA papers (not papers FAU, FTM or FFM), in addition to the conventional paper based examination.

Computer based examinations must be taken at an ACCA CBE Licensed Centre.

How does CBE work?

* Questions are displayed on a monitor

* Candidates enter their answer directly onto the computer

* Candidates have two hours to complete the examination

* When the candidate has completed their examination, the final percentage score is calculated and displayed on screen

* Candidates are provided with a Provisional Result Notification showing their results before leaving the examination room

* The CBE Licensed Centre uploads the results to the ACCA (as proof of the candidate's performance) within 72 hours

* Candidates can check their exam status on the ACCA website by logging into myACCA.

Benefits

* **Flexibility** as a CBE can be sat at any time.

* **Resits** can also be taken at any time and there is no restriction on the number of times a candidate can sit a CBE.

* **Instant feedback** as the computer displays the results at the end of the CBE.

* Results are notified to ACCA **within 72 hours**.

CBE question types

* Multiple choice – choose one answer from four options

* Number entry – key in a numerical response to a question

* Multiple response – select more than one response by clicking the appropriate tick boxes

* Multiple response matching – select a response to a number of related part questions by choosing one option from a number of drop down menus

See the ACCA website for further information on computer based exams.

http://www.accaglobal.com

Tackling Multiple Choice Questions

MCQs are part of all FIA exams. They form the paper based exams and may appear in the CBE.

The MCQs in your exam contain four possible answers. You have to **choose the option that best answers the question**. The three incorrect options are called distracters. There is a skill in answering MCQs quickly and correctly. By practising MCQs you can develop this skill, giving you a better chance of passing the exam.

You may wish to follow the approach outlined below, or you may prefer to adapt it.

Step 1	Skim read all the MCQs and identify what appear to be the easier questions.
Step 2	Attempt each question – **starting with the easier questions** identified in Step 1. Read the question **thoroughly**. You may prefer to work out the answer before looking at the options, or you may prefer to look at the options at the beginning. Adopt the method that works best for you.
Step 3	Read the four options and see if one matches your own answer. Be careful with numerical questions as the distracters are designed to match answers that incorporate common errors. Check that your calculation is correct. Have you followed the requirement exactly? Have you included every stage of the calculation?
Step 4	You may find that none of the options matches your answer. • Re-read the question to ensure that you understand it and are answering the requirement • Eliminate any obviously wrong answers • Consider which of the remaining answers is the most likely to be correct and select the option
Step 5	If you are still unsure make a note and continue to the next question
Step 6	Revisit unanswered questions. When you come back to a question after a break you often find you are able to answer it correctly straight away. If you are still unsure have a guess. You are not penalised for incorrect answers, so **never leave a question unanswered!**

After extensive practice and revision of MCQs, you may find that you recognise a question when you sit the exam. Be aware that the detail and/or requirement may be different. If the question seems familiar read the requirement and options carefully – do not assume that it is identical.

Using your BPP products

This Kit gives you the question practice and guidance you need in the exam. Our other products can also help you pass:

- **Passcards** provide you with clear topic summaries and exam tips
- **i-Pass CDs** are a vital revision tool for anyone taking FIA CBEs and offer tests of knowledge against the clock in an environment similar to that encountered in a computer based exam

You can purchase these products by visiting www.bpp.com/learningmedia

Questions

Do you know? – The business organisation, its stakeholders and the external environment

Check that you can fill in the blanks in the statements below before you attempt any questions. If in doubt, you should go back to your BPP Interactive Text and revise first.

- Organisations can achieve results which **i**......... cannot achieve by themselves.

- A .... organisation (NGO) is an independent voluntary association of people acting together for some common purpose (other than achieving government office or making money).

- Stakeholders are those individuals or groups that, potentially, have an **interest** in what the organisation does. These stakeholders can be **w**....... the organisation, **c**..... to the organisation or external to the organisation.

- **G**............. **p**...... influences the economic environment, the framework of laws, industry structure and certain operational issues. Political **i**........ is a cause of risk.

- P....... is the right of the individual not to suffer unauthorised disclosure of information.

- The (UK) **Data Protection Act 1998** protects **i**........ about whom data is held. Both manual and computerised information must comply with the Act.

- A contract is a **l**...... **b**....... agreement.

- O....... is the contracting out of specified operations or services to an external vendor.

- The v.... c..... describes those activities of the organisation that add value to purchased inputs.

- The **c**...... **e**........ is structured by five forces: barriers **to entry; substitute products**; the bargaining power of c.........; the bargaining power of **suppliers**; c......... **rivalry**.

- Equilibrium **n**........ **i**...... is determined using aggregate supply and aggregate demand analysis.

- Demand pull **i**....... arises from an excess of aggregate demand over the productive capacity of the economy.

- C.... p.... **inflation** arises from increases in the costs of production.

- Economic .... may be measured by increases in the **real** gross national product (GNP) per head of the population.

- **Macroeconomic policy objectives** relate to economic growth, **i**........., unemployment and the **b**...... **of p**........

- If a government decides to use fiscal policy to influence demand in the economy, it can choose either **e**.......... changes or **t**.. changes as its policy instrument.

- **M**...... **p**..... uses money supply, interest rates or credit controls to influence **aggregate demand**.

- A surplus or deficit on the balance of payments usually means a **surplus or deficit on the** c....... a.......

- The m..... e.............. refers to the immediate operational environment including suppliers, competitors, customers, stakeholders and intermediaries.

- Elasticity, in general, refers to the relationship between two variables. Price elasticity of demand explains the relationship between **change in** q.....demanded and **changes in** p......

- I...... e........ of demand measures the responsiveness of demand to changes in household income. **C**.....**elasticity of demand** is determined by the availability of substitute (competitors') products.

- The effects of **demand and supply** conditions on markets can be analysed by studying the behaviour of both demand and supply c........

Could you fill in the blanks? The answers are in bold. Use this page for revision purposes as you approach the exam.

- Organisations can achieve results which **individuals** cannot achieve by themselves.

- A **non-governmental** organisation (NGO) is an independent voluntary association of people acting together for some common purpose (other than achieving government office or making money).

- Stakeholders are those individuals or groups that, potentially, have an **interest** in what the organisation does. These stakeholders can be **within** the organisation, **connected** to the organisation or external to the organisation.

- **Government policy** influences the economic environment, the framework of laws, industry structure and certain operational issues. Political **instability** is a cause of risk.

- **Privacy** is the right of the individual not to suffer unauthorised disclosure of information.

- The (UK) **Data Protection Act 1998** protects **individuals** about whom data is held. Both manual and computerised information must comply with the Act.

- A contract is a **legally binding** agreement.

- Outsourcing is the contracting out of specified operations or services to an external vendor.

- The value chain describes those activities of the organisation that add value to purchased inputs.

- The **competitive environment** is structured by five forces: barriers **to entry; substitute products**; the bargaining power of customers; the bargaining power of **suppliers; competitive rivalry**.

- Equilibrium **national income** is determined using aggregate supply and aggregate demand analysis.

- Demand pull **inflation** arises from an excess of aggregate demand over the productive capacity of the economy.

- Cost push **inflation** arises from increases in the costs of production.

- Economic **growth** may be measured by increases in the **real** gross national product (GNP) per head of the population.

- **Macroeconomic policy objectives** relate to economic growth, **inflation**, unemployment and the **balance of payments.**

- If a government decides to use fiscal policy to influence demand in the economy, it can choose either **expenditure** changes or **tax** changes as its policy instrument.

- **Monetary policy** uses money supply, interest rates or credit controls to influence **aggregate demand**.

- A surplus or deficit on the balance of payments usually means a **surplus or deficit on the** current account.

- The micro environment refers to the immediate operational environment including suppliers, competitors, customers, stakeholders and intermediaries.

- Elasticity, in general, refers to the relationship between two variables. Price elasticity of demand explains the relationship between **change in** quantity demanded and **changes in** price.

- Income elasticity of demand measures the responsiveness of demand to changes in household income. **Cross elasticity of demand** is determined by the availability of substitute (competitors') products.

- The effects of **demand and supply** conditions on markets can be analysed by studying the behaviour of both demand and supply **curves**.

1 Business organisations and their stakeholders   20 mins

1.1   'An organisation is a social arrangement which pursues collective.., which controls its own performance and which has a boundary separating it from its environment.'

Which of the following words best completes this sentence?

    A   Profits
    B   Stakeholders
    C   Goals
    D   Tactics   **(2 marks)**

1.2   What is the term given to the idea that the combined output of a number of individuals working together will exceed that of the same individuals working separately?

    A   Sympathy
    B   Specialisation
    C   Synergy
    D   Systems thinking   **(2 marks)**

1.3   Which of the following statements is true?

    A   Limited company status means that a company is only allowed to trade up to a predetermined turnover level in any one year.

    B   For organisations that have limited company status, ownership and control are legally separate.

    C   The benefit of being a sole trader is that you have no personal liability for the debts of your business.

    D   Ordinary partnerships offer the same benefits as limited companies but are usually formed by professionals such as doctors and solicitors.   **(2 marks)**

1.4   An organisation is owned and run by central government agencies. The organisation is best described as which of the following statements?.

    A   A voluntary sector organisation
    B   A private sector organisation
    C   A local government organisation
    D   A public sector organisation   **(2 marks)**

1.5   Which of the following groups may be considered to be stakeholders in the activities of a nuclear power station?

    (i)   The government
    (ii)   Friends of the Earth
    (iii)   Employees
    (iv)   Local residents

    A   (i), (iii) and (iv)
    B   (i), (ii), (iii) and (iv)
    C   (iii) only
    D   (i) and (iii) only   **(2 marks)**

1.6   Secondary stakeholders is another term for which group of stakeholders?

    A   Internal stakeholders
    B   Connected stakeholders
    C   External stakeholders
    D   Contractual stakeholders   **(2 marks)**

1.7 Which of the following organisations would rely most heavily on value for money indicators and efficiency rather than information on performance and profitability?

    A   A private accountancy college
    B   A local authority
    C   A small retailer
    D   A pension fund   **(2 marks)**

1.8 ADB is a business which is owned by its workers. The workers share the profits and they each have a vote on how the business is run.

Which of the following best describes ADB?

    A   Public sector
    B   Private sector
    C   Not-for-profit
    D   Co-operative   **(2 marks)**

(Total = 16 marks)

2 The business environment   41 mins

2.1 What is an acronym used to describe the key elements of an organisation's external environment?

    A   SWOT
    B   SMART
    C   PEST
    D   WTO   **(2 marks)**

2.2 Which of the following is *not* a legitimate method of influencing government policy in the interests of a business?

    A   Employing lobbyists to put the organisation's case to ministers or civil servants
    B   Giving lawmakers non-executive directorships
    C   Offering financial incentives to public officials to use their influence on the organisation's behalf
    D   Attempting to influence public opinion, to put pressure on the legislative agenda   **(2 marks)**

2.3 .... is an analysis of statistics on birth and death rates, age structures of people and ethnic groups within a community.

Which word correctly completes the sentence?

    A   Ergonomics
    B   Economics
    C   Psychographics
    D   Demographics   **(2 marks)**

2.4 A recent trend in organisation and management is the rise in 'virtual organisation' and 'virtual teamworking'. To which of the following environmental (PEST) factors is this most directly attributed?

    A   Economic
    B   Socio-cultural
    C   Technological
    D   Political   **(2 marks)**

2.5   The stationery and printing company S Co, has recently upgraded its computers and printers so that more production has become automated. Many middle managers will now be made redundant. This is known as:

A   Downsizing
B   Delayering
C   Outsourcing
D   Degrading   **(2 marks)**

2.6   In the context of 'best practice' employment protection law, in which of the following circumstances is dismissal of an employee automatically considered unfair?

A   Selection for redundancy on the basis of age
B   Misconduct
C   Marriage to a key competitor
D   Incompetence   **(2 marks)**

2.7   Which of the following socio-cultural trends will have a direct impact on most business organisations?

(i)   Increasing ethnic and religious diversity in populations
(ii)   Falling birthrates
(iii)   Focus on 'green' issues
(iv)   Increase in single-member households

A   (iii) only
B   (i) and (iii) only
C   (i), (ii) and (iii) only
D   (i), (ii), (iii) and (iv)   **(2 marks)**

2.8   Porter's five forces model identifies factors which determine the nature and strength of competition in an industry. Which of the following is *not* one of the five forces identified in Porter's model?

A   Substitute products or services
B   New entrants to the industry
C   Bargaining power of customers
D   Government regulation of the industry   **(2 marks)**

2.9   For what function in an organisation would demographic information about social class be most relevant?

A   Finance
B   Human Resources
C   Marketing
D   Purchasing   **(2 marks)**

2.10 Which of the following is a *support* activity in Porter's value chain model?

A   Procurement
B   Operations
C   Marketing and sales
D   Inbound logistics   **(2 marks)**

2.11 Which of the following statements about the impact of technological developments is *not* true?

A   Technology developments have supported corporate delayering
B   Technology developments tend to adversely affect employee relations
C   Technology developments creates risk for long-range product/market planning
D   Technology developments offer significant advantages for corporate communications   **(2 marks)**

2.12 BCD Co is a large trading company. Steve is the administration manager and is also responsible for legal and compliance functions. Sheila is responsible for after sales service and has responsibility for ensuring that customers who have purchased goods from BCD Co are fully satisfied. Sunny deals with suppliers and negotiates on the price and quality of inventory. He is also responsible for identifying the most appropriate suppliers of plant and machinery for the factory. Sam is the information technology manager and is responsible for all information systems within the company.

According to Porter's value chain, which of the managers is involved in a primary activity as opposed to a support activity?

 A   Steve
 B   Sheila
 C   Sunny
 D   Sam   **(2 marks)**

2.13 What is the latest stage at which a new recruit to a company should first be issued with a copy of the company's health and safety policy statement?

 A   On accepting the position with the company
 B   As early as possible after employment
 C   After the first few weeks of employment
 D   During the final selection interview   **(2 marks)**

2.14 In Porter's five forces model, which of the following would not constitute a 'barrier to entry'?

 A   Scale economies available to existing competitors
 B   High capital investment requirements
 C   Low switching costs in the market
 D   Loyalty to existing brands   **(2 marks)**

2.15 Three of the following strategies are closely related. Which is the exception?

 A   Downsizing
 B   Delegating
 C   Delayering
 D   Outsourcing   **(2 marks)**

2.16 Which of the following would be identified as a cultural trend?

 A   Health and safety legislation
 B   Concern with health and diet
 C   Data protection legislation
 D   Increasing age of the population   **(2 marks)**

2.17 For demographic purposes, which of the following is not a variable in the identification of social class?

 A   Income level
 B   Lifestyle
 C   Occupation
 D   Education   **(2 marks)**

(Total = 34 marks)

3 The macro-economic environment

34 mins

3.1 Which of the following is *not* an element of fiscal policy?

    A   Government spending
    B   Government borrowing
    C   Taxation
    D   Exchange rates   **(2 marks)**

3.2 Which of the following is associated with a negative Public Sector Net Cash Requirement?

    A   The government is running a budget deficit
    B   The government's expenditure exceeds its income
    C   The government is running a budget surplus
    D   Public Sector Debt Repayment (PSDR) is high.   **(2 marks)**

3.3 .... taxes are collected by the Revenue authority from an intermediary, which attempts to pass on the tax to consumers in the price of goods.

Which word correctly completes this statement?

    A   Regressive
    B   Progressive
    C   Direct
    D   Indirect   **(2 marks)**

3.4 If a government has a macro-economic policy objective of expanding the overall level of economic activity, which of the following measures would *not* be consistent with such an objective?

    A   Increasing public expenditure
    B   Lowering interest rates
    C   Increasing taxation
    D   Decreasing taxation   **(2 marks)**

3.5 The currency in country X is the Krone while country Y uses the Euro. Country Y has recently experienced an increase in its exchange rate with Country X. Which of the following effects is likely to result in Country Y?

    A   A stimulus to exports in Country Y
    B   An increase in the costs of imports from Country X
    C   Reducing demand for imports from Country X
    D   A reduction in the rate of cost push inflation   **(2 marks)**

3.6 The following, *with one exception*, are 'protectionist measures' in international trade. Which is the exception?

    A   Import quotas
    B   Harmonisation of technical standards
    C   Customs procedures
    D   Tariffs   **(2 marks)**

3.7 Are the following statements true or false?

    1   Frictional unemployment will be short term
    2   Governments can encourage labour mobility if they want to reduce unemployment

    A   Both statements are true
    B   Statement 1 is true and statement 2 is false.
    C   Statement 1 is false and statement 2 is true.
    D   Both statements are false.   **(2 marks)**

3.8 Monetary policy is a government economic policy relating to:

1 Interest rates
2 Taxation
3 Public borrowing and spending
4 Exchange rates

Which of the above are correct?

A 1 and 4
B 2 and 3
C 2 and 4
D 3 and 4

(2 marks)

3.9 Which of the following organisations might benefit from a period of high price inflation?

A An organisation which has a large number of long term payables

B An exporter of goods to a country with relatively low inflation

C A supplier of goods in a market where consumers are highly price sensitive and substitute goods are available

D A large retailer with a high level of inventory on display and low rate of inventory turnover

(2 marks)

3.10 Which of the following are the goals of macroeconomic policy?

1 Encouraging economic growth
2 Low and stable inflation
3 Achievement of a balance between exports and imports
4 Encouraging stagnation

A 1 and 2
B 2 and 3
C 2, 3 and 4
D 1, 2 and 3

(2 marks)

3.11 Which of the following is an example of cyclical unemployment?

A The entry of school leavers into the labour pool each year
B Lay-offs among agricultural labourers in winter
C Automation of ticketing services in tourism
D Recession in the building industry

(2 marks)

3.12 A surplus on the balance of payments usually means a surplus or deficit on the .... account.

Which word correctly complete this statement?

A Current
B Capital
C Financial
D Income statement

(2 marks)

3.13 Northland, Southland, Eastland and Westland are four countries of Asia. The following economic statistics have been produced for the year 2007.

Country	Northland	Southland	Eastland	Westland
Change in GDP (%)	−0.30	+2.51	−0.55	+2.12
Balance of payments current account ($m)	+5550.83	−350.47	−150.90	+220.39
Change in consumer prices (%)	+27.50	+15.37	+2.25	+2.15
Change in working population employed (%)	−4.76	+3.78	+1.76	−8.76

Which country experienced stagflation in the relevant period?

A   Northland
B   Southland
C   Eastland
D   Westland   **(2 marks)**

3.14   .... economic growth is determined by supply-side rather than by demand side factors.

Which word correctly completes this statement?

A   Actual
B   Potential
C   National
D   Inflationary   **(2 marks)**

(Total = 28 marks)

4   Micro economic factors   70 mins

4.1   In a free market economy, the price mechanism:

A   Aids government control
B   Allocates resources
C   Reduces unfair competition
D   Measures national wealth   **(2 marks)**

4.2   The supply curve of a firm operating in a competitive market is its

A   Marginal cost curve above the average variable cost curve
B   Marginal cost curve above the average total cost curve
C   Average total cost curve beyond the point where the marginal cost curve cuts it from below
D   Average variable cost curve below the average revenue curve   **(2 marks)**

4.3   A legal minimum price is set which is below the equilibrium price. What will be the impact of this?

A   Excess of demand over supply
B   Excess of supply over demand
C   An increase in price
D   Nothing   **(2 marks)**

4.4   Which one of the following would cause the supply curve for a good to shift to the right (outwards from the origin)?

A   A fall in the price of the good
B   An increase in the demand for the good
C   A fall in production costs of the good
D   The imposition of a minimum price   **(2 marks)**

4.5   When the price of a good is held above the equilibrium price, the result will be

    A   Excess demand
    B   A shortage of the good
    C   A surplus of the good
    D   An increase in demand   **(2 marks)**

4.6   Which one of the following would *not* lead directly to a shift in the demand curve for overseas holidays?

    A   An advertising campaign by holiday tour operators
    B   A fall in the disposable incomes of consumers
    C   A rise in the price of domestic holidays
    D   A rise in the price of overseas holidays   **(2 marks)**

4.7   Which of the following is likely to lead to a fall in the price of good Q which is a normal good?

    A   A rise in the price of good P, a substitute for good Q
    B   A fall in the level of household incomes generally
    C   A fall in the price of good T, a complement to good Q
    D   A belief that the price of good Q is likely to double in the next 3 months   **(2 marks)**

4.8   The demand curve for a product will shift to the left when there is:

    A   A rise in household income
    B   An increase in the product's desirability from the point of view of fashion
    C   A fall in the price of a substitute
    D   A fall in the price of a complement   **(2 marks)**

4.9   Which of the following is not a substitute for carpet?

    A   Ceramic floor tiles
    B   Wooden floorboard
    C   Vinyl flooring
    D   Carpet underlay   **(2 marks)**

4.10   Which of the following is not a complement to cars?

    A   Petrol
    B   Tyres
    C   Holidays
    D   Satellite navigation systems   **(2 marks)**

4.11   The demand for fashion goods is not influenced by:

    A   Price
    B   Allocative inefficiency among producers
    C   The distribution of income among households
    D   Expectation of future price changes   **(2 marks)**

4.12   Which *one* of the following would normally cause a rightward shift in the demand curve for a product?

    A   A fall in the price of a substitute product
    B   A reduction in direct taxation on incomes
    C   A reduction in price of the product
    D   An increase in the price of a complementary product   **(2 marks)**

4.13   If the price of coffee falls, which *one* of the following outcomes would be expected to occur?

    A   A fall in the quantity of coffee demanded
    B   A rise in the price of tea
    C   A fall in the demand for drinking cups
    D   A fall in the demand for tea   **(2 marks)**

4.14 What is an inferior good?

    A   A good of such poor quality that demand for it is very weak

    B   A good of lesser quality than a substitute good, so that the price of the substitute is higher

    C   A good for which the cross elasticity of demand with a substitute product is greater than 1

    D   A good for which demand will fall as household income rises   **(2 marks)**

4.15 Consider the price and demand for flower vases. The price of cut flowers goes up sharply. Which of the following would you expect to happen?

    A   The demand curve for flower vases will shift to the left and their price will rise

    B   The demand curve for flower vases will shift to the right and their price will rise

    C   There will be a movement along the demand curve for flower vases and their price will go down

    D   The demand curve for flower vases will shift to the left and their price will go down   **(2 marks)**

4.16 Consider the price and demand for tickets to travel by sea ferry. The price of travelling by hovercraft (a substitute form of travel) goes up. Which of the following would you expect to happen?

    A   The demand curve for sea ferry tickets will shift to the left, and their price will go down. More sea ferry tickets will be sold.

    B   The demand curve for sea ferry tickets will shift to the right, and their price will go up. More ferry tickets will be sold.

    C   The demand curve for sea ferry tickets will shift to the right and their price will go down. More sea ferry tickets will be sold.

    D   The demand curve for sea ferry tickets will shift to the right and their price will go up. Fewer sea ferry tickets will be sold.   **(2 marks)**

4.17 The summer demand for hotel accommodation in London comes mainly from foreign tourists. Demand for hotel rooms in London in summer could be reduced by a fall in the price or value of which of the following?

    1   US dollars

    2   Aeroplane tickets

    3   Sterling

    A   Item 1 only

    B   Items 1 and 2 only

    C   Items 2 and 3 only

    D   Item 3 only   **(2 marks)**

4.18 Which of the following changes will cause the demand curve for chocolate to shift to the left?

    1   A fall in the price of chocolate

    2   A health campaign which claims that chocolate makes you fat

    3   A rise in the price of chocolate substitutes

    4   A fall in consumers' income

    A   Change 1 only

    B   Changes 2 and 3 only

    C   Changes 2 and 4 only

    D   Changes 3 and 4 only   **(2 marks)**

4.19   Suppose that, in a certain advanced industrialised country, the government has applied price controls over rents of both public and private rented accommodation for a number of years, and a serious problem of widespread homelessness has built up. Just recently, the rent price controls have been eased. Which of the following consequences should now occur?

1   An increase in homelessness
2   In the longer term, an increase in new building work
3   The provision of more rented accommodation
4   Fewer owner-occupied dwellings

A   Consequences 1 and 2
B   Consequences 2 and 3
C   Consequences 3 and 4
D   Consequences 1 and 4   **(2 marks)**

4.20   The demand curve for a resource may shift because of

A   A change in the demand for a good whose production is dependent on the resource
B   Concerns about potential harmful pollution from the resource
C   A change in the price of a substitute resource
D   All of the above   **(2 marks)**

4.21   The income elasticity of demand for a product is high. This means that:

A   Sales will increase sharply if the price is reduced
B   Sales will fall only slightly when incomes of households fall
C   Sales will rise sharply when incomes of households rise
D   The good is inferior good   **(2 marks)**

4.22   All of the following are likely to lead an outward shift in the supply curve for a good, except

A   The introduction of cost-reducing technology
B   An increase in the price of the good
C   A decrease in the price of a resource used to make the good
D   A decrease in taxes on producers   **(2 marks)**

4.23   The supply curve for sofas has moved to the right. Which of the following could have caused this shift?

A   A decrease in the price of sofas
B   A decrease in the price of futons (a substitute)
C   A decrease in the cost of horsehair (a raw material used in making sofas)
D   A decrease in the wage rate in the futon industry   **(2 marks)**

4.24   Using the point method, what is the price elasticity of demand of product X as price falls from its current price of $20 to $15?

	Old	New
Price	20	15
Quantity	10	15

A   0.5
B   1
C   1.5
D   2   **(2 marks)**

4.25 Consumer surplus is:

    A   The excess between what consumers are prepared to pay for a good or service, and the prevailing market price

    B   The indirect tax producers pay on a good or service

    C   The marginal utility gained by consuming one more unit of a good or service

    D   The indirect tax consumers pay on a good or service   **(2 marks)**

4.26 Which combination of demand and supply curves would be appropriate for a firm attempting to increase its profits by increasing its market share?

    A   Inelastic demand, inelastic supply
    B   Elastic demand, elastic supply
    C   Inelastic demand, elastic supply
    D   Elastic demand, inelastic supply   **(2 marks)**

4.27 Which one of the following would *not* cause a supply curve to shift to the left?

    A   A rise in the cost of factors of production
    B   A rise in household income
    C   A rise in indirect taxes imposed on the good or service being supplied
    D   A rise in the price of other, substitute goods   **(2 marks)**

4.28 If the absolute value of the price elasticity of demand for dry white wine is greater than one, a decrease in the price of all wine would result in:

    A   A more than proportional decrease in the quantity of dry white wine purchased
    B   A less than proportional decrease in the quantity of dry white wine purchased
    C   A less than proportional increase in the quantity of dry white wine purchased
    D   A more than proportional increase in the quantity of dry white wine purchased **(2 marks)**

4.29 Mr Smith has a limited income which restricts the number of different goods he can buy. Which one of the following best describes the position at which Mr Smith's utility from purchasing different goods is maximised?

    A   Total utility from each good is equal
    B   Marginal utility from each good is equal
    C   Marginal utility from each good is 0
    D   Ratio of marginal utility to price is equal for each good   **(2 marks)**

(Total = 58 marks)

Do you know? – Business organisation structure, functions and governance

Check that you can fill in the blanks in the statements below before you attempt any questions. If in doubt, you should go back to your BPP Interactive Text and revise first.

- An .... **organisation** always exists alongside the formal one.

- Organisations can be **d...........** on a **functional** basis, a **geographical** basis, a **product** basis, a **brand** basis, or a **matrix** basis. Organisation structures often feature a variety of these types, as **h......** structures.

- In a **d.......** **structure** some activities are **decentralised** to business units or regions.

- The strategic apex exerts a pull to centralise, leading to the **s.......** **structure**.

- **Span of control** or **'span of management'** refers to the number of s.......... responsible to a s.......

- Recent trends have been towards **d.........** organisations of levels of management.

- R........... may be **pure**, **applied** or **development**. It may be intended to improve **products** or **processes**.

- The .... **function** plans, organises, directs and controls the necessary activities to provide products and services, creating outputs which have added value over the value of inputs.

- The .... **function** manages an organisation's relationships with its customers.

- .... (HRM) is concerned with the most effective use of human resources. It deals with organisation, staffing levels, motivation, employee relations and employee services.

- Organisation c...... is 'the way we do things round here'.

- **Harrison** classified four types of culture, to which **Handy** gave the names of Greek deities.

  - **Power** culture (....) is shaped by one individual
  - **Role** culture (......) is a bureaucratic culture shaped by rationality, rules and procedures
  - **Task** culture (.......) is shaped by a focus on outputs and results
  - **Existential** or person culture (Dionysus) is shaped by the interests of individuals

- Within an organisation, c.............. can consist entirely of executives or may be instruments for joint consultation between employers and employees.

- Good c........ g........... involves **risk management** and **internal control, accountability** to stakeholders and other shareholders and conducting business in an **ethical and effective way.**

- The b..... should be responsible for taking major **policy** and **strategic** decisions.

- **Division of responsibilities** at the head of an organisation is most simply achieved by separating the roles of C....and c..... e..........

- Audit committees of **independent n...- ....** **directors** should liaise with **external audit, supervise internal audit,** and **review** the **annual accounts** and **internal controls**.

- Annual reports must **convey** a **f... and b....... view** of the organisation. They should state whether the organisation has complied with governance regulations and codes, and give specific disclosures about the board, internal control reviews, going concern status and relations with stakeholders.

Did you know? – Business organisation structure, functions and governance

Could you fill in the blanks? The answers are in bold. Use this page for revision purposes as you approach the exam.

- An **informal organisation** always exists alongside the formal one.

- Organisations can be **departmentalised** on a **functional** basis, a **geographical** basis, a **product** basis, a **brand** basis, or a **matrix** basis. Organisation structures often feature a variety of these types, as **hybrid** structures.

- In a **divisional structure** some activities are **decentralised** to business units or regions.

- The strategic apex exerts a pull to centralise, leading to the **simple structure**.

- **Span of control** or **'span of management'** refers to the number of subordinates responsible to a superior.

- Recent trends have been towards **delayering** organisations of levels of management.

- Research may be **pure**, **applied** or **development**. It may be intended to improve **products** or **processes**.

- **The production function** plans, organises, directs and controls the necessary activities to provide products and services, creating outputs which have added value over the value of inputs.

- The **marketing function** manages an organisation's relationships with its customers.

- **Human resource management** (HRM) is concerned with the most effective use of human resources. It deals with organisation, staffing levels, motivation, employee relations and employee services.

- Organisation culture is 'the way we do things round here'.

- **Harrison** classified four types of culture, to which **Handy** gave the names of Greek deities.

  - **Power** culture (Zeus) is shaped by one individual
  - **Role** culture (Apollo) is a bureaucratic culture shaped by rationality, rules and procedures
  - **Task** culture (Athena) is shaped by a focus on outputs and results
  - **Existential** or person culture (Dionysus) is shaped by the interests of individuals

- Within an organisation, committees can consist entirely of executives or may be instruments for joint consultation between employers and employees.

- Good corporate governance involves **risk management** and **internal control, accountability** to stakeholders and other shareholders and conducting business in an **ethical and effective way.**

- The board should be responsible for taking major **policy** and **strategic** decisions.

- **Division of responsibilities** at the head of an organisation is most simply achieved by separating the roles of Chair and chief executive.

- **Independent non-executive directors** have a key role in governance. Their number and status should mean that their views carry significant weight.

- Audit committees of **independent non-executive directors** should liaise with **external audit, supervise internal audit**, and **review** the **annual accounts** and **internal controls**.

- Annual reports must **convey** a **fair and balanced view** of the organisation. They should state whether the organisation has complied with governance regulations and codes, and give specific disclosures about the board, internal control reviews, going concern status and relations with stakeholders.

5 Business organisation, structure and strategy 20 mins

5.1 Which of the following statements about an organisation chart is not true?

- A An organisation chart provides a summary of the structure of a business.
- B An organisation chart can improve internal communications within a business.
- C An organisation chart can improve employees' understanding of their role in a business.
- D An organisation chart can indicate functional authority but not line authority within a business.

(2 marks)

5.2 Which of the following is a correct definition of 'span of control'?

- A The number of employees subordinate in the hierarchy to a given manager
- B The number of levels in the hierarchy 'below' a given manager's
- C The length of time between a manager's decision and the evaluation of it by his superior
- D The number of employees directly responsible to a manager (2 marks)

5.3 Which of the following terms is not used by Mintzberg in his description of organisational structure?

- A Strategic apex
- B Support base
- C Technostructure
- D Operating core (2 marks)

5.4 Y plc is a growing organisation which has recently diversified into a number of significant new product markets. It has also recently acquired another company in one of its overseas markets.

What would be the most appropriate form of organisation for Y plc?

- A Geographical departmentation
- B Divisionalisation
- C Functional departmentation
- D Hybrid structure (2 marks)

5.5 Which of the following principles of classical management is challenged by matrix management?

- A Structuring the organisation on functional lines
- B Structuring the organisation on geographical lines
- C Unity of command
- D Decentralisation of decision-making (2 marks)

5.6 Which of the following statements about the informal organisation is not true?

- A The influence of the informal organisation was highlighted by the Hawthorne Studies, in the way group norms and dynamics affected productivity.
- B Informal organisation can pose a threat to employee health and safety.
- C Informal organisation can stimulate innovation.
- D Managers in positions of authority generally cannot be part of the informal organisation (2 marks)

5.7 Which one of the following is an advantage of centralisation?

- A It helps to develop the skills of junior managers
- B It avoids overburdening top managers in terms of workload and stress
- C Senior managers can take a wider view of problems and consequences
- D Controls and accountability are better (2 marks)

5.8 Which of the following statements is/are true?

(i) An informal organisation exists with every formal organisation

(ii) The objectives of the informal organisation are broadly the same as those of the formal organisation

(iii) A strong, close-knit informal organisation is desirable within the formal organisation

A Statement (i) only
B Statements (i) and (iii) only
C Statements (ii) and (iii) only
D Statement (iii) only

(2 marks)

(Total = 16 marks)

6 Organisational culture and committees 44 mins

6.1 BZ Ness Ltd is an organisation with a strongly traditional outlook. It is structured and managed according to classical principles: specialisation, the scalar chain of command, unity of command and direction. Personnel tend to focus on their own distinct tasks, which are strictly defined and directed. Communication is vertical, rather than lateral. Discipline is much prized and enshrined in the rule book of the company.

From the scenario, what sort of culture does BZ Ness Ltd have, using Harrison's classifications?

A Role culture
B Task culture
C Existential culture
D Power culture

(2 marks)

6.2 Which of the following statements is true?

A Strong values improve corporate performance
B Strong values can replace rules and controls in an organisation
C Strong values minimise conflict within an organisation
D Strong values are dangerous if they filter out 'uncomfortable' environmental information

(2 marks)

6.3 Culture is the collective programming of the mind which distinguishes the members of one .... from another.

Which word or phrase most accurately completes the definition.

A Nation
B Ethnic group
C Category of people
D Social class

(2 marks)

6.4 Which of the following is *not* one of the terms used by Hofstede to describe a key dimension of culture?

A Power-distance
B Acquisitive/giving
C Individualism/collectivism
D Uncertainty avoidance

(2 marks)

6.5 Which is the 'deepest' set of underlying factors which determine culture, and the hardest to manage?

A Values
B Beliefs
C Rituals
D Assumptions

(2 marks)

6.6 Who defined organisational culture as 'the set of shared, taken-for-granted implicit assumptions that a group holds and that determines how it perceives, thinks about and reacts to its environment.'

A   Maslow
B   Schein
C   Porter
D   Mintzberg   **(2 marks)**

6.7 Research has indicated that workers in country A display characteristics such as toughness and the desire for material wealth and possessions, while workers in country B value personal relationships, belonging and the quality of life.

According to Hofstede's theory, these distinctions relate to which of the following cultural dimensions?

A   Masculinity – femininity
B   Power – distance
C   Individualism – collectivism
D   Uncertainty avoidance   **(2 marks)**

6.8 The research and development (R & D) function of a business:

(i)   is primarily concerned with market research
(ii)   can improve existing products as well as developing completely new products
(iii) has been less important for firms manufacturing computers to meet an industry standard than for those firms developing the next generation of computers
(iv)   is always undertaken under contract by specialist external consultancies

Which of the above statements are correct?

A   (i) and (ii) only
B   (ii) and (iii) only
C   (i), (iii) and (iv) only
D   (ii) and (iv) only   **(2 marks)**

6.9 Services have certain qualities which distinguish them from products. Because of their
.... , physical elements such as vouchers, tickets, confirmations and merchandise are an important part of service provision.

Which of the following words most accurately completes the sentence?

A   Intangibility
B   Inseparability
C   Variability
D   Perishability   **(2 marks)**

6.10 U Ltd produces a portfolio of products and focuses its efforts and resources on persuading customers to buy them.

This is an example of which type of 'orientation'?

A   Production
B   Sales
C   Marketing
D   Purchasing   **(2 marks)**

6.11 Which of the following is/are objectives of human resource management?

1   To meet the organisation's social and legal responsibilities relating to the human resource.
2   To manage an organisation's relationship with its customers
3   To develop human resources that will respond effectively to change.

A   1 and 2
B   1 and 3
C   1
D   1,2 and 3   **(2 marks)**

6.12 Jeff, Jane and Jaitinder work in different departments in the firm XYZ Co. They are members of the permanent 'staff committee' which meets on a monthly basis to discuss staff issues such as pensions and benefits. Their purpose is to listen to communication from staff within their department and raise issues on behalf of their department at committee meetings. What is the name given to this type of committee?

A   Joint committee
B   Task force
C   Ad hoc committee
D   Standing committee   **(2 marks)**

6.13 Josh, Joanne, Ed, and Sue all work for D Co. Josh works in the finance department. Joanne works in the human resources department. Ed is Sue's line manager in the purchasing department. Which one of the staff members would be involved with payroll administration?

A   Josh
B   Joanne
C   Ed
D   Sue   **(2 marks)**

6.14 Managers Jill and Paul are talking about how to resolve a business problem. Jill suggests that a committee should be formed to discuss the issues. Paul argues that committees are:

(i)   time-consuming and expensive
(ii)   they invite a compromise instead of a clear-cut decision.

Which of these statements is true?

A   Both (i) and (ii)
B   (i) only
C   (ii) only
D   Neither statement is true   **(2 marks)**

6.15 Diane carries out routine processing of invoices in the purchasing department of L Co. Joanne is Diane's supervisor. Lesley is trying to decide how many staff will be needed if some proposed new technology is implemented. Tracey is considering the new work that L Co will be able to offer and the new markets it could enter, once the new technology is well established.

Which member of L Co carries out tactical activities?

A   Diane
B   Joanne
C   Lesley
D   Tracey   **(2 marks)**

6.16 Mr Q is manager of a division which is undergoing a business downturn. He tries to shelter the workforce from the effects of downsizing: taking time for consultation, organising counselling and refusing to institute compulsory redundancies.

Which one of the following cultural types identified in the Hofstede model is this manager most likely to represent?

A   Low power-distance
B   Low masculinity
C   Low uncertainty avoidance
D   High individuality   **(2 marks)**

6.17 Which of the following would *not* be an objective of stakeholder management in relation to major suppliers?

    A   Continuity of supply
    B   Mutual trust
    C   Mutual dependency
    D   Information sharing   **(2 marks)**

6.18 Janet works for a toy company called K Co. She telephones Mary at P Co on a daily basis to order parts. Janet has no contact with customers but does deal with complaint letters from D Group, an organisation against slave labour. D Group believe that K Co use slave labour in the toy manufacturing factories.

Which of the following are internal stakeholders of K Co?

    A   Janet only
    B   Janet and Mary at P Co
    C   Janet and D Group
    D   Janet, Mary and D Group   **(2 marks)**

(Total = 36 marks)

7   Corporate governance and social responsibility   32 mins

7.1 Which of the following statements about corporate social responsibility is true?

    (i)   CSR guarantees increased profit levels
    (ii)   CSR adds cost to organisational activities and reduces profit levels
    (iii)   Social responsibility may have commercial benefits
    (iv)   Social responsibility is a concern confined to business organisations

    A   (i), (ii), (iii) and (iv)
    B   (i) and (iii)
    C   (ii) and (iv)
    D   (iii) only   **(2 marks)**

7.2 Calum, Heidi and Jonas are managers for Zip Co. They have been told that their salary will be based on company performance and that a bonus scheme will also be introduced. The bonus will also be related to company performance. Which of the following best describes the approach to governance that Zip Co is using?

    A   Stewardship theory
    B   Agency theory
    C   Stakeholder theory
    D   None of the above   **(2 marks)**

7.3 Michael has been asked to prepare a presentation for the company directors on good corporate governance. Which one of the following is he likely to exclude from his presentation?

    A   Risk management
    B   Internal controls
    C   Maximising shareholder wealth
    D   Accountability to stakeholders   **(2 marks)**

7.4 Corporate governance is essentially of what significance?

    A   Control system
    B   Strategic importance
    C   Risk management
    D   All of the above   **(2 marks)**

7.5 Which of the following is a feature of poor corporate governance?

A   Domination of the board by a single individual
B   Critical questioning of senior managers by external auditors
C   Supervision of staff in key roles
D   Lack of focus on short-term profitability   **(2 marks)**

7.6 The tasks of which body include: monitoring the chief executive officer; formulating strategy; and ensuring that there is effective communication of the strategic plan?

A   The audit committee
B   The Public Oversight Board
C   The board of directors
D   The nomination committee   **(2 marks)**

7.7 Which of the following would be included in the principles of Corporate Social Responsibility?

(i)   Human rights
(ii)   Employee welfare
(iii)   Professional ethics
(iv)   Support for local suppliers

A   (ii) and (iii) only
B   (i) only
C   (ii), (iii) and (iv) only
D   (i), (ii) and (iv) only   **(2 marks)**

7.8 Which of the following is subject to the least direct regulation?

A   Employment protection
B   Corporate social responsibility
C   Professional ethics
D   Corporate governance   **(2 marks)**

7.9 In most countries , what is the usual purpose of codes of practice on corporate governance?

A   To establish legally binding requirements to which all companies must adhere
B   To set down detailed rules to regulate the ways in which companies must operate
C   To provide guidance on the standards of the best practice that companies should adopt
D   To provide a comprehensive framework for management and administration   **(2 marks)**

7.10 Who should set directors' reward and incentive packages, according to corporate governance provisions?

A   The board of directors
B   The nomination committee
C   A remuneration committee made up of independent non-executive directors
D   A remuneration committee made up of a balance of executive and non-executive directors
                                                                                  (2 marks)

7.11 What is the purpose of an Operating and Financial Review (OFR)?

A   To provide the board of directors with a narrative statement by the audit committee of its findings on the efficacy of internal operational and financial controls.

B   To provide the London Stock Exchange with a statement as to whether or not they complied through the accounting period with the provisions set out in the Combined Code.

C   To set out the directors' analysis of the business, in order to provide investors with a historical and prospective view through the eyes of management.

D   To provide a statement that the company is a going concern.   **(2 marks)**

7.12 Which of the following are advantages of having non-executive directors on the company board?

    1   They can provide a wider perspective than executive directors.

    2   They provide reassurance to shareholders.

    3   They may have external experience and knowledge which executive directors do not possess.

    4   They have more time to devote to the role.

    A   1 and 3

    B   1, 2 and 3

    C   1, 3 and 4

    D   2 and 4   **(2 marks)**

7.13 What is implied by an 'accommodation' strategy, in the context of corporate social responsibility?

    A   The business is prepared to take full responsibility for its actions and plans in advance to minimise its adverse impacts on stakeholders and the environment.

    B   The business recognises that it has a problem, and attempts to minimise or avoid additional obligations arising from it.

    C   The business sites its facilities in areas which will benefit from economic activity, while minimising environmental impacts at the sites.

    D   The business takes responsibility for its actions in response to pressure from interest groups or the risk of government interference if it does not.   **(2 marks)**

(Total = 26 marks)

Do you know? – Accounting and reporting systems, controls and compliance

Check that you can fill in the blanks in the statements below before you attempt any questions. If in doubt, you should go back to your BPP Interactive Text and revise first.

- A........ is a way of recording, analysing and summarising transactions of a business.

- The two most important e............ financial statements are the statement of financial position and the income statement. Reports produced for internal purposes include budgets and costing schedules.

- The **income statement** is a record of i..... generated and e........ incurred over a given period.

- The **statement of financial position** is a list of all the ....owned by a business and all the .... owed by a business at a particular date.

- The **statement of ....** shows sources of cash generated during a period and how these funds have been spent.

- The p....... and s.... systems will be the most important components of most company accounting systems.

- C...... should be regularly checked and any problems reported to management.

- A **d**....... may be described as a 'pool' of data, which can be used by any number of applications. Its use is not restricted to the accounts department.

- **S**........, too, are often used both in financial accounting and cost accounting.

- **Internal controls** should help organisations counter risks, maintain the quality of reporting and comply with laws and regulations. They provide r........ a....... that the organisations will fulfil their objectives.

- Controls can be classified in various ways including administrative and accounting; p......, detect and correct; discretionary and non-discretionary; v....... and mandated; manual and automated.

- **Internal auditors** are e........ of the organisation whose work is designed to **add value** and who report to the **audit committee. External auditors** are from a....... f...... and their role is to **report on the financial statements to shareholders**.

- An **a**..... **t**...... shows who has accessed a system and the operations performed.

- In a corporate context f..... can fall into one of two main categories: **removal of funds or assets** from a business or the **intentional misrepresentation of the financial position of a business**.

- There are three broad **pre-requisites** or 'pre-conditions' that must exist in order to make fraud a possibility: d........, m......... and ....

- It is the responsibility of the .... to take such steps as are reasonably open to them to **prevent and detect** fraud.

- The growth of globalisation has created more opportunities for m..... l......... which governments and international bodies are trying to combat with legislation.

Did you know? – Accounting and reporting systems, controls and compliance

Could you fill in the blanks? The answers are in bold. Use this page for revision purposes as you approach the exam.

- Accounting is a way of recording, analysing and summarising transactions of a business.

- The two most important external financial statements are the statement of financial position and the income statement. Reports produced for internal purposes include budgets and costing schedules.

- The **income statement** is a record of income generated and expenditure incurred over a given period.

- The **statement of financial position** is a list of all the assets owned by a business and all the liabilities owed by a business at a particular date.

- The **statement of cash flows** shows sources of cash generated during a period and how these funds have been spent.

- The purchases and sales systems will be the most important components of most company accounting systems.

- Controls should be regularly checked and any problems reported to management.

- A **database** may be described as a 'pool' of data, which can be used by any number of applications. Its use is not restricted to the accounts department.

- **Spreadsheets**, too, are often used both in financial accounting and cost accounting.

- **Internal controls** should help organisations counter risks, maintain the quality of reporting and comply with laws and regulations. They provide reasonable assurance that the organisations will fulfil their objectives.

- Controls can be classified in various ways including **administrative** and **accounting; prevent**, **detect** and **correct**; **discretionary** and **non-discretionary**; **voluntary** and **mandated**; **manual** and **automated**.

- **Internal auditors** are **employees** of the organisation whose work is designed to **add value** and who report to the **audit committee**. **External auditors** are from **accountancy firms** and their role is to **report on the financial statements to shareholders**.

- An **audit trail** shows who has accessed a system and the operations performed.

- In a corporate context fraud can fall into one of two main categories: **removal of funds or assets** from a business or the **intentional misrepresentation of the financial position of a business**.

- There are three broad **pre-requisites** or 'pre-conditions' that must exist in order to make fraud a possibility: dishonesty, motivation and opportunity.

- It is the responsibility of the directors to take such steps as are reasonably open to them to **prevent and detect** fraud.

- The growth of globalisation has created more opportunities for money laundering which governments and international bodies are trying to combat with legislation.

8 The role of accounting ⬛ 60 mins

8.1 Joseph has just started his first job in an accountancy department. A qualified senior member of staff explains to him what the main aim of accounting is. Which of the following options is the correct aim of accounting?

    A   To maintain ledger accounts for every asset and liability
    B   To provide financial information to users of such information
    C   To produce a trial balance
    D   To record every financial transaction individually   **(2 marks)**

8.2 Luca Pacioli wrote the first printed explanation of double entry bookkeeping in which year?

    A   1024
    B   1494
    C   1884
    D   1924   **(2 marks)**

8.3 Which of the following statements about accounting information is *incorrect?*

    A   Some companies voluntarily provide specially-prepared financial information to employees.

    B   Accounting information should be relevant, reliable, complete, objective and timely.

    C   Accountants have a strong obligation to ensure that company accounts conform to accounting standards

    D   Charities and professional bodies do not have to produce financial statements in the same way as businesses.   **(2 marks)**

8.4 In a typical finance function, preparation of budgets and budgetary control would usually be the responsibility of which of the following roles?

    A   The Financial Controller
    B   The Management Accountant
    C   The Treasurer
    D   The Finance Director   **(2 marks)**

8.5 Three of the following are outputs of a payroll system, and one is an input to the system. Which is the input?

    A   Credit transfer forms
    B   Time sheets
    C   Payroll analysis
    D   Pay slips   **(2 marks)**

8.6 Which of the following is an aim of the control system relating to accounts payable and purchases?

    A   To ensure that all credit notes received are recorded in the general and payables ledger

    B   To ensure that goods and services are only supplied to customers with good credit ratings

    C   To ensure that all credit notes that have been issued are recorded in the general and receivables ledgers

    D   To ensure that potentially doubtful debts are identified   **(2 marks)**

8.7 Which of the following does company law require a statement of financial position to give?

  A A true and fair view of the profit or loss of the company for the financial year

  B An unqualified (or 'clean') report on the statement of affairs of the company as at the end of the financial year

  C A true and fair view of the statement of affairs of the company as at the end of the financial year

  D A qualified report, setting out matters on which independent auditors disagree with management

  (2 marks)

8.8 The following, with one exception, are areas in which an integrated accounting software package has advantages compared to a series of separate (stand-alone) dedicated programs. Which is the exception?

  A Efficiency in updating data
  B Flexibility in preparing reports
  C Data integrity
  D Specialised capabilities **(2 marks)**

8.9 A .... is a program which deals with one particular part of a computerised business accounting system.

  Which of the following terms correctly completes this definition?

  A Suite
  B Module
  C Spreadsheet
  D Database **(2 marks)**

8.10 All the following, with one exception, are examples of advantages of a computer-based accounting system over a manual system. Which statement is the exception?

  A Financial calculations can be performed more quickly and accurately
  B Financial information can be presented to other business departments in a variety of forms
  C There is much stronger provision for data security
  D The system is easier to update as new information becomes available **(2 marks)**

8.11 A spreadsheet software application may perform all of the following business tasks *except one*. Which one of the following is the exception?

  A The presentation of numerical data in the form of graphs and charts
  B The application of logical tests to data
  C The application of 'What if?' scenarios
  D Automatic correction of all data entered by the operator into the spreadsheet **(2 marks)**

8.12 The preparation and filing of accounts by limited companies each year is required by which of the following?

  A Codes of corporate governance
  B National legislation
  C International Accounting Standards
  D Local Accounting Standards **(2 marks)**

8.13 All the following statements *except one* are examples of the advantages that a computer-based accounting system used by a management accountant has over a manual system.

Which statement is the exception?

A   A computer-based accounting system is easier to update as new information becomes available

B   A computer-based accounting system will always reject inaccurate financial information input to the system's database

C   Financial calculations can be performed more quickly and accurately

D   The management accountant can more readily present financial information to other business departments in a variety of forms   **(2 marks)**

8.14 Gordon works in the accounts department of a retail business. He and his colleagues are looking at the sales figures for various types of clothing. The director asks them to use exception reporting to summarise their findings. Which of the following correctly defines the concept of 'exception reporting' within a business context?

A   The reporting of unusual events, outside the normal course of events
B   The analysis of those items where performance differs significantly from standard or budget
C   The preparation of reports on routine matters on an 'ad hoc' basis
D   The scrutiny of all data as a matter of course, save in exceptional circumstances

(2 marks)

8.15 A small company's computer system comprises five desktop personal computers located in separate offices linked together in an intranet within the same building. The computers are not connected to the Internet and employees are not allowed to take storage media into or out of the building. Information which the business' owner wishes to keep confidential to herself is stored in one of the computers.

Which one of the following statements can be concluded from this information?

A   This company's computer system does not need a back-up storage system
B   This company's computer system does not need a password access system
C   This company's computer system does not receive e-mail from customers or suppliers
D   This company's computer system does not need virus detection software   **(2 marks)**

8.16 .... Systems pool data from internal and external sources and make information available to senior managers, for strategic, unstructured decision-making.

Which word or phrase correctly completes this sentence?

A   Expert
B   Decision Support
C   Executive Support
D   Management Support   **(2 marks)**

8.17 All the following statements *except one* describe the relationship between data and information. Which *one* is the exception?

A   Information is data which has been processed in such a way as to be meaningful to the person who receives it.

B   The relationship between data and information is one of inputs and outputs

C   Information from one process can be used as data in a second process

D   Data is always in numerical form whereas information is always in text form.   **(2 marks)**

8.18

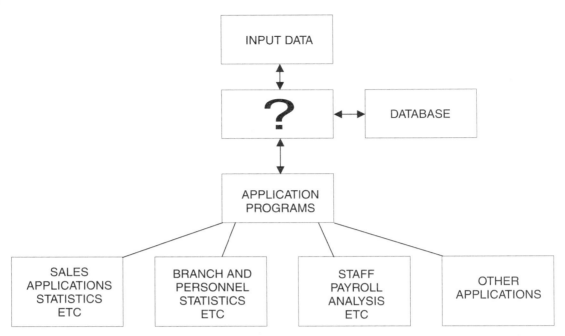

What element of a database system is represented by the question mark in the above diagram?

A   Database administrator
B   Electronic point of sale system
C   Data storage
D   Database management system   **(2 marks)**

8.19   Which of the following statements about data security is *not* true?

A   Loss or corruption of data is almost always non-deliberate.
B   New staff in particular pose a threat.
C   It is impossible to prevent all threats cost-effectively.
D   Smoke detectors are a form of data protection.   **(2 marks)**

8.20   Office Automation Systems are designed mainly to increase the .... of data and information workers.

Which word correctly completes this sentence.

A   Expertise
B   Productivity
C   Flexibility
D   Decision-making capability   **(2 marks)**

8.21   Which of the following user groups of financial and accounting information are likely to need, and have access to, this information most?

A   Managers of the company
B   Shareholders of the company
C   Tax authorities
D   Financial analysis advisers   **(2 marks)**

8.22   To whom should the internal audit department of an organisation report?

A   The Finance Director
B   The Management Accountant
C   The audit committee of the board of directors
D   The shareholders   **(2 marks)**

8.23 Which of the following statements, in the context of computerised accounting systems, is *not* true?

   A   A database is a structured, centralised pool of data which can be accessed by a number of applications.

   B   A spreadsheet is particularly useful for creating financial models.

   C   Computerised systems reduce the risk of errors in financial calculations

   D   Information and Communication Technology (ICT) systems are more efficient than manual systems for any task an accountant may have to perform   **(2 marks)**

8.24 Which function in an organisation is responsible for ensuring that only properly authorised purchases which are necessary for the business are made?

   A   Goods inwards
   B   Finance/accounts
   C   Purchasing/procurement
   D   Production/operations   **(2 marks)**

8.25 There is a need for co-ordinated information flow between sections and departments in accounting management. To which of the following should the receivables ledger section give information about overdue debts?

   A   Cost accounting staff
   B   The credit control department
   C   The payables ledger section
   D   The cashier   **(2 marks)**

(Total = 50 marks)

9   Control, security and audit   34 mins

9.1 Which of the following is *not* an aim of internal controls?

   A   To enable the organisation to respond appropriately to business, operational and financial risks
   B   To eliminate the possibility of impacts from poor judgement and human error
   C   To help ensure the quality of internal and external reporting
   D   To help ensure compliance with applicable laws and regulations   **(2 marks)**

9.2 Some controls are provided automatically by the system and cannot be by-passed, ignored or overridden: for example, having to input a password to enter a computer system. These are classified as .... controls.

Which term correctly completes this statement?

   A   Detect
   B   Mandated
   C   Non-discretionary
   D   Administrative   **(2 marks)**

9.3 The mnemonic SPAMSOAP is often used to remember the range of financial control procedures. What does the 'O' stand for in this mnemonic?

   A   Operations
   B   Organisation
   C   Oversight
   D   Openness   **(2 marks)**

9.4 Which of the following is *not* an internal check?

   A   Separation of duties for authorising, custody and recording
   B   Pre-lists, post-lists and control totals
   C   Bank reconciliations
   D   Systems for authorising transactions within specified spending limits   **(2 marks)**

9.5 Which of the following statements about internal audit is true?

   A   Internal audit is an independent appraisal activity
   B   Internal audit is separate from the organisation's internal control system
   C   Internal audit is carried out solely for the benefit of the organisation's stakeholders
   D   The internal audit function reports to the finance director   **(2 marks)**

9.6 The use of uninterruptible (protected) power supplies is a method of protecting data and IT systems from what sort of security threat?

   A   Fire
   B   Accidental damage
   C   Weather
   D   Hacking   **(2 marks)**

9.7 Which of the following would be classed as a contingency control in an information system?

   A   Password-only access to the system
   B   System recovery procedures
   C   Audit trails
   D   Data validation procedures   **(2 marks)**

9.8 All of the following, with one exception, are inherent limitations of internal control systems. Which is the exception?

   A   The costs of control
   B   Potential for human error and deliberate override
   C   The types of transactions controls are designed to cope with
   D   The independence of controls from the method of data processing   **(2 marks)**

9.9 Which of the following statements about external auditors is *not* correct?

   A   External auditors are appointed by the shareholders of a company

   B   The primary responsibility of external auditors is to investigate financial irregularities and report them to shareholders

   C   External auditors may rely on the work of internal auditors, if they first assess its worth

   D   External auditors are concerned with the financial records and statements of the organisation
          (2 marks)

9.10 In the context of audit, what are 'substantive tests' designed to accomplish?

   A   To establish whether internal controls are being applied as prescribed
   B   To identify errors and omissions in financial records
   C   To establish the causes of errors or omissions in financial records
   D   To establish an audit trail   **(2 marks)**

9.11 Backing up computer files and storing copies of software in separate locations to the main system are examples of which type of controls?

   A   Prevent
   B   Detect
   C   Correct
   D   Automated   **(2 marks)**

9.12 In the context of data security controls, ... are records showing who has accessed a computer system and what operations he or she has performed.

Which word or phrase correctly completes this definition?

   A   Passwords
   B   Audit trails
   C   Archives
   D   Cookies   **(2 marks)**

9.13 Which type of audit is concerned with the monitoring of management's performance, concentrating on the outputs of the system and the efficiency of the organisation?

   A   Systems audit
   B   Operational audit
   C   Probity audit
   D   Social audit   **(2 marks)**

9.14 Which of the following circumstances would cast doubt on the external auditor's ability to rely on the work of internal auditors?

   A   There is evidence that management and directors consistently act on internal audit recommendations

   B   The internal audit function has a direct line of communication to the audit committee

   C   No audit manuals or working papers are available for inspection

   D   Internal auditors are recruited on technical qualifications and demonstrated proficiency   **(2 marks)**

(Total = 28 marks)

10 Identifying and preventing fraud   34 mins

10.1 What is the term given to a method of fraud in the accounts receivable area, by which cash or cheque receipts are stolen, and the theft concealed by setting subsequent receipts against the outstanding debt?

   A   Collusion
   B   Misrepresentation
   C   Teeming and lading
   D   Fictitious sales   **(2 marks)**

10.2 Which of the following activities create vulnerability to fraud?

   (i)   Calculating payslips
   (ii)   Preparing delivery notes
   (iii)   Paying supplier invoices
   (iv)   Meeting budgets and performance targets

   A   (iii) only
   B   (i) and (iii) only
   C   (i) and (ii) only
   D   (i), (ii), (iii) and (iv)   **(2 marks)**

10.3 X plc has a bad debt policy whereby aged receivables who are obviously not going to pay, are written off. The financial accountant does not enforce this policy.

This might be fraudulent insofar as it creates which of the following effects?

A   It removes funds from the business
B   It results in the understatement of profits and net assets
C   It results in the overstatement of profits and net assets
D   It results in the intentional overstatement of profits and net assets   **(2 marks)**

10.4 Dishonesty is a .... to act in ways which contravene accepted ethical, social, organisational or legal norms for fair and honest dealing.

Which word correctly completes this statement?

A   Motivation
B   Pre-disposition
C   Opportunity
D   Unwillingness   **(2 marks)**

10.5 All of the following, with one exception, are internal factors which might increase the risk profile of a business. Which is the exception?

A   Increased competition
B   Corporate restructuring
C   Upgraded management information system
D   New personnel   **(2 marks)**

10.6 Which of the following would most clearly present a personnel risk of fraud?

A   Segregation of duties
B   High staff morale
C   Staff not taking their full holiday entitlements
D   Consultative management style   **(2 marks)**

10.7 All of the following, with one exception, are potential impacts on a business of removal of significant funds or assets. Which is the exception?

A   Fall in returns to shareholders
B   Reduction in profits
C   Increase in working capital
D   Reputational damage   **(2 marks)**

10.8 Which of the following internal controls might be least effective in preventing fraud, if staff are in collusion with customers?

A   Physical security
B   Requiring signatures to confirm receipt of goods or services
C   Sequential numbering of transaction documents
D   Authorisation policies   **(2 marks)**

10.9 In a limited company, or plc, it is the ultimate responsibility of the .... to take reasonable steps to prevent and detect fraud.

Which word or phrase correctly completes this statement?

A   The board of directors
B   The fraud officer
C   The external auditor
D   The audit committee   **(2 marks)**

10.10 Which of the following is *not* a key risk area for computer fraud?

    A   Hackers
    B   Lack of managerial understanding
    C   Inability to secure access to data
    D   Integration of data systems   **(2 marks)**

10.11 Which *two* of the following stakeholders will be most directly affected if a business overstates its financial position?

    (i)   Staff
    (ii)   Customers
    (iii)   Investors
    (iv)   Suppliers

    A   (i) and (ii)
    B   (ii) and (iii)
    C   (iii) and (iv)
    D   (ii) and (iv)   **(2 marks)**

10.12 Which of the following would *not* form part of a fraud response plan?

    A   Suspending staff suspected of fraudulent activity
    B   Investigating the activities and contacts of a suspected fraudster
    C   Changing passwords for computer access
    D   Fraud awareness training and recruitment controls.   **(2 marks)**

10.13 Only allowing purchasing staff to choose suppliers from an approved list is an example of what sort of fraud prevention measure?

    A   Segregation of duties
    B   Appropriate documentation
    C   Limitation control
    D   Check control   **(2 marks)**

10.14 Which of the following statements about fraud prevention is *not* true?

    A   Cash sales are an area of high risk of fraud.
    B   Performance-based rewards for managers reduce the risk of fraud.
    C   Emphasis on the autonomy of operational management may weaken controls.
    D   Fraud awareness and ethics education can reduce the risk of fraud   **(2 marks)**

(Total = 28 marks)

Do you know? – Leading and managing individuals and teams

Check that you can fill in the blanks in the statements below before you attempt any questions. If in doubt, you should go back to your BPP Interactive Text and revise first.

- M......... is responsible for using the organisation's resources to meet its goals. It is accountable to the owners: shareholders in a business, or government in the public sector.

- There are three basic **schools of leadership theory**: ..... ('qualities') theories, s.... theories and ....(including situational and functional) theories.

- Effective r......... practices ensure that a firm has enough **people with the right skills**.

- **Recruitment** is a systematic process of (a) i......... and defining skill needs and (b) attracting suitably skilled candidates.

- S......... **tests** can be used before or after interviews. Intelligence tests measures the candidate's general intellectual ability, and personality tests identify character traits and behavioural preferences. Other tests are more specific to the job (eg proficiency tests).

- E..... o......... is an approach to the management of people at work based on equal access to benefits and fair treatment.

- **Recruitment and s.......** are areas of particular sensitivity to claims of d........... – as well as genuine (though often unintended) inequality.

- The concept of **'managing diversity'** is based on the belief that the dimensions of i......... difference on which organisations currently focus are crude and performance-irrelevant classifications of the most obvious differences between people.

- P........n is the process by which the brain selects and organises information in order to make sense of it. People behave according to what they perceive – not according to what really is.

- A ..... is a collection of individuals who perceive themselves as a group. It thus has a sense of **identity**.

- A team **develops in stages**: forming, s......., n......., performing (**Tuckman**) and d...... or mourning/adjourning.

- M......... is 'a decision-making process through which the individual chooses desired outcomes and sets in motion the behaviour appropriate to acquiring them'. (*Huczynski and Buchanan*).

- **McGregor** suggested that a manager's approach is based on attitudes somewhere on a scale between two extreme sets of assumptions: Theory ... (workers have to be coerced) and Theory ... (workers want to be empowered).

- The main **purpose** of t...... and development is to raise competence and therefore performance standards. It is also concerned with personal development, helping and motivating employees to fulfil their potential.

- I....... is the process whereby a person is formally introduced and integrated into an organisation or system.

- A...... is part of the system of performance management, including goal setting, performance monitoring, feedback and improvement planning.

Did you know? – Leading and managing individuals and teams

Could you fill in the blanks? The answers are in bold. Use this page for revision purposes as you approach the exam.

- **Management** is responsible for using the organisation's resources to meet its goals. It is accountable to the owners: shareholders in a business, or government in the public sector.

- There are three basic **schools of leadership theory**: trait ('qualities') theories, style theories and contingency (including situational and functional) theories.

- Effective recruitment practices ensure that a firm has enough **people with the right skills**.

- **Recruitment** is a systematic process of (a) identifying and defining skill needs and (b) attracting suitably skilled candidates.

- **Selection tests** can be used before or after interviews. Intelligence tests measures the candidate's general intellectual ability, and personality tests identify character traits and behavioural preferences. Other tests are more specific to the job (eg proficiency tests).

- **Equal opportunities** is an approach to the management of people at work based on equal access to benefits and fair treatment.

- **Recruitment and selection** are areas of particular sensitivity to claims of discrimination – as well as genuine (though often unintended) inequality.

- The concept of '**managing diversity**' is based on the belief that the dimensions of individual difference on which organisations currently focus are crude and performance-irrelevant classifications of the most obvious differences between people.

- **Perception** is the process by which the brain selects and organises information in order to make sense of it. People behave according to what they perceive – not according to what really is.

- A **group** is a collection of individuals who perceive themselves as a group. It thus has a sense of **identity**.

- A team **develops in stages**: forming, storming, norming, performing (**Tuckman**) and dorming or mourning/adjourning.

- **Motivation** is 'a decision-making process through which the individual chooses desired outcomes and sets in motion the behaviour appropriate to acquiring them'. (*Huczynski and Buchanan*).

- **McGregor** suggested that a manager's approach is based on attitudes somewhere on a scale between two extreme sets of assumptions: Theory X (workers have to be coerced) and Theory Y (workers want to be empowered).

- The main **purpose** of training and development is to raise competence and therefore performance standards. It is also concerned with personal development, helping and motivating employees to fulfil their potential.

- **Induction** is the process whereby a person is formally introduced and integrated into an organisation or system.

- Appraisal is part of the system of performance management, including goal setting, performance monitoring, feedback and improvement planning.

11 Leading and managing people   41 mins

11.1 Leaders may be distinguished from managers by the fact that they do not depend on.................................... power in the organisation.

Which of the following types of power correctly completes this statement?

    A   Person power
    B   Expert power
    C   Position power
    D   Physical power   **(2 marks)**

11.2 Which of the following writers is *not* a member of the school of management thought to which the others belong?

    A   FW Taylor
    B   Elton Mayo
    C   Abraham Maslow
    D   Frederick Herzberg   **(2 marks)**

11.3 Monica is a manager in the finance department of P Co and she has several staff working for her. She has become quite friendly with most of her staff and they like her and appreciate that she does everything she can to attend to their needs. Which type of managerial style does Monica have?

    A   Impoverished
    B   Task management
    C   Country club
    D   Dampened pendulum   **(2 marks)**

11.4 According to Fielder, which of the following are true of psychologically distant managers?

    1   They judge their staff on the basis of performance
    2   They are primarily task-oriented
    3   They prefer formal consultation methods rather than seeking staff opinions
    4   They are closer to their staff

    A   1 and 2
    B   2 and 3
    C   1,2 and 3
    D   1,2,3 and 4   **(2 marks)**

11.5 What is delegated by a superior to a subordinate?

    A   Authority
    B   Power
    C   Responsibility
    D   Accountability   **(2 marks)**

11.6 Which of the following is *not* a technique of scientific management or Taylorism?

    A   Micro-design of jobs
    B   Work study techniques to establish efficient methods
    C   Multi-skilled teamworking
    D   Financial incentives   **(2 marks)**

11.7 What is the key contribution of the human relations approach to management?

   A   Awareness of the importance of group dynamics and worker attitudes as an influence on productivity

   B   Concern for productivity and efficiency

   C   Awareness of the many different variables that influence and constrain a manager's behaviour

   D   Proof of a clear link between job satisfaction, worker motivation and business success

   (2 marks)

11.8 Which of the following leadership styles gives the most discretion or decision-making power to subordinates?

   A   Autocratic
   B   Consultative
   C   Democratic
   D   Persuasive   **(2 marks)**

11.9 Of Mintzberg's nine managerial roles, which is being exercised by a manager who gathers information from contacts within and outside the organisation?

   A   Leader
   B   Monitor
   C   Spokesperson
   D   Disseminator   **(2 marks)**

11.10 .... is the role at the interface between the operational core (non-managerial workers) and management.

   Which word or phrase correctly completes this definition?

   A   Middle line
   B   Junior management
   C   Employee communications
   D   Supervision   **(2 marks)**

11.11 According to research, which of the following statements is true of a consultative style of management, compared to other styles?

   A   It is most popular among subordinates
   B   It is most popular among leaders
   C   It encourages the highest productivity
   D   It provokes most hostility in groups   **(2 marks)**

11.12 Which of the following terms is used to describe the 'right' to perform an action in an organisation?

   A   Responsibility
   B   Authority
   C   Influence
   D   Power   **(2 marks)**

11.13 Which of the following is an 'interpersonal' role of management, in Mintzberg's classification of nine managerial roles?

   A   Spokesperson
   B   Figurehead
   C   Negotiator
   D   Resource allocator   **(2 marks)**

11.14 John Adair's action-centred leadership model is part of which school of thought?

    A   Trait theories
    B   Style theories
    C   Contingency theories
    D   Management theories   **(2 marks)**

11.15 Are the following statements true or false?

    1   Adair's leadership model focuses on what leaders do and not what they are
    2   The Ashridge leadership model proposes a democratic approach to leadership

    A   Both statements are true
    B   Statement 1 is true; statement 2 is false
    C   Statement 1 is false; statement 2 is true
    D   Both statements are false   **(2 marks)**

11.16 Which leadership approach sees the leadership process in a context made up of three interrelated variables: task needs, the individual needs of group members and the needs of the group as a whole?

    A   Action-centred leadership
    B   Contingency theory
    C   The managerial grid
    D   Dispersed leadership   **(2 marks)**

11.17 .... is the managerial function concerned with establishing a structure of tasks; grouping and assigning them to appropriate units; and establishing lines of information and reporting to support performance.

    Which managerial function is referred to in this definition?

    A   Planning
    B   Organising
    C   Commanding
    D   Controlling   **(2 marks)**

(Total = 34 marks)

12 Recruitment and selection   44 mins

12.1 Which of the following would be classed as a 'selection' rather than a 'recruitment' activity?

    A   Job description
    B   Designing application forms
    C   Screening application forms
    D   Advertising vacancies   **(2 marks)**

12.2 A recruitment manager has prepared a statement of the key duties, tasks and reporting responsibilities involved in a particular job, as the basis for job interviewing.

    What name would be given to such a statement?

    A   Job analysis
    B   Job description
    C   Job advertisement
    D   Personnel specification   **(2 marks)**

12.3 In the context of personnel specifications, the Seven Point Plan (Rodger) does *not* explicitly include which of the following headings?

    A   Physical make-up
    B   Interests
    C   Motivation
    D   Circumstances   **(2 marks)**

12.4 What is the current trend in human resource management?

    A   Centralise recruitment and selection within HR
    B   Devolve recruitment and selection to line managers
    C   Devolve recruitment and selection to the Board
    D   None of the above   **(2 marks)**

12.5 Selection tests such as IQ tests and personality tests may not be effective in getting the right person for the job for several reasons. Which of the following criticisms of the tests is *not* justified, however?

    A   Test results can be influenced by practice and coaching rather than genuine ability
    B   Subjects are able to deliberately falsify results
    C   Tests do not completely eliminate bias and subjectivity
    D   Tests are generally less accurate predictors of success than interviews   **(2 marks)**

12.6 In a selection interview, the interviewer asks: 'Surely you'd agree that objectivity is a key requirement for an auditor?'

What sort of question is this?

    A   Open
    B   Closed
    C   Problem-solving
    D   Leading   **(2 marks)**

12.7 Which of the following is a disadvantage of a large panel or selection board interview compared to individual or one-to-one interviews?

    A   A number of people see the candidate at one sitting
    B   Specialists can ask a questions about technical areas of the work
    C   Questions tend to be more varied and more random
    D   There is less opportunity for personal rapport with the candidate   **(2 marks)**

12.8 In the context of selection interviews, which of the following describes the 'halo effect'?

    A   A tendency for people to make an initial judgement based on first impressions, and then letting this colour their later perceptions.

    B   An effect whereby the interviewer changes the behaviour of the applicant by suggestion

    C   A tendency to mentally assign people to a group and then attribute to them the traits assumed to be characteristic of the group as a whole

    D   An effect whereby the interviewer attributes to the applicant beliefs, attitudes or feelings which he has himself   **(2 marks)**

12.9 Selection tests which focus on aptitude, intelligence and personality factors are called
.... tests.

Which word correctly completes this sentence?

    A   Proficiency
    B   Psychometric
    C   Standardised
    D   Sensitive   **(2 marks)**

12.10 In the context of selection, what is an assessment centre?

    A   A place where candidates are taken to undergo group assessments

    B   A series of tests and interviews undergone by an individual candidate over several days

    C   A series of tests, interviews and activities undergone by a group of candidates over several days

    D   A technique for assessing large numbers of candidates, usually for junior positions, in a cost-effective manner   **(2 marks)**

12.11 Which of the following statements about reference checking is true?

    A   References provide objective information about a job candidate

    B   Written references help to minimise the inaccuracy of references

    C   Personal references are particularly valuable in assessing the qualities of a candidate

    D   At least two employer references are desirable   **(2 marks)**

12.12 Job descriptions have advantages for use in all but *one* of the following areas of human resource management. Which is the exception?

    A   Job evaluation

    B   Training needs analysis

    C   Recruitment

    D   Employee flexibility   **(2 marks)**

12.13 A financial consultancy firm has a job vacancy for a junior office assistant at one of its offices. Which of the following would be the most suitable external medium for the job advertisement?

    A   Accountancy journal

    B   National newspapers

    C   Local newspapers

    D   The company web site   **(2 marks)**

12.14 A policy of internal promotion, as opposed to external recruitment, can have positive and negative effects. Which *one* of the following would be *negatively* effected by such a policy?

    A   Innovation

    B   Succession planning

    C   Induction times

    D   Accuracy of selection decision**s**   **(2 marks)**

12.15 Which of the following is *not* a primary aim of a job selection interview?

    A   Comparing the applicant against job requirements

    B   Getting as much information as possible about the applicant

    C   Giving the applicant information about the job and organisation

    D   Making the applicant feel (s)he has been treated fairly   **(2 marks)**

12.16 In which of the following circumstances would an organisation be better off carrying out its own recruitment, rather than using recruitment consultants?

    A   The organisation has a strong, traditional culture, but is now looking to introduce greater innovation and flexibility

    B   The organisation does not have a specialist recruitment function, but is looking to recruit on a large scale for the first time

    C   The organisation uses outside consultants in many areas of its business, and is used to managing their services effectively

    D   The organisation has complex cultural, business and technical selection criteria for its staff, but is considering using a consultancy for the first time, because it requires new people urgently in order to exploit an opportunity   **(2 marks)**

12.17 .... are capacities that lead to behaviours that meet job demands within the parameters of the organisational environment.

Which word correctly completes this sentence?

A   Attributes

B   Skills

C   Competences

D   Attainments   **(2 marks)**

12.18 The first stage in the recruitment process is:

A   To write a job description

B   To write a person specification

C   To identify a vacancy

D   To liaise with recruitment consultants   **(2 marks)**

(Total = 36 marks)

13   Diversity and equal opportunities   24 mins

13.1   Sound business arguments can be made for having an equal opportunities policy. Which of the following reasons apply?

1   To show common decency and fairness in line with business ethics

2   To widen the recruitment pool

3   To attract and retain the best people for the job

4   To improve the organisation's image as a good employer

A   1,2 and 3

B   2 and 3

C   1 and 3

D   1,2,3 and 4   **(2 marks)**

13.2   Which of the following correctly describes the purpose of current Equal Pay regulations?

A   To ensure that there is no element of sexual or racial discrimination in determining pay rates

B   To provide that job evaluation must be used in determining pay rates

C   To provide that women have the right to equal pay to work of equal value to that of men

D   To ensure that women have the right to equal pay to men in the same job   **(2 marks)**

13.3   Which of the following statements are true?

1   Taking active steps to encourage people from disadvantaged groups to apply for jobs and training is classed as positive discrimination.

2   Diversity in the workplace means implementing an equal opportunities policy.

A   They are both true

B   1 is true and 2 is false

C   1 is false and 2 is true

D   They are both false.   **(2 marks)**

13.4 Members of a religious minority in a workplace are frequently subjected to jokes about their dress and dietary customs, and a bit of name-calling, by non-religious workmates. They find this offensive and hurtful – even though their colleagues say it is 'just a bit of fun'.

What type of discrimination (if any) would this represent?

A   Victimisation
B   Indirect discrimination
C   Harassment
D   No discrimination is involved   **(2 marks)**

13.5 Which of the following is a potential business benefit of a corporate diversity policy?

A   Compliance with equal opportunities legislation
B   Respect for individuals
C   Better understanding of target market segments
D   Efficiency in managing human resources   **(2 marks)**

13.6 Which of the following statements about disability discrimination law is *not* true?

A   The requirements only effect employers of more than 20 employees

B   Employers must adjust working arrangements or the physical features of premises to remove any disadvantage to disabled people

C   For an individual to be defined as a disabled person, the physical or mental impairment must have an adverse effect of more than 12 months duration

D   Public bodies have additional duties to protect and promote equality for disabled people
                                                                                      (2 marks)

13.7 Which of the following would constitute direct discrimination?

A   Setting age limits or ranges in an employment advertisement

B   Offering less favourable terms to workers on flexible hours contracts

C   Using word-of-mouth recruitment in a predominantly male workforce

D   Offering staff benefits to the spouses of heterosexual employees, but not to the partners of gay employees   **(2 marks)**

13.8 A job interviewer asks a woman about her plans to have a family. She eventually does not get the job, because she lacks qualifications which are listed as essential in the person specification. However, she later finds out that men who attended interviews were not asked questions about their plans to have a family.

Which of the following statements correctly describes the situation?

A   The woman would have a successful claim of direct sexual discrimination

B   The woman would have a successful claim of indirect sexual discrimination

C   The organisation has laid itself open to a claim of indirect sexual discrimination, but such a claim would not be successful

D   The organisation has not laid itself open to any claim of discrimination   **(2 marks)**

13.9 The concept of .... is based on the belief that the dimensions of individual difference on which organisations currently focus are crude and performance-irrelevant, and that an organisation should reflect the range of differences within its customer and labour markets.

Which words correctly complete this sentence?

    A   Equal opportunity
    B   Cultural divergence
    C   Managing diversity
    D   Market segmentation   **(2 marks)**

13.10 Which of the following is an example of 'positive discrimination' rather than 'positive action' on equal opportunities?

    A   Selecting a certain number of people from ethnic minorities for jobs, regardless of job-relevant selection criteria

    B   Using ethnic languages in job advertisements

    C   Implementing training for women in managerial skills

    D   Setting targets for the number of people from ethnic minorities that the organisation would like to see in managerial positions   **(2 marks)**

(Total = 20 marks)

14 Individuals, groups and teams   36 mins

14.1 Which of the following is most clearly a sign of an ineffective group?

    A   There is disagreement and criticism within the group
    B   There is competition with other groups
    C   Members passively accept work decisions
    D   Individuals achieve their own targets   **(2 marks)**

14.2 A team leader is having difficulties with conflict in the team, due to 'clashes' or incompatibilities in the personalities of two of its members. The leader draws up a list of options for managing the problem.

Which option, from the following list, would be the least practicable?

    A   Educate the members about personality differences
    B   Encourage the members to modify their behaviours
    C   Encourage the members to modify their personalities
    D   Remove one of the members from the team   **(2 marks)**

14.3 At the Soli-Darretty Bros factory, a project team has been put together by management. The team are engaged in debating how they are going to approach the task, and who is going to do what. Some of their first ideas have not worked out but they are starting to put forward some really innovative ideas: they get quite excited in brainstorming sessions, and are uninhibited in putting forward their views and suggestions. Factions are emerging, not only around different ideas, but around two dominating individuals who always seem to disagree.

At what stage of Tuckman's group development model is this team?

    A   Forming
    B   Storming
    C   Norming
    D   Performing   **(2 marks)**

14.4 .... are mental states (made up of thoughts, feelings and intentions) which influence an individual's response to all objects and situations with which they are related.

Which word correctly completes this definition?

A   Personality traits
B   Perceptions
C   Attitudes
D   Emotional intelligences   **(2 marks)**

14.5   For which of the following applications is teamworking *not* best suited?

A   Ideas generation for innovation
B   Co-ordination of different functions
C   Crisis decision-making
D   Co-ordination of geographically dispersed workers   **(2 marks)**

14.6   If a team is bogged down in argument, and discussion is turning hostile, which of the following types of contribution would the team leader seek to discourage?

A   Bringing-in
B   Blocking
C   Summarising
D   Testing understanding   **(2 marks)**

14.7   Which of the following is *not* a key tool of team building?

A   Members identify with the team
B   Members are as alike as possible
C   Members have solidarity with one another
D   Members commit to shared objectives   **(2 marks)**

14.8   Grant is a member of a project team. His colleagues in the team rely on him to read and check complex project documentation. Grant has a keen eye for detail and often identifies minor details in documents that others miss but may be of significance. Despite the diligent approach, Grant always meets his deadlines. However, some of Grant's colleagues feel frustrated when he refuses to involve others. He can hold up progress as he will not agree to the team signing off project documents until all of his concerns are fully discussed.

According to Belbin's team roles theory, Grant is an example of which of the following?

A   Implementer
B   Completer – finisher
C   Monitor – evaluator
D   Shaper   **(2 marks)**

14.9   What is the most important attribute of a 'group', which distinguishes it from a random crowd of people?

A   Leadership
B   Purpose
C   Conformity
D   Identity   **(2 marks)**

14.10 In Belbin's model of team roles, which of the following is most important for a well-functioning team?

A   A mix and balance of team roles
B   Nine members, so that all roles are filled
C   A focus on functional/task roles, not process roles
D   As few members as possible   **(2 marks)**

14.11 A team is winding up a challenging project that it has been working on for some time. Next week, the same team will go on to a new project with quite different challenges.

Which stage of the group development model is this team likely to be going through?

A   Norming
B   Dorming
C   Mourning
D   Adjourning   **(2 marks)**

14.12 Which of the following would be an effective technique for encouraging healthy team solidarity?

A   Discouraging competition with other groups
B   Encouraging competition within the group
C   Encouraging members to express disagreements
D   Discouraging members from expressing disagreements   **(2 marks)**

14.13 Which of the following theories suggests that people behave according to other people's expectations of how they should behave in that situation?

A   Group think theory
B   Team identity theory
C   Role theory
D   Hero theory   **(2 marks)**

14.14 An organisation has set up a team in which any member of the team can perform the full range of its tasks. The manager is able to share out tasks between members according to who is available to do a given job when it is required.

What sort of team organisation does this describe?

A   Multi-disciplinary team
B   Multi-skilled team
C   Self-managed team
D   Virtual team   **(2 marks)**

14.15 Team-member Tom is one of those people who is dynamic and thrives on pressure. He tends to be the one who challenges and pushes other team members, sometimes annoying or upsetting them – but also getting the team past difficult periods.

Which of Belbin's team roles does Tom exercise?

A   Plant
B   Co-ordinator (chair)
C   Implementer
D   Shaper   **(2 marks)**

(Total = 30 marks)

15 Motivating individuals and groups   41 mins

15.1   Phil T Luker & Son offers its employees a reward package which includes salary and company car. Its factory is safe and clean and rather smart. The work is technically challenging and employees are encouraged to produce innovative solutions to problems.

Which of the rewards offered by the firm is a form of intrinsic reward?

A   The salary
B   The car
C   The factory environment
D   The work   **(2 marks)**

15.2   Which of the following is not a category in Maslow's hierarchy of needs theory?

A   Physiological needs
B   Freedom of inquiry and expression needs
C   Need for affiliation
D   Safety needs   **(2 marks)**

15.3   Keepham (Hungary) Co offers its employees:

(i)   Sensible company policies
(ii)   Good salaries and bonuses
(iii)   Considerate supervision
(iv)   Training programmes

According to Herzberg's two-factor theory, which of these things will satisfy employees in such a way as to motivate them to superior effort in the long-term?

A   (ii) only
B   (iv) only
C   (ii) and (iv) only
D   (i), (ii), (iii) and (iv)   **(2 marks)**

15.4   What term is given, in motivation theory, to the things people value and choose to pursue?

A   Goals
B   Innate needs
C   Drives
D   Satisfaction   **(2 marks)**

15.5   Willy Dewitt-Ornott works in Sales. There is always a sales competition at the year end and the winner is likely to be made team leader. Willy's quite certain that he will be able to win and that he will have more responsibility, which he would like. But he would also have to work much longer hours, and he is quite reluctant to do this for family reasons.

If an expectancy equation were used to assess Willy's motivation to work hard at the end of the year, based on the information given, which of the following results would you expect to see?

A   Valence would be high, expectancy high, motivation high
B   Valence would be high, expectancy low, motivation low
C   Valence would be around 0, expectancy high, motivation low
D   Valence would be around 0, expectancy high, motivation high   **(2 marks)**

15.6   All of the following, with one exception, are alternative terms for the same thing. Which is the exception?

A   Motivator factor
B   Hygiene factor
C   Environmental factor
D   Maintenance factor   **(2 marks)**

15.7 The five core dimensions which contribute to job satisfaction are skill variety, task identity, task significance, ... and feedback.

Which of the following is the dimension missing from the above list?

A   Recognition
B   Advancement
C   Autonomy
D   Rewards   **(2 marks)**

15.8 Participation can motivate employees by making them take 'ownership' of the task and increasing their commitment. In which of the following circumstances, however, would this *not* happen?

A   Participation is genuine
B   The purpose of participation is made clear
C   Everyone is allowed to participate equally
D   Efforts at participation are maintained for a reasonable period   **(2 marks)**

15.9 The management of Guenguiss Cans Co runs a 'tight ship', with clocking-on timekeeping systems, close supervision and rules for everything. 'Well,' says the general manager, 'if you allow people to have any freedom at work, they will take advantage and their work rate will deteriorate'.

Which of Douglas McGregor's 'theories' does this management team subscribe to?

A   Theory X
B   Theory Y
C   Theory W
D   Theory Z   **(2 marks)**

15.10 Application of process theories to motivation in practice involves all but one of the following measures. Which is the exception?

A   Clarifying intended results
B   Giving feedback on actual results
C   Immediacy of reward following results
D   Consistency of reward for results   **(2 marks)**

15.11 Which of the following is a potential problem with individual performance-related pay (PRP) as a motivator?

A   Its effect on organisational communication
B   Its relevance to business objectives
C   The fact that it does not relate to individuals' wage or salary grades
D   Its effect on team motivation   **(2 marks)**

15.12 The following, with one exception, are claimed as advantages for job enrichment as a form of job re-design. Which is the exception?

A   It increases job satisfaction
B   It enhances quality of output
C   It replaces monetary rewards
D   It reduces supervisory costs   **(2 marks)**

15.13 According to Maslow's hierarchy of needs, which of the following is the final 'need' to be satisfied?

A   Self-realisation
B   Self-actualisation
C   Esteem needs
D   Physiological needs   **(2 marks)**

15.14 Job evaluation puts a relative value on jobs primarily on the basis of which of the following factors?

    A   Equity
    B   Job content
    C   Negotiated pay scales
    D   Market rates of pay   **(2 marks)**

15.15 In Vroom's expectancy theory, what is meant by 'valence'?

    A   The strength of an individual's preference for a given outcome
    B   The strength of an individual's motivation to act in a certain way
    C   The strength of an individual's belief that acting in a certain way will obtain the desired outcome
    D   The values an individual applies to the motivation decision   **(2 marks)**

15.16 Eva Moor-Drudgery used to pack chocolate bars into boxes of three dozen. Her job has been redesigned, so that she now packs them, applies a 'sell-by' date stamp, cellophanes the box and applies a promotional sticker.

Of which form of job redesign is this an example?

    A   Job rotation
    B   Job evaluation
    C   Job enlargement
    D   Job enrichment   **(2 marks)**

15.17 Which job design technique was advocated by the scientific management school?

    A   Empowerment
    B   Micro-division of labour
    C   Division of labour
    D   Job enlargement   **(2 marks)**

(Total = 34 marks)

16 Training and development   39 mins

16.1 Trainee Sara is unhappy in her current training programme, because it is too 'hands on': she is required to attempt techniques before she has had a chance to study the underlying principles first. She spends the evenings trying to read ahead in the course text-book.

Which of Honey and Mumford's learning styles is probably Sara's preferred style?

    A   Reflector
    B   Pragmatist
    C   Theorist
    D   Activist   **(2 marks)**

16.2 Which of the following is *not* a characteristic of a 'learning organisation'?

    A   The generation and transfer of knowledge
    B   Support for learning and development by all members
    C   A scientific approach to problem-solving, in order to minimise risk and error
    D   Willingness to continuously transform itself in response to a changing environment   **(2 marks)**

16.3 Which of the following statements about training is most likely to be the foundation of an effective training policy?

A   Training is the responsibility of the HR department
B   Training is all cost and no quantifiable benefit
C   The important thing is to do lots of training
D   Training can be an effective solution to some performance problems   **(2 marks)**

16.4 .... is 'the planned and systematic modification of behaviour through learning events, programmes and instruction which enable individuals to achieve the level of knowledge, skills and competence to carry out their work effectively'.

Which word correctly completes this definition?

A   Conditioning
B   Training
C   Education
D   Development   **(2 marks)**

16.5 The learning cycle developed by David Kolb is a process for .... learning.
Which of the following words correctly completes this sentence?

A   Programmed
B   Experiential
C   Action
D   Reflection   **(2 marks)**

16.6 All the following, with one exception, are clear benefits of training and development for an organisation. Which is the exception?

A   Increased organisational flexibility
B   Less need for detailed supervision
C   Enhanced employability of staff members
D   Improved succession planning   **(2 marks)**

16.7 Which of the following are 'on the job' training methods?

(i)   Day-release
(ii)   Job rotation
(iii)   Coaching
(iv)   Temporary promotion

A   Method (iii) only
B   Methods (i) and (iii) only
C   Methods (ii), (iii) and (iv) only
D   Methods (i), (ii), (iii) and (iv)   **(2 marks)**

16.8 You have been asked to comment on the most effective approach for training accounts staff in the use of a new payroll system. Which of the following arguments would you put forward for choosing an *on*-the-job approach?

A   Ability of learners to concentrate on the learning process
B   Risk of errors
C   Relevance to the informal customs and practices of the department
D   Application of learned skills to the job   **(2 marks)**

16.9 The effectiveness of a training scheme may be measured at different levels. Which of the following levels would be most appropriate for a team leader seeking to evaluate a training programme designed to improve the productivity of her section?

A   Level 1: trainee reactions
B   Level 2: trainee learning
C   Level 3: job behaviour
D   Level 5: ultimate value   **(2 marks)**

16.10 .... development is a process whereby employees are offered a wide range of developmental opportunities, rather than focusing on skills required in the current job.

Which word or phrase correctly completes this sentence?

A   Management
B   Career
C   Continuing professional
D   Personal   **(2 marks)**

16.11 Peter has been identified, using Honey & Mumford's learning styles questionnaire, as a Pragmatist learner. He is now preparing a personal development plan to improve his sales skills. Which of the following training methods is he most likely to include in his plan?

A   On-the-job coaching by his supervisor
B   A group workshop in 'interpersonal skills practice'
C   Personal development journaling
D   A computer-based training module on sales   **(2 marks)**

16.12 The HR manager of a firm has been asked to explain to the finance director the quantifiable benefits of training programmes. Which of the following might she hesitate to put forward?

A   Increased speed of working
B   Increased accuracy of work
C   Increased employee satisfaction
D   Decreased accident rates   **(2 marks)**

16.13 1   The growth or realisation of a person's ability and potential through the provision of learning and educational experiences.

       2   The planned and systematic modification of behaviour through learning events, programmes and instruction which enable individuals to achieve the level of knowledge, skills and competences to carry out their work effectively.

Which of the following is correct?

A   1 is the definition of development and 2 is the definition of training
B   1 is the definition of education and 2 is the definition of development
C   1 is the definition of training and 2 is the definition of development
D   1 is the definition of education and 2 is the definition of training **(2 marks)**

16.14 Which of the following documents would be part of a formal training needs analysis exercise?

A   An e-mail reminding you that a new piece of legislation is about to come into effect

B   A health and safety officer's report showing that a department failed its assessment in a recent fire evacuation drill

C   A set of competence standards for your job or department

D   Feedback from a colleague about the standard of your work   **(2 marks)**

16.15 .... is learning through a network of computers or the Internet (but not stand-alone CD-Rom or tuition software), so that learning support is available from on-line tutors, moderators and discussion groups.

What term is used for this important new learning technology?

A   E-learning
B   Computer based training
C   Blended learning
D   Computer based assessment   **(2 marks)**

16.16 The stages of Kolb's experiential learning cycle are as follows.

1   Draw conclusions from the experience
2   Have an experience
3   Plan the next steps
4   Reflect on the experience

Which is the correct order?

A   2, 4, 1, 3
B   2, 3, 4, 1
C   2, 4, 3, 1
D   2, 1, 4, 3   **(2 marks)**

(Total = 32 marks)

17 Performance appraisal   32 mins

17.1 Which of the following is *not* a purpose of performance appraisal?

A   Job evaluation
B   Reward review
C   Identification of training needs
D   Succession planning   **(2 marks)**

17.2 A manager is assessing the performance of her team members. In accordance with the appraisal system of the organisation, she has been given a list of characteristics and performance elements, with notes on how to interpret and apply the terms: 'integrity', 'punctuality' and so on. She is required to comment on how each appraisee measures up in terms of each factor.

Which appraisal technique is this organisation using?

A   Overall assessment
B   Grading
C   Behavioural incident
D   Guided assessment   **(2 marks)**

17.3 All of the following, except one, are sound principles for devising performance measures. Which is the exception?

A   They should be related to actual key tasks of the job
B   They should be easily achievable
C   They should be within the control of the individual
D   They should be observable or measurable   **(2 marks)**

17.4 In an appraisal interview, the manager tells the subordinate how he has been assessed – good and bad – and then gives him a chance to put questions, suggest improvement targets, explain shortcomings and identify problems.

Using Maier's classification, what is the name given to this approach to appraisal interviewing?

A   Tell and sell
B   Tell and listen
C   Problem solving
D   Sell and listen   **(2 marks)**

17.5 Which of the following is likely to be the most objective approach to appraisal?

A   Self appraisal
B   Peer appraisal
C   Upward appraisal
D   360-degree feedback   **(2 marks)**

17.6 .... is 'a process to establish a shared understanding about what is to be achieved, and an approach to managing and developing people in order to achieve it'.

Which two words correctly completes this definition?

A   Performance appraisal
B   Disciplinary action
C   Performance management
D   Peer appraisal   **(2 marks)**

17.7 Which of the following are meaningful criteria for measuring the effectiveness of an appraisal scheme?

(i)   Serious intent
(ii)   Fairness
(iii) Efficiency
(iv)   Co-operation
(v)   Results

A   (ii), (iii) and (v) only
B   (iii) and (v) only
C   (i), (ii), (iii) and (iv) only
D   (i), (ii), (iii), (iv) and (v)   **(2 marks)**

17.8 .... is the name given to gathering of appraisals from the individual, superiors, subordinates, peers and co-workers and customers.

Which word or phrase correctly completes this sentence?

A   Multi-source feedback
B   360-degree management
C   Management by objectives
D   Performance management   **(2 marks)**

17.9 Appraisal is a complex human relations and political exercise. Which of the following is *not* necessarily a helpful factor in the design of an appraisal scheme?

A   The purpose of the system is positive and clearly expressed
B   There is reasonable standardisation throughout the organisation
C   Time is allowed for appraisee preparation and appraiser training
D   There is an implied link between assessment and reward   **(2 marks)**

17.10 Which of the following is *not* a barrier to effective appraisal?

A	Appraisal is seen as a way of wrapping up unfinished business for the year
B	Appraisal is seen as conforming to Human Resource procedures
C	Appraisal is seen as an opportunity to raise workplace problems and issues
D	Appraisal is seen as an annual event

(2 marks)

17.11 Which *one* of the following criteria would *not* be suitable for evaluating an appraisal system?

A	Serious intent
B	Fairness
C	Bonuses awarded
D	Equality

(2 marks)

17.12 Which of the following is an advantage to all employees of having a formal appraisal system?

A	Suitable promotion candidates are identified
B	It provides a basis for medium-to-long term HR planning
C	Individual objectives are related to the objectives of the whole organisation
D	It provides a basis for reviewing recruitment and selection decisions

(2 marks)

17.13 A sales team is assessed according to the number of sales calls made, number of leads generated, and number and value of sales made.

Which appraisal technique is described in this example?

A	Behavioural incident
B	Rating scale
C	Guided assessment
D	Results-oriented

(2 marks)

(Total = 26 marks)

Do you know? – Personal effectiveness and communication in business

Check that you can fill in the blanks in the statements below before you attempt any questions. If in doubt, you should go back to your BPP Interactive Text and revise first.

- **T...** is a scarce resource and managers' time must be used to the best effect.

- The **c..... of c........n** will impact on the effectiveness of the communication process. The characteristics of the message will determine what communication tool is best for a given situation.

- **C..........** is an interpersonal interview, the aim of which is to facilitate another person in identifying and working through a problem.

- Counselling is facilitating others through the process of **d...... and e.......g their own problems**: it is primarily a non-directive role.

- **Communication** is a two-way process involving the t...... or e....... of information and the provision of feedback. It is necessary to direct and co-ordinate activities.

- Communication in an organisation **flows** d......, u......, s....... and d..........

- Data and **information** come from **s.......** both **inside** and **outside** an organisation. An organisation's information systems should be designed so as to obtain – or **capture** – all the relevant data and information required.

- I........ communication supplements the f....... system.

- B......... to communication include 'noise' from the environments, poorly constructed or coded/decoded messages (distortion) and failures in understanding caused by the relative position of the senders and receivers.

Did you know? – Personal effectiveness and communication in business

Could you fill in the blanks? The answers are in bold. Use this page for revision purposes as you approach the exam.

- **Time** is a scarce resource and managers' time must be used to the best effect.

- The **channel of communication** will impact on the effectiveness of the communication process. The characteristics of the message will determine what communication tool is best for a given situation.

- **Counselling** is an interpersonal interview, the aim of which is to facilitate another person in identifying and working through a problem.

- Counselling is facilitating others through the process of **defining and exploring their own problems**: it is primarily a non-directive role.

- **Communication** is a two-way process involving the transmission or exchange of information and the provision of feedback. It is necessary to direct and co-ordinate activities.

- Communication in an organisation **flows** downwards, upwards, sideways and diagonally.

- Data and **information** come from **sources** both **inside** and **outside** an organisation. An organisation's information systems should be designed so as to obtain – or **capture** – all the relevant data and information required.

- Informal communication supplements the formal system.

- Barriers to communication include 'noise' from the environments, poorly constructed or coded/decoded messages (distortion) and failures in understanding caused by the relative position of the senders and receivers.

18 Personal effectiveness and communication 39 mins

18.1 If a supervisor in the Sales department requests the help of the HR Director in a complex disciplinary matter, what direction is the communication flow?

    A   Vertical
    B   Horizontal
    C   Lateral
    D   Diagonal   (2 marks)

18.2 What name is give to the process whereby an individual defines objectives and formulates action plans for learning with a view to improving his or her own effectiveness?

    A   Coaching
    B   Mentoring
    C   Counselling
    D   Personal development planning   (2 marks)

18.3 The following, with one exception, are potential problems for time management. Which is the exception?

    A   An open door policy of management
    B   A sociable work group
    C   An assertive style of communication
    D   Reading and acting on e-mails as they are received   (2 marks)

18.4 Jared is the leader of a virtual team which stays in contact via e-mail. Team members send all messages to Jared, who forwards them to the rest of the network.

Which communication pattern is reflected in this situation?

    A   The circle
    B   The 'Y'
    C   The wheel
    D   The all-channel   (2 marks)

18.5 You are a sales representative who routinely visits customers in their homes and places of business to present the latest products and take orders (where inventory is available).

Which of the following technology tools will most directly enhance your effectiveness?

    A   Computer telephony integration
    B   Asymmetric Digital Subscriber Line (ADSL) broadband
    C   Electronic Data Interchange (EDI)
    D   Mobile communications   (2 marks)

18.6 Which of the following areas is *not* an advantage of using e-mail as a communication tool?

    A   Security
    B   Speed
    C   Multiple recipients
    D   Versatility   (2 marks)

18.7 Counselling is essentially a/an .... role.

Which of the following words correctly completes this statement.

    A   Advisory
    B   Non-directive
    C   Task-related
    D   Non-advisory   (2 marks)

18.8 Which of the following is *not* an attribute of communication through an informal organisational network or 'grapevine'?

    A   Fast
    B   Selective
    C   Accurate
    D   Up-to-date   **(2 marks)**

18.9 The following, apart from one statement, are measures for encouraging upward communication in an organisation. Which is the incorrect statement?

    A   Suggestion schemes
    B   Management by Walking Around
    C   Quality circles
    D   Exception reporting   **(2 marks)**

18.10 In the radio signal model, which of the following shows the correct order in which a message is transmitted?

    A   Feedback, Sender, Decoded message, Coded message, Receiver
    B   Sender, Decoded message, Coded message, Feedback, Receiver
    C   Coded message, Sender, Decoded message, Receiver, Feedback
    D   Sender, Coded message, Decoded message, Receiver, Feedback   **(2 marks)**

18.11 Which of the following communication mechanisms is designed to improve upward communication?

    A   Notice boards
    B   Organisation manual
    C   Team meetings
    D   Team briefings   **(2 marks)**

18.12 What is the technical term given to a fault in the communication process where the meaning of the message is lost 'in translation' from intention to language, or from language to understanding?

    A   Noise
    B   Redundancy
    C   Distortion
    D   Feedback   **(2 marks)**

18.13 According to Leavitt, which one of the following communication patterns is the fastest in terms of problem solving?

    A   Y
    B   Circle
    C   Chain
    D   Wheel   **(2 marks)**

18.14 Which of the following best defines coaching?

    A   Developing the individual by helping to build on skills and overcome weaknesses
    B   Provision of one-way instruction on formal tasks required to carry out the immediate job
    C   Offering career guidance in order to maximise the individual's potential
    D   Provision of objective advice to overcome the individual's personal problems   **(2 marks)**

18.15 Which of the following statements about non-verbal communication is *not* true?

    A   Non-verbal cues can be used to reinforce or undermine spoken messages
    B   People pay less attention to non-verbal cues than to what is being said
    C   Non-verbal cues include tone of voice and silences
    D   Non-verbal cues are a key source of feedback   **(2 marks)**

18.16 In the context of work planning and personal development planning, a SMART framework is often used as a checklist of the characteristics of effective goals.

What does the 'M' in SMART stand for?

A   Manageable
B   Measurable
C   Motivational
D   Memorable

(2 marks)

(Total = 32 marks)

Do you know? – Professional ethics in accounting and business

Check that you can fill in the blanks in the statements below before you attempt any questions. If in doubt, you should go back to your BPP Interactive Text and revise first.

- Organisations are not autonomous; they exist to serve some e...... p......, usually manifested in a group such as shareholders in a company or trustees of a charity. In particular, the **strategic apex must not lose sight of this accountability**.

- All managers have a **duty of f.... s......** to the external purpose of the organisation and this lies most heavily on the shoulders of those at the strategic apex.

- E.... and .... are about right and wrong behaviour. Western thinking tends to be based on ideas about **duty** and **consequences**. Unfortunately, such thinking often fails to indicate a single clear course of action.

- E.....thinking is also influenced by the concepts of **virtue** and **rights**.

- Ethical c....... by all members should be a major concern for management. Inside the organisation, a **c......... based** approach highlights **conformity with the law**.

- An **i....... based** approach suggests a **wider remit**, incorporating ethics in the organisation's **values and culture**.

- Organisations sometimes issue codes of conduct to ....

- As an accountant, your values and attitudes **flow through** everything you do professionally. They contribute to the **trust** the wider c......... puts in the profession and the **perception** it has of it.

- The .... (IFAC) is an international body representing all the major accountancy bodies across the world. Its mission is to develop the **high standards** of professional accountants and enhance the quality of services they provide.

Did you know? – Professional ethics in accounting and business

Could you fill in the blanks? The answers are in bold. Use this page for revision purposes as you approach the exam.

- Organisations are not autonomous; they exist to serve some external purpose, usually manifested in a group such as shareholders in a company or trustees of a charity. In particular, the **strategic apex must not lose sight of this accountability**.

- All managers have a **duty of faithful service** to the external purpose of the organisation and this lies most heavily on the shoulders of those at the strategic apex.

- Ethics and morality are about right and wrong behaviour. Western thinking about ethics tends to be based on ideas about **duty** and **consequences**. Unfortunately, such thinking often fails to indicate a single clear course of action.

- Ethical thinking is also influenced by the concepts of **virtue** and **rights**.

- Ethical conduct by all members should be a major concern for management. Inside the organisation, a **compliance based** approach highlights **conformity with the law**.

- An **integrity based** approach suggests a **wider remit**, incorporating ethics in the organisation's **values and culture**.

- Organisations sometimes issue codes of conduct to employees.

- As an accountant, your values and attitudes **flow through** everything you do professionally. They contribute to the **trust** the wider community puts in the profession and the **perception** it has of it.

- The **International Federation of Accountants** (IFAC) is an international body representing all the major accountancy bodies across the world. Its mission is to develop the **high standards** of professional accountants and enhance the quality of services they provide.

19 Ethical considerations 24 mins

19.1 Managers are said to have a .... responsibility (or duty of faithful service) in respect of the entities whose purposes they serve.

Which term correctly completes this sentence?

A Financial
B Ethical
C Fiduciary
D Fiscal (2 marks)

19.2 What is the name given to an approach to ethical decision-making which considers the 'right' decision to be the one which results in the greatest good to the greatest number of people in a given situation?

A Utilitarianism
B Deontology
C Virtue ethics
D Corporate social responsibility (2 marks)

19.3 X plc is trying to get a trading permit, for which it qualifies. Unfortunately, there is a backlog at the issuing office, and X plc has been notified that there will be a delay in the processing of its permit. The divisional manager offers a donation to the issuing office's staff welfare fund, if the official concerned will expedite the paperwork.

Which of the following statements is true of this action?

A It is not unethical, because the money is offered for positive purposes.
B It is not unethical, because X plc is legally entitled to the benefit it is claiming.
C It constitutes bribery.
D It constitutes grease money. (2 marks)

19.4 Which of the following is an approach to ethics which combines a concern for the law with an emphasis on managerial responsibility?

A Compliance based
B Integrity based
C Environmental based
D Economic based (2 marks)

19.5 Farrah works in the sales tax section of the accounts department of BCD Co. When the finance director is on holiday, Farrah notices that BCD Co has not been paying the correct quarterly amounts to the authorities. Farrah had suspected this for some time and decides to contact the authorities to tell them about the fraud. This disclosure is known as....................................

What two words correctly complete the sentence?

A Organisational accountability
B Confidentiality breach
C Corporate conscience
D Whistle blowing (2 marks)

19.6 Which of the following would raise ethical issues for a manufacturer of fast-moving consumer goods?

    (i)   The materials used in manufacture of the goods
    (ii)   The quality of the goods
    (iii)   How the goods are advertised
    (iv)   How much its raw materials suppliers pay their staff
    (v)   How the goods are packaged

    A   (ii) and (iii) only
    B   (i), (ii) and (iii) only
    C   (ii), (iii) and (v) only
    D   (i), (ii), (iii), (iv) and (v)   **(2 marks)**

19.7 Reliability, responsibility,.. , courtesy and respect are the personal qualities expected of an accountant.

Which of the following words correctly complete this statement?

    A   Accountability
    B   Social responsibility
    C   Timeliness
    D   Ambition   **(2 marks)**

19.8 You have been asked to work on a major investment decision that your company will be making, and discover that your brother-in-law is the managing director of a firm that may benefit from the outcome of the decision. You have no intention of allowing this to influence the advice you give your firm, and you know that your brother-in-law will not try to influence you in any way.

What professional quality would make you consider handing this task to a colleague, or otherwise raising questions with your superiors?

    A   Scepticism
    B   Accountability
    C   Independence of mind
    D   Independence in appearance   **(2 marks)**

19.9 Which of the following would *not* represent an ethical objective in relation to employment practices?

    A   Guarantee of minimum wages
    B   Proactive health, safety and welfare promotion
    C   Promotion of workforce diversity
    D   Employability training   **(2 marks)**

19.10 Of the three main sources of rules that regulate the behaviour of businesses, the minimum level of acceptable behaviour is set by which?

    A   Non-legal rules and regulations
    B   Ethics
    C   The law
    D   Society   **(2 marks)**

(Total = 20 marks)

20 Mixed Bank 1   56 mins

20.1 Systems are sometimes described as either open or closed.

When a system is closed it is:

A   Incapable of further technical enhancement
B   Protected from unauthorised access
C   Isolated from its external environment
D   Shut down   **(2 marks)**

20.2 Homer and Marge work for similar companies but at Marge's company a mechanistic system of management exists, in contrast to the organic approach at Homer's firm. They are discussing some of the characteristics of each system, which are outlined below.

(i)   Managers are responsible for co-ordinating tasks
(ii)   Insistence on loyalty to the organisation
(iii)   Job description are less precise, it is harder to 'pass the buck'.
(iv)   Hierarchical structure of control in an impersonal organisation

Which three would Marge recognise from her workplace?

A   (i), (ii) and (iii)
B   (i), (ii) and (iv)
C   (ii), (iii) and (iv)
D   (i), (iii) and (iv)   **(2 marks)**

20.3 What is the main focus and role of the accounting function?

A   To pay employee salaries
B   To provide information to external auditors
C   To record financial information
D   To estimate how much to spend on production   **(2 marks)**

20.4 Which of the following is a benefit of decentralisation?

A   Decisions are made at one place in the organisation
B   Reductions in bureaucracy
C   Better crisis management
D   Improves the motivation of junior managers   **(2 marks)**

20.5 A narrow span of control would be suitable where.

A   The team is not dispersed across a wide area
B   The work is of a routine nature
C   There is little similarity between team members' work
D   The team is very experienced   **(2 marks)**

20.6 When analysing the current situation in a business, a consultant will review the general environment surrounding it.

Which of the following would not be included in this analysis?

A   New legislation coming into effect in 6 months' time
B   Activities of overseas competitors
C   Interest rates
D   Independence of the non-executive directors   **(2 marks)**

20.7   How might the purchasing manager work closely with the accounting function?

    A   Processing expense claims
    B   Seeking prompt payment from customers
    C   Managing the prompt payment of suppliers
    D   Recording staff salaries   **(2 marks)**

20.8   Many organisations are described as bureaucratic. When the team, was first coined, bureaucracy was regarded as being highly efficient and there are still cases where a bureaucratic approach is appropriate. However, bureaucracy has some undesirable features. Can you identify three from the list below?

    (i)   It relies on the expertise of its members – not through standardised skills but by the importance of the mix of skills

    (ii)   Committees and reports slow down the decision-making process

    (iii)   Innovation is difficult

    (iv)   Over-prescriptive rules produce a simplistic approach to problems

    A   (i), (ii) and (iii)
    B   (i), (iii) and (iv)
    C   (ii), (iii) and (iv)
    D   (i), (ii) and (iv)   **(2 marks)**

20.9   Mr Warner, your department manager, is weighting up the benefits and disadvantages of off-the-shelf packages that have been customised so that they fit the organisation's specific requirements. From his list below can you identify two disadvantages of customisation?

    (i)   It may delay delivery of the software
    (ii)   The user is dependent on the supplier for maintenance of the package
    (iii)   The company will not be able to buy 'add-ons' to the basic package
    (iv)   It may introduce bugs that do not exist in the standard version

    A   (i) and (ii)
    B   (i) and (iii)
    C   (i) and (iv)
    D   (ii) and (iii)   **(2 marks)**

20.10   Which of the following is an external stakeholder?

    A   Professional body
    B   Customer
    C   Supplier
    D   Bank   **(2 marks)**

20.11   Which of the following is not an advantage of a matrix structure?

    A   Dual authority
    B   Greater flexibility
    C   Employee motivation
    D   Improved communications   **(2 marks)**

20.12   Which of the following parties has the main responsibility for good corporate governance?

    A   The board of directors
    B   The internal auditor
    C   The audit committee
    D   The non-executive directors   **(2 marks)**

20.13 Which of the following statements is not true in respect of the relationships between directors, shareholders and auditors?

    A   Auditors are the agents of shareholders

    B   Shareholders are accountable to auditors

    C   Auditors report to shareholders on the financial statements prepared by directors

    D   Directors are accountable to shareholders   **(2 marks)**

20.14 Which of the following statements correctly describes the principal purpose of the external audit of a company within the UK?

    A   To assist management in the preparation of the company's periodic financial statements

    B   To examine and express an opinion on the company's periodic financial statements

    C   To assist management in the maintenance of the company's accounting records

    D   To prevent and detect fraud within the company   **(2 marks)**

20.15 A record showing who has accessed a computer system is called:

    A   A fraud trail

    B   An audit trail

    C   A computer trail

    D   A password trail   **(2 marks)**

20.16 Alf Sparks is a manager of a small team designing and building a new management information system. The various levels of management that will be using the system will all have different information requirements but the qualities of good information are the same at each level. He is describing these qualities to his team.

Which of the following would be included in his explanation?

    (i)   Comprehensive

    (ii)   Relevant

    (iii)   Accurate

    (iv)   Authoritative

    A   (i), (ii) and (iii)

    B   (ii), (iii) and (iv)

    C   (i), (ii) and (iv)

    D   (i), (iii) and (iv)   **(2 marks)**

20.17 External auditors may place reliance on internal auditors' work.

Is this statement correct?

    A   External auditors need to assess the work of internal audit first

    B   Internal auditors are not independent and so cannot be relied upon

    C   Yes, always

    D   No, external auditors must always do their own work   **(2 marks)**

20.18 Which of the following costs, which might be incurred before or during the development of an information system, are capital costs?

    (i)   Hardware purchase costs

    (ii)   Costs of testing the system

    (iii)   Software purchase costs

    (iv)   Installation costs

    A   (i), (ii) and (iii)

    B   (i), (ii) and (iv)

    C   (ii), (iii) and (iv)

    D   (i), (iii) and (iv)   **(2 marks)**

20.19 Who appoints external auditors?

    A   Chairman
    B   Finance director
    C   Shareholders
    D   Trade Union   **(2 marks)**

20.20 Control over cash receipts will concentrate on three main areas.

Receipts must be .... promptly

The record of receipts must be ....

The loss of receipts through theft or accident must be ....

    A   Banked, complete, prevented
    B   Counted, accurate, reported
    C   Banked, accurate, avoided
    D   Reported, accurate, prevented   **(2 marks)**

20.21 There are three broad pre-requisites or 'pre-conditions' that must exist in order to make fraud a possibility.

What are they?

    A   Deception, criminality and opportunity
    B   Dishonesty, criminality and opportunity
    C   Dishonesty, motivation and opportunity
    D   Deception, motivation and opportunity   **(2 marks)**

20.22 The identification within a client company of financial problems, a dominant chief executive, poor internal control, unusual transactions, or a high-technology environment, are ALL indicative of:

    A   Increased scope for potential fraud
    B   A higher than normal risk audit
    C   Inadequacies in the systems of reporting
    D   The presence of going concern problems   **(2 marks)**

20.23 Data and information come from sources both inside and outside an organisation.

Which of the following represent data or information captured from within the organisation?

    (i)   Information about personnel from the payroll system
    (ii)   Market information on buying habits of potential customers from the marketing manager
    (iii)   Information on decisions taken from the minutes of a meeting
    (iv)   Value of sales from the accounting records

    A   (i), (ii) and (iii)
    B   (i), (ii) and (iv)
    C   (ii), (iii) and (iv)
    D   (i), (iii) and (iv)   **(2 marks)**

(Total = 46 marks)

21 Mixed Bank 2   58 mins

21.1 Which three of the following did *Henri Fayol* include in his five functions of management?

(i) Motivating
(ii) Co-ordinating
(iii) Commanding
(iv) Controlling

A (i), (ii) and (iii)
B (ii), (iii) and (iv)
C (i), (ii) and (iv)
D (i), (iii) and (iv)   **(2 marks)**

21.2 Which one of the statements below **best** describes contingency theory?

A Theory states that there is one best way to design an organisation

B Organisational design will be determined by a number of factors all of which depend on the others

C Companies must plan for changes to their organisation

D Companies should focus on the short-term as the future is uncertain   **(2 marks)**

21.3 *Peter Drucker* grouped management activities or operations into five categories.

Which of the following is not one of those categories?

A Setting objectives
B The job of measurement
C Planning and control
D Motivation   **(2 marks)**

21.4 Different types of power may be exercised within an organisation any different individuals.

Which type of power is associated with formal authority?

A Resource power
B Expert power
C Personal power
D Position power   **(2 marks)**

21.5 *Rensis Likert* identifies four management styles. What are they?

A Benevolent autocratic, participative, democratic, exploitative autocratic
B Benevolent authoritative, participative, exploitative authoritative, democratic
C Exploitative autocratic, benevolent autocratic, participative, laissez faire
D Benevolent autocratic, consultative participative, exploitative, laissez faire   **(2 marks)**

21.6 A company has established a project team to design a new information system. The team has had a few meetings to discuss how they are going to tackle the work, and who would do what, but some early ideas have been unsuccessful. Group members are still putting forward a number of very innovative ideas, but they often disagree strongly with each other. The group members appear to be dividing into two 'camps' each of which has an unofficial 'leader'. These two individuals agree about very little and appear to dislike each other. According to *Tuckman*, which stage in development has the project team reached?

A Forming
B Norming
C Performing
D Storming   **(2 marks)**

21.7 Which three of the following are typical of informal groups within an organisation?

(i)   Membership is voluntary
(ii)   Tasks are assigned by management
(iii)   Communication is open and informal
(iv)   Tasks are not assigned by management

A   (i), (ii) and (iii)
B   (ii), (iii) and (iv)
C   (i), (ii) and (iv)
D   (i), (iii) and (iv)   **(2 marks)**

21.8 Belbin described the most effective character mix in a team. This involves eight necessary roles, which should ideally be balanced and spread in a team.

A person who is highly strung, extrovert and passionate about the task fits into which of Belbin's roles?

(i)   Plant
(ii)   Completer Finisher
(iii)   Resource investigator
(iv)   Shaper

A   (i), (ii) and (iii)
B   (ii), (iii) and (iv)
C   (i), (ii) and (iv)
D   (i), (iii) and (iv)   **(2 marks)**

21.9 Which three of the following five team member roles do you recognise from Belbin's list of group rules?

A   Shaper
B   Plant
C   Attacker
D   Finisher   **(2 marks)**

21.10 Which of the following are positive aspects of teamworking?

(i)   Control
(ii)   Work organisation
(iii)   Knowledge generation
(iv)   Decision making

A   (i), (ii) and (iii)
B   (i) and (ii)
C   (i), (ii) and (iv)
D   All four   **(2 marks)**

21.11 Tuckman identified four stages in group development, which occur in a particular order. What is the order in which the stages occur?

A   Forming, norming, storming, performing
B   Forming, storming, performance, norming
C   Storming, norming, forming, performance
D   Storming, forming, performing, norming   **(2 marks)**

21.12 'The justification for empowering workers, or removing levels in hierarchies that restrict freedom, is that not only will the job be done more effectively but the people who do the job will get more out of it in terms of growth, challenge, responsibility and self-fulfilment'.

The thinking is in line with which management writer?

A   Herzberg
B   Fayol
C   Taylor
D   Weber   **(2 marks)**

21.13 Bruce has been on a training course to help him develop his negotiation skills and learn some new techniques.

He has been practising three of these back in the office – can you identify them?

(i)   Look for a wide variety of possible solutions
(ii)   Try to develop options that would result in mutual gain
(iii)   Create a trusting supportive atmosphere in group
(iv)   Define the problem carefully

A   (i), (ii) and (iii)
B   (ii), (iii) and (iv)
C   (i), (ii) and (iv)
D   (i), (iii) and (iv)   **(2 marks)**

21.14 There are many different methods of communication, each with its own features and limitations. Can you identify the three features/advantages of conversation as a communication technique from the list below?

(i)   Requires little or no planning
(ii)   Gives a real impression of feelings
(iii)   Complex ideas can be communicated
(iv)   Usually unstructured so can discuss a wide range of topics

A   (i), (ii) and (iii)
B   (ii), (iii) and (iv)
C   (i), (ii) and (iv)
D   (i), (iii) and (iv)   **(2 marks)**

21.15 Some meetings achieve very little because of hindrances. Sally is learning about these problems and how she can avoid them in her role as chairperson at the next project team meeting. Which two of the following are ways of avoiding participants being unclear about the purpose of the meeting?

(i)   Name the person responsible for completing each action point, and assign a completion date
(ii)   Agree goals in advance
(iii)   Include all actions required and the assigned dates in the minutes
(iv)   Prepare a focused agenda and ensure people stick to it

A   (i) and (ii)
B   (ii) and (iii)
C   (iii) and (iv)
D   (ii) and (iv)   **(2 marks)**

21.16 Vocabulary and style should contribute to the clarity of message in a presentation. It is recommended that short simple sentences are used and the presenter should avoid certain expressions. Which three from the following list should be avoided?

(i)   Acronyms
(ii)   Jargon
(iii)   Colloquialisms
(iv)   Double meanings

A   (i), (ii) and (iii)
B   (ii), (iii) and (iv)
C   (i), (ii) and (iv)
D   (i), (iii) and (iv)   **(2 marks)**

21.17 Electronic mail has so many features and advantages that it is easy to forget that there may be limitations associated with it. Can you identify the disadvantages of e-mail from the list below?

(i)   People may not check their email regularly
(ii)   Complex images do not transmit well
(iii) Requires some computer literacy to use effectively
(iv)   Lack of privacy – can be forwarded without your knowledge

A   (i), (ii) and (iii)
B   (ii), (iii) and (iv)
C   (i), (ii) and (iv)
D   (i), (iii) and (iv)   **(2 marks)**

21.18 For a formal meeting, in which order would you expect the following items to appear on the agenda?

1   Subjects for discussion
2   Minutes of previous meeting
3   Date of next meeting
4   Any other business
5   Apologies for absence
6   Matters arising

A   The sequence is 5, 2, 6, 1, 4, 3
B   The sequence is 5, 2, 1, 6, 3, 4
C   The sequence is 2, 5, 1, 6, 3, 4
D   The sequence is 2, 5, 6, 1, 4, 3   **(2 marks)**

21.19 A 360° (or multi-source) appraisal collects feedback on an individual's performance from sources such as the person's immediate superior and also his or her immediate subordinates. Identify these other sources from the list below.

(i)   Peers
(ii)   Customers
(iii) Self-appraisal
(iv)   Family and friends

A   (i), (ii) and (iii)
B   (ii), (iii) and (iv)
C   (i), (ii) and (iv)
D   (i), (iii) and (iv)   **(2 marks)**

21.20 What type of appraisal occurs when employees judge managers?

A   Peer
B   Traditional
C   Upward
D   Customer   **(2 marks)**

21.21 Which one of the following is not a general aim of an appraisal system?

A   Identify potential
B   Deal with grievances
C   Reward attainment
D   Measure performance   **(2 marks)**

21.22 Which one of the following is the person least likely to be requested to fill out feedback forms for use in a 360 degree appraisal of a sales account manager?

A   Accounts payable clerk
B   Credit sales clerk
C   Direct customer
D   Sales director   **(2 marks)**

21.23 Which of the following is not a characteristic of a learning organisation?

- A   Learning climate
- B   Enabling accounting
- C   Reward flexibility
- D   Internal exchange   **(2 marks)**

21.24 Upward appraisal is used by some businesses. This involves staff giving their opinions on the performance of their managers. There are problems with this method, which include three of the following.

Can you identify them?

- (i)   Employee point scoring
- (ii)   Fear of reprisal
- (iii)   The chance of bias is increased
- (iv)   Lack of authority

- A   (i), (ii) and (iii)
- B   (ii), (iii) and (iv)
- C   (i), (ii) and (iv)
- D   (i), (iii) and (iv)   **(2 marks)**

(Total = 48 marks)

22   Mixed Bank 3   58 mins

22.1   Which of the following is an acronym used to describe the key elements of an organisation's external environment?

- A   PERT
- B   PEST
- C   SWOT
- D   SPAM   **(2 marks)**

22.2   Henry Mintzberg categorised five basic components of an organisation.

Which TWO the following statements describes the work cf the technostructure of an organisation?

- 1   Designing systems
- 2   Organising and controlling work
- 3   Standardising work
- 4   Securing inputs

- A   1 and 2
- B   1 and 3
- C   2 and 3
- D   3 and 4   **(2 marks)**

22.3   Which of the following is a correct definition of the term 'span of control'?

- A   The number of employees reporting to one manager
- B   The number of managers to whom one employee reports
- C   The number of levels in the hierarchy
- D   The number of employees at each level of the organisation   **(2 marks)**

22.4 To whom is the internal auditor accountable?

A The directors of the company
B The employees of the company
C The shareholders of the company
D The external auditors of the company

(2 marks)

22.5 SPAMSOAP is a mnemonic for the types of internal control employed by an organisation.

Which TWO of the following are types of internal control included in SPAMSOAP?

1 Output
2 Arithmetic
3 Preventative
4 Physical

A 1 and 2
B 1 and 3
C 2 and 3
D 2 and 4

(2 marks)

22.6 Which of the following are typical responsibilities of the financial accountant in a large organisation?

1 Inventory valuation
2 Sales invoicing
3 Project appraisal
4 Payroll

A 1 and 2
B 2 and 4
C 1 and 4
D 3 and 4

(2 marks)

22.7 Who was responsible for developing the 'Situational Leadership' model?

A Blake and Mouton
B Katz and Kahn
C Hersey and Blanchard
D Tannenbaum and Schmidt

(2 marks)

22.8 Which of the following statements accurately describes a multi-disciplinary team?

A All team members collaboratively decide how to organise their work
B All team members have different skills and specialisms which they pool
C All team members can perform any and all of the group's tasks
D All team members are jointly responsible for the leadership of the team

(2 marks)

22.9 Which TWO of the following are examples of content theories of motivation?

1 Maslow's hierarchy of needs
2 Vroom's expectancy theory
3 Herzberg's two factor theory
4 Adam's equity theory

A 1 and 2
B 2 and 4
C 3 and 3
D 1 and 3

(2 marks)

22.10 Which TWO of the following are examples of 'on the job' training

    1   Formal training courses
    2   Mentoring by a colleague
    3   Self study courses
    4   Secondments to other departments

    A   1 and 2
    B   2 and 3
    C   3 and 4
    D   2 and 4   **(2 marks)**

22.11 If a manager in the purchasing department requests the help of the Human Resources Director in preparing for a difficult appraisal, what direction is the communication flow?

    A   Vertical
    B   Horizontal
    C   Lateral
    D   Diagonal   **(2 marks)**

22.12 Honey and Mumford classified four different learning styles.

Which of the following statements accurately describes the reflector?

    A   Prefers to understand principles
    B   Prefers to think things through first
    C   Prefers to try things 'hands on'
    D   Prefers to see practical examples   **(2 marks)**

22.13 'An organisation is a social arrangement which pursues collective.., which controls its own performance and which has a boundary separating it from its environment.'

Which of the following words best completes this sentence?

    A   Ambitions
    B   Stakeholders
    C   Goals
    D   Duties   **(2 marks)**

22.14 From the list below, pick out two of Mintzberg's organisational components

    (i)   Strategic apex
    (ii)   Technicians
    (iii)   Specialists
    (iv)   Support staff

    A   (i) and (ii)
    B   (ii) and (iii)
    C   (i) and (iv)
    D   (ii) and (iv)   **(2 marks)**

22.15 Which of the following are examples of weak financial control procedures?

    A   Suppliers not being paid on time
    B   Debtors not paying within credit limits
    C   Excessive bad or doubtful debts
    D   All of the above   **(2 marks)**

22.16 In a typical finance function, budgets and budgetary control would usually be the responsibility of which of the following roles?

- A   The Financial Controller
- B   The Management Accountant
- C   The Chief Executive
- D   The auditors   **(2 marks)**

22.17 Which function in an organisation is responsible for ensuring that only properly authorised purchases which are necessary for the business are made?

- A   Dispatch
- B   Internal audit
- C   Purchasing/procurement
- D   Production/operations   **(2 marks)**

22.18 What is the term given to a method of fraud in the accounts receivable area, by which cash or cheque receipts are stolen, and the theft concealed by setting subsequent receipts against the outstanding debt?

- A   Collaboration
- B   Topping and tailing
- C   Teeming and lading
- D   Understating sales   **(2 marks)**

22.19 Which of the following are purposes of a receivables control account?

- (i)   A sales ledger control account provides a check on the arithmetical accuracy of the personal ledger

- (ii)   A sales ledger control account helps to improve separation of duties

- (iii) A sales ledger control account ensures that there are no errors in the personal ledger

- (iv)   Control accounts deter fraud

- A   (i), (ii) and (iii)
- B   (ii), (iii) and (iv)
- C   (i), (ii) and (iv)
- D   (i), (iii) and (iv)   **(2 marks)**

22.20 A .... is a program which deals with one particular part of a computerised business accounting system.

Which of the following terms correctly completes this definition?

- A   Suite
- B   Module
- C   Spreadsheet
- D   Algorithm   **(2 marks)**

22.21 Power arising from an individual's formal position in the organisation is called:

- A   Coercive power
- B   Legitimate power
- C   Expert power
- D   Negative power   **(2 marks)**

22.22 What is the most important attribute of a 'group', which distinguishes it from a random crowd of people?

- A   Leadership
- B   Goals
- C   Function
- D   Identity   **(2 marks)**

22.23 Which of Belbin's nine roles does the following description apply to? Single-minded, self-starting, dedicated.

    A   Chairman
    B   Specialist
    C   Co-ordinator
    D   Teamworker   **(2 marks)**

22.24 Which of the following is a category in Maslow's hierarchy of needs theory?

    A   Psychic needs
    B   Self determination
    C   Need for affiliation
    D   Safety needs   **(2 marks)**

(Total = 48 marks)

23   Mixed Bank 4   58 mins

23.1   William Ouchi identified three types of control.

    Which of the following is not one of those?

    A   Bureaucratic control
    B   Market control
    C   Output control
    D   Clan control   **(2 marks)**

23.2   From the list below, identify the one that doesn't have the attributes of a group.

    A   The finance department of an organisation
    B   An orchestra
    C   A football team
    D   Five pop fans   **(2 marks)**

23.3   Which of the following is most clearly a sign of an ineffective group?

    A   Internal disagreement and criticism
    B   Passive acceptance of work decisions
    C   Competition with other groups
    D   Achievement of individual targets   **(2 marks)**

23.4   A leader may be distinguished from a manager by lack of dependency on:

    A   Position power
    B   Expert power
    C   Personal power
    D   Physical power   **(2 marks)**

23.5   Delegation is needed in organisations to enable a distribution of work in the organisation. Select the two best reasons why managers may be reluctant to delegate.

    (i)   Doesn't trust staff to carry out delegated tasks
    (ii)   Wants to control all activities under his or her responsibility
    (iii)   The organisation is dynamic and turbulent with constant changes
    (iv)   Is new and doesn't know how competent staff are

    A   (i) and (ii)
    B   (ii) and (iii)
    C   (iii) and (iv)
    D   (i) and (iv)   **(2 marks)**

23.6 Bill has been on a training course to learn negotiation skills. Which of the following are negotiation skills.

    (i)   Look for a wide variety of possible solutions
    (ii)   Define the problem carefully
    (iii)   Evaluate progress towards objectives
    (iv)   Try to develop objectives resulting in mutual gains

    A   (i), (ii) and (iii)
    B   (ii), (iii) and (iv)
    C   (i), (ii) and (iv)
    D   (i), (iii) and (iv)   **(2 marks)**

23.7 Leadership involves activities that are generally people-centred. Which of the following doesn't fall into this category?

    A   Creating the culture
    B   Inspiring and motivating others
    C   Reconciling individual needs with the requirements of the organisation
    D   Allocating scarce resources   **(2 marks)**

23.8 Which of the following describes an employee duty, rather than an employer duty under Health and Safety legislation?

    A   To keep all plant and machinery up to a necessary standard
    B   To ensure all work practices are safe
    C   To take reasonable care of themselves
    D   To instruct subordinates in the safe processes of the company   **(2 marks)**

23.9 Every organisation has a boundary that separates it from its environment. From an organisation's point of view, which two of the following would be part of the organisation's environment?

    (i)   Shareholders
    (ii)   Customers
    (iii)   Sales team
    (iv)   Purchasing department

    A   (i) and (ii)
    B   (ii) and (iii)
    C   (iii) and (iv)
    D   (i) and (iv)   **(2 marks)**

23.10 Which of the following disciplinary actions may be used only if it is (they are) provided for in the employee's contract of employment?

    (i)   Suspension without pay
    (ii)   Dismissal
    (iii)   Demotion
    (iv)   Suspension with pay

    A   (i) and (ii)
    B   (ii) and (iii)
    C   (iii) and (iv)
    D   (i) and (iv)   **(2 marks)**

23.11 Which type of culture according to Handy's cultural models would best fit with a matrix structure?

    A   Person
    B   Role
    C   Power
    D   Task   **(2 marks)**

23.12 Who said 'Culture is the way we do things around here'.

    (i)   Handy
    (ii)   Schein
    (iii)   Harrison
    (iv)   Deal and Kennedy

    A   (i) only
    B   (i) and (ii)
    C   (i) and (iii)
    D   (iv) only   **(2 marks)**

23.13 Which of the following are external stakeholders to an organisation?

    1   Employees
    2   Suppliers
    3   Managers
    4   Customers

    A   1 and 3
    B   1 and 4
    C   2 and 4
    D   2 and 3   **(2 marks)**

23.14 Henry Mintzberg categorised five basic components of an organisation.

Which of the following statements describes the work of the strategic apex of an organisation?

    A   Ensuring the organisation pursues its objectives and serves the needs of its owners and stakeholders
    B   Securing inputs and processing and distributing them as outputs
    C   Organising, planning and controlling work and acting as an interface
    D   Offering technical support to the rest of the structure   **(2 marks)**

23.15 Which of the following are typical responsibilities of the management accountant in a large organisation?

    1   Processing sales invoices
    2   Reconciling cash balances with bank statements
    3   Planning and preparing budgets
    4   Appraisal of capital investment projects

    A   1 and 3
    B   2 and 4
    C   1 and 4
    D   3 and 4   **(2 marks)**

23.16 Lack of control over which of the following activities can lead to the fraudulent practice of teeming and lading?

    A   Non-current asset register
    B   Budgetary system
    C   Inventory management
    D   Sales ledger and receipts   **(2 marks)**

23.17 Which of the following statements identifies three broad requisites for fraud?

    A   Collusion, opportunity, motivation
    B   Dishonesty, opportunity, motivation
    C   Opportunity, collusion, dishonesty
    D   Dishonesty, collusion, motivation   **(2 marks)**

23.18 Which type of audit is concerned with the evaluation and testing of the internal controls within an organisation?

A   Systems
B   Management
C   Transactions
D   Social   **(2 marks)**

23.19 To which of the following cultural types did Charles Handy give the name of the Greek god Dionysus?

A   Power/club culture
B   Person culture
C   Role culture
D   Task culture   **(2 marks)**

23.20 Which of the following describes the 'impoverished' style of management identified by Blake and Mouton's managerial grid?

A   High degree of concern for both people and the task
B   High concern for people and a low concern for the task
C   Low concern for people and a high concern for the task
D   Low concern for people and low concern for the task   **(2 marks)**

23.21 According to Belbin, the success of a group can depend on the balance of individual skills and personality types.

Which of the following statements are characteristics of the 'shaper'?

A   Calm, self confident and controlled – coordinating and operating through others
B   Concerned with the relationships within the group, supportive and tends to diffuse conflict
C   Highly-strung, outgoing and dynamic and committed to the task
D   Orderly, conscientious, anxious and ensures that timetables are met   **(2 marks)**

23.22 Which of the following statements describes the correct sequence between sender and receiver within the communication cycle?

A   Encoded message, medium, decoded message
B   Medium, encoded message, decoded message
C   Decoded message, encoded message, medium
D   Medium, decoded message, encoded message   **(2 marks)**

23.23 Which of the following should be the purposes of an appraisal interview?

1   To discuss employee performance
2   To discipline an employee
3   To agree an employee's salary review
4   To identify an employee's development needs

A   1 and 3
B   1 and 4
C   3 and 4
D   1 and 2   **(2 marks)**

23.24 Which of the following must be in a job description?

    1   Reporting lines
    2   Salary
    3   Hours of work
    4   Job content

    A   1 and 3
    B   2 and 4
    C   1 and 4
    D   2 and 3   **(2 marks)**

(Total = 48 marks)

24   Mixed Bank 5   58 mins

24.1   Which TWO of the following are advantages of computerised accounting packages over manual systems?

    1   They make it easier to see where a mistake has been made
    2   They can be used by non-specialists
    3   They provide more consistent processing than manual systems
    4   They are less expensive to implement

    A   1 and 2
    B   1 and 4
    C   3 and 4
    D   2 and 3   **(2 marks)**

24.2   Which of the following is normally subject to the most direct government regulation?

    A   Employment protection
    B   Corporate social responsibility
    C   Business ethics
    D   Corporate governance   **(2 marks)**

24.3   Which part of SWOT analysis considers external environmental factors?

    A   Strengths and weaknesses
    B   Strengths and threats
    C   Opportunities and threats
    D   Opportunities and weaknesses   **(2 marks)**

24.4   For which TWO of the following does the external auditor have responsibility?

    1   Evaluating the efficiency of systems and procedures
    2   Reporting to shareholders
    3   Detecting fraud
    4   Giving an opinion on financial statements

    A   1 and 2
    B   1 and 3
    C   2 and 4
    D   3 and 4   **(2 marks)**

24.5 A medium sized manufacturing firm produces a number of reports, for example, production and materials reports, marketing reports, personnel reports and financial reports.

Which TWO of the following would you expect to see in a production and materials report?

1 Transport costs
2 Wastage rates
3 Labour utilisation figures
4 Sales analyses

A 1 and 2
B 2 and 3
C 2 and 4
D 3 and 4 **(2 marks)**

24.6 Which of the following is a feature of a structured decision?

A There is a formal process for decision-making
B The decision variables are very complex
C The information needed for decision-making is unpredictable
D The manager's experience and intuition play a large part in making the decision **(2 marks)**

24.7 Who was responsible for developing the 'two-factor theory' of motivation?

A Herzberg
B Maslow
C Vroom
D Dams **(2 marks)**

24.8 Which of the following statements describes coercive power?

A Power associated with a particular role or status
B Power associated with physical force or punishment
C Power associated with control over physical resources
D Power associated with individual personality and attitudes **(2 marks)**

24.9 Which TWO of the following are parts of the job of a supervisor?

1 Managing team performance
2 Coordinating departmental objectives
3 Developing strategic plans
4 Organising the work of others

A 1 and 3
B 1 and 4
C 2 and 4
D 2 and 3 **(2 marks)**

24.10 Which of the following statements is an example of lateral communication?

A Communication between shareholders and directors
B Communication between middle managers and their first line supervisors
C Communication between heads of department reporting to the same divisional manager
D Communication between supervisors and their team members **(2 marks)**

24.11 Which TWO of the following are best shown using a bar chart?

1   The nature of activities within an action plan
2   A sequence of activities within a project
3   The time required for different activities
4   Quantitative relationships between activities

A   1 and 2
B   2 and 3
C   2 and 4
D   3 and 4   **(2 marks)**

24.12 Kolb provides a useful descriptive model of adult learning

Which of the following is the correct sequence of the four stages of the learning cycle?

A   Active experimentation, observation and reflection, abstract conceptualisation, concrete experience

B   Concrete experience, abstract conceptualisation, active experimentation, observation and reflection

C   Abstract conceptualisation, observation and reflection, active experimentation, concrete experience

D   Concrete experience, observation and reflection, abstract conceptualisation, active experimentation   **(2 marks)**

24.13 Which of the following features of organisational structure is *not* associated with flexibility and adaptability?

A   Horizontal structure
B   Shamrock organisation
C   Scalar chain
D   Project te   **(2 marks)**

24.14 Which of the following is the role of the secretary of a committee?
A   Guiding discussion in committee meetings
B   Selecting members of the committee
C   Taking and circulating minutes of the meeting
D   Determining the agenda of the meeting   **(2 marks)**

24.15 Which of Handy's 'gods' is associated with 'power culture'?

A   Zeus
B   Apollo
C   Athena
D   Dionysus   **(2 marks)**

24.16 Which of the following factors help shape an organisation's culture?

(i)   The person who founded the organisation
(ii)   The failures and successes experienced by the organisation
(iii)   Recruitment and selection
(iv)   The industry the organisation is in
(v)   Labour turnover

A   (ii) and (iv) only
B   (i), (ii) and (iv) only
C   (ii), (iii) and (iv) only
D   (i), (ii), (iii), (iv) and (v)   **(2 marks)**

24.17 In the context of the different levels of objectives that an organisation may pursue, environmental protection regulations would represent which of the following categories?

    A   Primary economic objective
    B   Non-economic, social objective
    C   Responsibility
    D   Boundary   **(2 marks)**

24.18 Three of the following are recognised advantages of a framework-based approach to ethical codes. Which is the exception?

    A   Encourages proactive discussion of issues
    B   Encourages consistent application of rules
    C   Suits complex situations and evolving environments
    D   Encourages professional development   **(2 marks)**

24.19 While out to lunch, you run into a client at the sandwich bar. In conversation, she tells you that she expects to inherit from a recently deceased uncle, and asks you how she will be affected by inheritance tax, capital gains tax and other matters – which you have not dealt with, in detail, for some years.

Which of the following principles of the ACCA Code of Ethics is raised by this scenario?

    A   Due care
    B   Integrity
    C   Professional behaviour
    D   Confidentiality   **(2 marks)**

24.20 Which one of the following would be identified as a problem with the role of non-executive director?

    A   External stakeholder security
    B   Time available to devote to the role
    C   Objective viewpoint
    D   Dual nature as full board members *and* strong, independent element   **(2 marks)**

24.21 In the context of corporate social responsibility, which two of the following might 'sustainability' involve?

    (i)   Using local suppliers
    (ii)   Maintaining long-term relationships with suppliers
    (iii)   Minimising energy consumption
    (iv)   Ethical employment practices

    A   (i) and (ii) op
    B   (i) and (iii)
    C   (ii) and (iv)
    D   (iii) and (iv)   **(2 marks)**

24.22 Which type of unemployment arises from a permanent reduction in demand for the products supplied by a single industry or group of industries with traditionally large workforces?

    A   Frictional
    B   Structural
    C   Cyclical
    D   Seasonal   **(2 marks)**

24.23 Government can directly affect an organisation by influencing

    1   Demand
    2   Capacity expansion
    3   Competition

    A   1 and 2
    B   1 and 3
    C   2 and 3
    D   1,2 and 3   **(2 marks)**

24.24 In relation to fraud prevention, what objective should external auditors have in designing and implementing their audit procedures?

    A   A reasonable prospect of detecting irregular statements or records

    B   The identification of every inconsistency or error within the records

    C   To provide a systematic check of every recorded transaction

    D   To verify pre-determined samples of all types of records   **(2 marks)**

(Total = 48 marks)

25   Mixed Bank 6   56 mins

25.1 Which of the following groups are the owners of a limited company?

    A   Executive directors

    B   Non-executive directors

    C   Stakeholders

    D   Shareholders   **(2 marks)**

25.2 Which of the following correctly describes the meaning of Mintzberg's term: 'technostructure'?

    A   Analysts such as accountants and workplanners, whose objective is to effect standardisation in the organisation

    B   The range of technology needed for effective organisational performance

    C   The organisation of shopfloor workers and their supervisors in a manufacturing environment

    D   The central strategy-setting component of organisation structure   **(2 marks)**

25.3 Z plc sources a range of complex components from suppliers which are critical to the quality of Z plc's final product. Any disruption to the supply of these components will mean that Z plc cannot maintain its service levels to its own customers.

In the purchasing of these components, which *two* of the following are *least* likely to be a component of Z plc's supply strategy?

    (i)   Long-term partnership relations with key suppliers of the components

    (ii)   A small number of suppliers of the components

    (iii)   Outsourcing production of the product to low-cost countries

    (iv)   Consolidating purchases of the components and sourcing from a single supplier to reduce sourcing costs

    A   (i) and (ii)

    B   (ii) and (iii)

    C   (iii) and (iv)

    D   (i) and (iv)   **(2 marks)**

25.4 In Robert Anthony's hierarchy, which of the following is the term given to the process of establishing means to corporate ends, mobilising resources and innovating?

    A   Strategic management

    B   Tactical management

    C   Operational management

    D   Ordinary management   **(2 marks)**

25.5 .... is the system by which organisations are directed and controlled by their senior officers.

Which two words correctly complete this definition?

A   Corporate governance
B   Strategic management
C   Executive directorship
D   Internal controls   **(2 marks)**

25.6 Which of the following statements is true of a 'progressive tax'.

A   It takes a higher proportion of a poor person's salary than of a rich person's.
B   It takes the same proportion of income in tax from all levels of income.
C   It takes a higher proportion of income in tax as income rises.
D   It is charged as a fixed percentage of the price of the good.   **(2 marks)**

25.7 In employment protection law, which of the following would constitute unfair dismissal?

A   Dismissal because the employer has ceased to carry on the business
B   Dismissal because the employer has relocated the place of work
C   Dismissal because demand for the type of work done by the employee(s) is expected to decline
D   Dismissal because the employee is pregnant   **(2 marks)**

25.8 Various groups of people might be interested in financial information about an organisation, for various reasons.

Match up each of the following groups with the primary nature of their interest in financial information.

	Groups		Interest
(i)	Shareholders	1	Ability to maintain and repay loans
(ii)	Financiers	2	Potential social contributions and impacts
(iii)	Employees	3	Management stewardship
(iv)	Public	4	Attainment of performance objectives

A   (i)2, (ii)4, (iii)1, (iv)3
B   (i)4, (ii)3, (iii)2, (iv)1
C   (i)1, (ii)2, (iii)3, (iv)4
D   (i)3, (ii)1, (iii)4, (iv)2   **(2 marks)**

25.9 The web site of a university contains a dedicated site for academic researchers, giving them access to the university's archived material, if they register and obtain a password to enter the site.

Of which type of network is this an example?
A   Internet
B   Intranet
C   Extranet
D   Local   **(2 marks)**

25.10 Business .... are a set of moral principles to guide behaviour in business contexts.

Which of the following words correctly completes the sentence?

A   Objectives
B   Controls
C   Ethics
D   Disciplines   **(2 marks)**

25.11 There are three pre-requisites for fraud: motivation, opportunity and dishonesty. Match each of these with the most immediate control strategy from the following list.

Control strategies

1   Recruitment reference checking
2   Disciplinary codes
3   Internal checks and controls

(i)   Motivation
(ii)   Opportunity
(iii) Dishonesty

A   1(i), 2(ii), 3(iii)
B   1(iii), 2(i), 3(ii)
C   1(ii), 2(iii), 3(i)
D   1(iii), 2(ii), 3(i)   **(2 marks)**

25.12 In which *one* of the following areas does a database system have significant advantages?

A   Data security
B   Data privacy
C   Development cost
D   Data management   **(2 marks)**

25.13 The .... Studies is the name given to experimental social research initiated by Elton Mayo, which identified the influence exercised by social needs and informal groups in the workplace, and gave rise to the human relations school of management.

Which word correctly completes the sentence?

A   Hofstede
B   Hawthorne
C   Ashridge
D   Minzberg   **(2 marks)**

25.14 In strategic planning, what is the purpose of environmental scanning?

A   To monitor PEST factors
B   To appraise SWOT factors
C   To monitor competitive forces
D   To audit the environmental impacts of the organisation   **(2 marks)**

25.15 What is the main focus of International Accounting Standards (IASs)?

A   Financial control
B   Accountancy training
C   Financial reporting
D   Corporate governance   **(2 marks)**

25.16 A large supermarket chain has purchased land for a new out-of-town shopping development in an area of recognised natural beauty. The organisation is now preparing plans for infrastructure development (road access, parking, power) and construction.

Level of interest

	Low	High
Low	A	B
Power		
High	C	D

Into which quadrant of the above power/interest matrix would the organisation place local nature appreciation groups, and what strategy does this indicate?

A   Consult and involve
B   Keep informed
C   Keep satisfied
D   Minimal effort   **(2 marks)**

25.17 What is a fraud response plan?

A   A strategy for preventing and controlling fraud
B   A framework of disciplinary rules and sanctions to be applied when fraud is discovered
C   The appointment of a fraud officer
D   A strategy for investigating and dealing with the consequences of suspected or identified fraud
     (2 marks)

25.18 In which *one* of the following areas is economic growth most clearly beneficial, as an objective of macro-economic policy?

A   Employment
B   Public services
C   Environment
D   Ethics   **(2 marks)**

25.19 According to Warren Bennis, which *two* of the following attributes distinguishes a leader, as opposed to a manager?

(i)   Administers and maintains
(ii)   Focuses on people
(iii)   Innovates
(iv)   Focuses on systems

A   (i) and (ii)
B   (ii) and (iii)
C   (iii) and (iv)
D   (i) and (iv)   **(2 marks)**

25.20 Comfy Dentiality, a large dental practice, is concerned with the security of its patient records. The manager amends the disciplinary rules of the practice, so that unauthorised disclosure of data by personnel can be made grounds for dismissal.

What type of approach to data security does this reflect?

A   Correction
B   Detection
C   Threat avoidance
D   Deterrence

(2 marks)

25.21

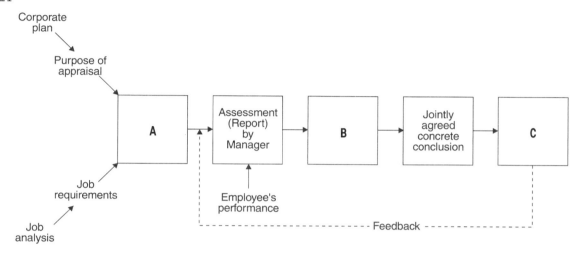

Referring to the above diagram of an appraisal system, identify which of the following labels correctly fills each of the missing labels A, B and C.

Labels:

1   Assessment interview
2   Follow up action
3   Criteria for assessment

A   A1, B2, C3
B   A2, B3, C1
C   A3, B1, C2
D   A1, B3, C2

(2 marks)

25.22 What set of environmental factors is most directly influenced by birth and mortality rates?

A   Political
B   Economic
C   Social
D   Technological

(2 marks)

25.23 In the context of rewarding team performance, team-based rewards and bonuses are more effective if individual team members' contributions and work patterns are largely ....

Which word correctly completes this sentence?

A   Independent
B   Interdependent
C   Isolated
D   Connected

(2 marks)

(Total = 46 marks)

26 Mixed Bank 7   60 mins

26.1 In a payroll system, which of the following actions would *not* require authorisation, as a standard control measure?

A Engagement or discharge of employees
B Changes in pay rates
C Statutory deductions from pay
D Overtime payments   **(2 marks)**

26.2 At a chocolate manufacturing company, one of the production mixers has recently been made redundant. Fellow shop-floor staff are outraged: he was 'the only one who knew anything about chocolate' and they had relied on his judgement for years. Protests are ignored. A week later, cement is found in a batch of crunchy bars. Two weeks later, staff refuse to work overtime. The mixer is finally reinstated.

Which *two* types of power are illustrated in this scenario by the mixer and the shop floor staff?

(i) Position power
(ii) Expert power
(iii) Personal power
(iv) Negative power

A (i) and (ii)
B (ii) and (iii)
C (ii) and (iv)
D (iii) and (iv)   **(2 marks)**

26.3 In a particular work team, Jemima is acknowledged to be the 'ideas' person who 'thinks outside the box' with creative solutions to difficult problems. However, she tends to look at the big picture, not at the details. Frank spots the gaps in Jemima's suggestions, and encourages the team to consider other options.

Match each character in this scenario with the role that they occupy in Belbin's team role model.

Characters		Roles	
A	Jemima	1	Monitor-Evaluator
B	Frank	2	Team worker
		3	Plant

A A1, B2
B A1, B3
C A2, B2
D A3, B1   **(2 marks)**

26.4 Which of the following statements about outsourcing is true?

A In order to maintain control, the organisation should outsource activities in areas of its own core competence.

B Outsourcing to external contractors harnesses specialist expertise, but at the cost of lost economies of scale.

C Outsourcing carries commercial and reputational risks.

D Outsourcing saves all the costs associated with performing a task in-house.   **(2 marks)**

26.5 Victor Vroom's 'expectancy theory' is an example of which type of motivational theory?

A Content theory
B Process theory
C Two-factor theory
D Hierarchy theory   **(2 marks)**

26.6 In the context of improving organisational communication, which *one* of the following would be helpful measures in addressing the problem of information overload on managers?

A   Using e-mail
B   Introducing reporting by exception
C   Holding regular staff meetings
D   Speed reading training for managers   **(2 marks)**

26.7 Which one of the following is represented by Blake and Mouton's managerial grid?

A   The balance in a manager's leadership style between concern for the task and concern for people and relationships

B   The success of a manager's performance, for the purposes of appraisal

C   A manager's position on the continuum between concern for task and concern for people and relationships

D   A matrix organisation structure, combining functional and line authority   **(2 marks)**

26.8 In the context of selection interviewing, which *two* of the following types of question might you use to pin down a candidate who seems reluctant or unable to give a definite answer?

(i)   Open
(ii)   Closed
(iii)   Leading
(iv)   Probing

A   (i) and (ii)
B   (i) and (iii)
C   (i) and (iv)
D   (ii) and (iv)   **(2 marks)**

26.9 In the context of motivation, workers may have the attitude that work is not an end in itself, but a means to other ends, through earning financial rewards.

What term is given to this attitude?

A   Theory Y
B   Job enrichment
C   Instrumental orientation
D   Performance-related pay   **(2 marks)**

26.10 In the context of performance appraisal, what does the term 'tell and listen' refer to?

A   An approach to appraisal interviewing
B   An approach to upward appraisal
C   A barrier to effective appraisal
D   None of the above   **(2 marks)**

26.11 Which of the following is likely to pose the *least* number of problems for effective time management?

A   Personal work patterns
B   Meetings
C   The telephone
D   Personal availability   **(2 marks)**

26.12 According to the hierarchy of needs (a motivational theory put forward by Maslow) which *two* of the following rewards might you pursue in order to have your esteem needs satisfied?

    (i)   Opportunity to undertake further professional development
    (ii)   Award of a departmental prize for your performance
    (iii)   Receiving praise on an achievement from your work team
    (iv)   Being invited to join colleagues for lunch

    A   (i) and (ii)
    B   (ii) and (iii)
    C   (iii) and (iv)
    D   (i) and (iv)   **(2 marks)**

26.13 If a team has been functioning for some time, it may grow complacent with its performance, and start to devote more attention to relationship and power issues with in the group.

    In the group development model, which of the following terms would be used for this stage of the team's development?

    A   Forming
    B   Norming
    C   Dorming
    D   Storming   **(2 marks)**

26.14 In a typical recruitment and selection process, in what order would the following steps be carried out. Assign each a number in the sequence, from 1 (first) to 5 (last).

    (i)   Preparing job descriptions
    (ii)   Selection interviewing
    (iii)   Reference checking
    (iv)   Selection testing
    (v)   Preparing person specifications

    A   1(i), 2(ii), 3(iii), 4(iv), 5(v)
    B   1(ii), 2(iv), 3(i), 4(iii), 5(iv)
    C   1(iii), 2(i), 3(v), 4(ii), 5(iv)
    D   1(i), 2(v), 3(ii), 4(iv), 5(iii)   **(2 marks)**

26.15 One of the distinctions between coaching and mentoring is that a .... is not usually the immediate superior of the person being helped.

    Which word correctly completes this sentence?

    A   Coach
    B   Mentor
    C   Coachee
    D   Mentoree   **(2 mark)**

26.16 A popular approach to self development is for employees to reflect on work incidents, and assess whether and how they might adjust their behaviour to gain more successful outcomes in future.

    On which school of learning theory is this approach based?

    A   Behaviourist psychology
    B   Cognitive psychology
    C   Contingency theory
    D   Learning styles   **(2 marks)**

26.17 Which *two* of the following factors establish the independence of an internal auditor?

    (i)   The auditor's mandatory authority

    (ii)   The auditor's involvement in the activities being appraised

    (iii)   The auditor's own professionalism

    (iv)   The auditor's freedom from accountability

    A   (i) and (ii)

    B   (i) and (iii)

    C   (i) and (iv)

    D   (ii) and (iv)   **(2 marks)**

26.18 A manager is coming up to retirement in a year's time. In which of the following circumstances would the organisation be most likely to consider external recruitment, rather than internal promotion, to fill the position?

    A   The organisation has a policy of staff development and succession planning

    B   The vacancy is a new skill requirement that would take time to develop in-house

    C   The organisation is looking to introduce a culture of innovation for the first time

    D   The organisation has a very strong managerial culture, which it wishes to preserve   **(2 marks)**

26.19 In which one of the following areas is there an advantage to using formal off-the-job training courses as opposed to on-the-job or experiential learning methods?

    A   Level of risk for acquiring new skills

    B   Relevance of learning to the job

    C   Application of learning to the job

    D   Continuity of work effort   **(2 marks)**

26.20 .... occurs when a person is penalised for giving information or taking action is pursuit of a claim of discrimination

Which word or words correctly complete this statement?

    A   Direct discrimination

    B   Indirect discrimination

    C   Victimisation

    D   Terrorisation   **(2 marks)**

26.21 Which of the following would be considered a potentially sensitive or negative element of an effective equal opportunities policy?

    A   Flexible working and career break programmes

    B   Monitoring numbers and performance of ethnic minority staff

    C   Diverse job interview panels

    D   Counselling and disciplinary policies on discrimination   **(2 marks)**

26.22 Which of the following checks would the external audit function be responsible for?

    A   Separation of duties for independent proving of work

    B   Arithmetic checks on the accuracy of data recording and calculation

    C   Creating and preserving records that confirm accounting entries

    D   Considering whether directors act on internal audit information   **(2 marks)**

26.23 The effectiveness of training programmes can be evaluated using a five-level model by Hamblin. Assign the correct number from 1 to 5 to each of the following levels.

- (i)   Ultimate value
- (ii) Changes in job behaviour
- (iii) Trainee reactions
- (iv) Trainee learning
- (v)   Impact on organisational results

- A   1(i), 2(ii), 3(iii), 4(iv), 5(v)
- B   1(iii), 2(iv), 3(ii), 4(v), 5(i)
- C   1(ii), 2(iii), 3(iv), 4(i), 5(v)
- D   1(iii), 2(i), 3(v), 4(ii), 5(iv)   **(2 marks)**

26.24 In the context of data security, which *two* of the following are examples of physical access controls to protect computer equipment or data storage media?

- (i)   Card entry systems
- (ii) Back-up controls
- (iii) Personal identification numbers
- (iv) Logical access systems

- A   (i) and (ii)
- B   (ii) and (iii)
- C   (i) and (iii)
- D   (ii) and (iv)   **(2 marks)**

26.25 An organisation's employees are one of its connected stakeholders.

Is this statement true or false?

- A   True
- B   False   **(2 marks)**

(Total = 50 marks)

27 Mixed Bank 8   120 mins

27.1   An organisation which restructures through a major de-layering exercise has as a result moved to a shorter scalar chain and a narrower span of control.

Is the above statement true or false?

- A   True
- B   False   **(2 marks)**

27.2   Which of the following is the main function of marketing?

- A   To maximise sales volume
- B   To identify and anticipate customer needs
- C   To persuade potential consumers to convert latent demand into expenditure
- D   To identify suitable outlets for goods and services supplied   **(2 marks)**

27.3   Which one of the following has become an established best practice in corporate governance in recent years?

- A   An increasingly prominent role for non-executive directors
- B   An increase in the powers of external auditors
- C   Greater accountability for directors who are in breach of their fiduciary duties
- D   A requirement for all companies to establish an internal audit function   **(2 marks)**

27.4 In a higher education teaching organisation an academic faculty is organised into courses and departments, where teaching staff report both to course programme managers and to subject specialists, depending on which course they teach and upon their particular subject specialism.

According to Charles Handy's four cultural stereotypes, which of the following describes the above type of organisational structure?

A Role
B Task
C Power
D Person **(2 marks)**

27.5 At what stage of the planning process should a company carry out a situation analysis?

A When converting strategic objectives into tactical plans
B When formulating a mission statement
C When validating the effectiveness of plans against outcomes
D When formulating strategic objectives **(2 marks)**

27.6 Which one of the following is a potential advantage of decentralisation?

A Greater control by senior management
B Risk reduction in relation to operational decision-making
C More accountability at lower levels
D Consistency of decision-making across the organisation **(2 marks)**

27.7 Which one of the following is an example of an internal stakeholder?

A A shareholder
B An non-executive director
C A manager
D A supplier **(2 marks)**

27.8 According to Mendelow, companies must pay most attention to the needs of which group of stakeholders?

A Those with little power and little interest in the company
B Those with a high level of power but little interest in the company
C Those with little power but a high level of interest in the company
D Those with a high level of power and a high level of interest in the company **(2 marks)**

27.9 What is the responsibility of a Public Oversight Board?

A The establishment of detailed rules on internal audit procedures
B The commissioning of financial reporting standards
C The creation of legislation relating to accounting standards
D The monitoring and enforcement of legal and compliance standards **(2 marks)**

27.10 The ageing population trend in many European countries is caused by a increasing birth rate and an increasing mortality rate.

A True
B False **(2 marks)**

27.11 Which one of the following is consistent with a government's policy objective to expand the level of economic activity?

A An increase in taxation
B An increase in interest rates
C An increase in personal savings
D An increase in public expenditure **(2 marks)**

27.12 Martin is an experienced and fully trained shipbuilder, based in a western European city. Due to significant economic change in supply and demand conditions for shipbuilding in Martin's own country, the shipyard he worked for has closed and he was made redundant. There was no other local demand for his skills within his own region and he would have to move to another country to obtain a similar employment, and could only find similar work locally through undertaking at least a year's retraining in a related engineering field.

Which of the following describes the type of unemployment that Martin has been affected by?

A   Structural unemployment
B   Cyclical unemployment
C   Frictional unemployment
D   Marginal unemployment   **(2 marks)**

27.13 When an organisation carries out an environmental scan, it analyses which of the following?

A   Strengths, weaknesses, opportunities and threats
B   Political, economic, social and technological factors
C   Strategic options and choice
D   Inbound and outbound logistics   **(2 marks)**

27.14 Which of the following is data protection legislation primarily designed to protect?

A   All private individuals and corporate entities on whom only regulated data is held
B   All private individuals on whom only regulated data is held
C   All private individuals on whom any data is held
D   All private individuals and corporate entities on whom any data is held   **(2 marks)**

27.15 Which of the following types of new legislation would provide greater employment opportunities in large companies?

A   New laws on health and safety
B   New laws to prevent discrimination in the workplace
C   New laws making it more difficult to dismiss employees unfairly
D   New laws on higher compensation for employer breaches of employment contracts   **(2 marks)**

27.16 The total level of demand in the economy is made up of consumption, ... , government expenditure and net gains from international trade.

Which of the following correctly completes the sentence above.

A   Savings
B   Taxation
C   Investment
D   None of the above   **(2 marks)**

27.17 Which set of environmental factors does a lobby group intend to directly influence?

A   Political
B   Technological
C   Demographic
D   Economic   **(2 marks)**

27.18 Adrian is the manager of a call centre. Consultants have advised him that by reorganising his teams to complete highly specific tasks the call centre will be able to increase the throughput of work significantly, as well as increasing the number of sales calls made to the public. The reorganisation proposals are unpopular with many workers, who feel that their jobs will become tedious and repetitive.

The proposal to reorganise the work of the call centre utilises principles put forward by which school of management thought?

A   The human relations school
B   The empirical school
C   The scientific school
D   The administrative school   **(2 marks)**

27.19 The original role of the accounting function was which one of the following?

A   Providing management information
B   Recording financial information
C   Maintaining financial control
D   Managing funds efficiently   **(2 marks)**

27.20 Tax avoidance is a legal activity whilst tax evasion is an illegal activity.

Is this statement true or false?

A   True
B   False   **(2 marks)**

27.21 The system used by a company to record sales and purchases is an example of which of the following?

A   A transaction processing system
B   A management information system
C   An office automation system
D   A decision support system   **(2 marks)**

27.22 The implementation of a budgetary control system in a large organisation would be the responsibility of the internal auditor.

Is this statement true or false?

A   True
B   False   **(2 mark)**

27.23 Which type of organisation would have the retail prices it charges to personal consumers subject to close scrutiny by a regulator?

A   A multinational corporation
B   A multi-divisional conglomerate
C   A national utilities company
D   A financial services provider   **(2 marks)**

27.24 The central bank has announced a 2% increase in interest rates.

This decision has the most direct impact on which department of a large company?

A   Marketing
B   Treasury
C   Financial accounting
D   Production   **(2 marks)**

27.25 The major purpose of the International Accounting Standards Board (IASB) is to ensure consistency in
....

Which two words complete this sentence?

A   Financial control
B   Corporate reporting
C   External auditing
D   Internal auditing   **(2 marks)**

27.26 Farrah, Gordon, Helene and Ian work in the finance department of X Co, which has separate financial
accounting and management accounting functions. Farrah deals with payroll, the purchase ledger and
sales invoicing. Gordon's duties involve inventory valuation, budgetary control and variance analysis.
Helene deals with fraud prevention and detection, and internal control. Ian carries out risk assessments,
investment appraisals and assists in project planning.

Which member of the department works in the financial accounts function?

A   Farrah
B   Gordon
C   Helene
D   Ian   **(2 marks)**

27.27 In an economic environment of high price inflation, those who owe money will gain and those who are
owed money will lose.

Is this statement true or false?

A   True
B   False   **(2 marks)**

27.28 To whom is the internal auditor primarily accountable?

A   The directors of the company
B   The company as a separate entity
C   The shareholders of the company
D   The employees of the company   **(2 marks)**

27.29 Which one of the following is a DISADVANTAGE of a computerised accounting system over a manual
accounting system?

A   A computerised system is more time consuming to operate
B   The operating costs of a computerised system are higher
C   The computerised system is more costly to implement
D   A computerised system is more error prone   **(2 marks)**

27.30 Calum works in the internal audit department of Z Co. His duties involve the identification, evaluation
and testing of internal controls. He produces reports to senior management on these activities.

For which type of audit is Calum responsible?

A   Operational audit
B   Transactions audit
C   Social responsibility audit
D   Systems audit   **(2 marks)**

27.31 What is the primary responsibility of the external auditor?

A   To verify all the financial transactions and supporting documentation of the client

B   To ensure that the client's financial statements are reasonably accurate and free from bias

C   To report all financial irregularities to the shareholders of the client

D   To ensure that all the client's financial statements are prepared and submitted to the relevant
authorities on time   **(2 marks)**

27.32 Which of the following are substantive tests used for in the context of external audit of financial accounts?

    A   To establish whether a figure is correct
    B   To investigate why a figure is incorrect
    C   To investigate whether a figure should be included
    D   To establish why a figure is excluded   **(2 marks)**

27.33 In the context of fraud, 'teeming and lading' is most likely to occur in which area of operation?

    A   Sales
    B   Quality control
    C   Advertising and promotion
    D   Despatch   **(2 marks)**

27.34 In order to establish an effective internal control system that will minimise the prospect of fraud, which one of the following should be considered first?

    A   Recruitment policy and checks on new personnel
    B   Identification of areas of potential risk
    C   Devising of appropriate sanctions for inappropriate behaviour
    D   Segregation of duties in critical areas   **(2 marks)**

27.35 The leadership style that least acknowledges the contribution that subordinates have to make is

....

Which word correctly completes this sentence?

    A   Authoritarian
    B   Autocratic
    C   Assertive
    D   None of the above   **(2 marks)**

27.36 Renata has attended a leadership development course in which she experienced a self-analysis exercise using the Blake and Mouton managerial grid. The course leader informed her that the results suggested that Renata demonstrated a 9.1 leadership style, which suggested that she is highly focused on achieving the objectives of the team.

What other conclusion may be drawn in relation to Renata's leadership style?

    A   She maximises the involvement of her team
    B   She demonstrates little concern for people in the team
    C   She balances the needs of the team with the need to complete the task.
    D   She favours psychologically close manager subordinate relationships   **(2 marks)**

27.37 Jackie leads an established team of six workers. In the last month, two have left to pursue alternative jobs and one has commenced maternity leave. Three new staff members have joined Jackie's team.

Which one of Tuckman's group stages will now occur?

    A   Norming
    B   Forming
    C   Performing
    D   Storming   **(2 marks)**

27.38 Richard is a highly enthusiastic member of his team. An extrovert by nature, he is curious and communicative. He responds to new challenges positively and has a capacity for contacting people exploring anything new. However, his attention span is short and he tends to become less involved in a task once his initial interest has passed.

According to Belbin's team roles theory, Richard displays the characteristics of which of the following?

A   Monitor-evaluator
B   Plant
C   Resource-investigator
D   Company worker   **(2 marks)**

27.39 Which one of the following statements is correct in relation to monetary rewards in accordance with Herzberg's Two-Factor theory?

A   Pay increases are a powerful long-term motivator
B   Inadequate monetary rewards are a powerful dissatisfier
C   Monetary rewards are more important than non-monetary rewards
D   Pay can never be used as a motivator   **(2 marks)**

27.40 Which one of the following is a characteristic of a team as opposed to a group?

A   Members agree with other members
B   Members negotiate personal roles and positions
C   Members arrive at decisions by consensus
D   Members work in cooperation   **(2 marks)**

27.41 According to Victor Vroom:

Force (or motivation) = ... × expectancy

Which of the following words completes Vroom's equation.

A   Needs
B   Valence
C   Opportunity
D   None of the above   **(2 marks)**

27.42 According to Handy's 'shamrock' organisation model, which one of the following is becoming progressively less important in contemporary organisations?

A   The permanent, full-time work force
B   The part-time temporary work force
C   The role of independent sub-contractors
D   The role of technical support functions   **(2 marks)**

27.43 Which pattern of communication is the quickest way to send a message?

A   The circle
B   The chain
C   The Y
D   The wheel   **(2 marks)**

27.44 Poor quality lateral communication will result in which of the following?

A   Lack of direction
B   Lack of coordination
C   Lack of delegation
D   Lack of control   **(2 marks)**

27.45 Role playing exercises using video recording and playback would be most effective for which type of training?

A   Development of selling skills
B   Regulation and compliance
C   Dissemination of technical knowledge
D   Introduction of new processes or procedures   **(2 marks)**

27.46 In the context of marketing, the 'four P's' are price, place, promotion and ....

Which word correctly completes this sentence?

A   Processes
B   Production
C   Product
D   Purchasing   **(2 marks)**

27.47 In relation to employee selection, which type of testing is most appropriate for assessing the depth of knowledge of a candidate and the candidate's ability to apply that knowledge?

A   Intelligence testing
B   Personality testing
C   Competence testing
D   Psychometric testing   **(2 marks)**

27.48 A company has advertised for staff who must be at least 1.88 metres tall and have been in continuous full-time employment for at least five years.

Which of the following is the legal term for this unlawful practice?

A   Direct discrimination
B   Indirect discrimination
C   Victimisation
D   Implied discrimination   **(2 marks)**

27.49 Gloria has the responsibility to work with selected management trainees in her organisation. Her objective is to help the trainees over the medium to long-term with their personal career development. Supporting and encouraging them to fulfil their potential is an integral part of her role. Gloria has no involvement in the technical content of the trainee managers' work.

Which of the following roles does Gloria fulfil?

A   Buddy
B   Counsellor
C   Mentor
D   Instructor   **(2 marks)**

27.50 Gils is conducting an appraisal interview with his assistant Jill. He initially invites Jill to talk about the job, her aspirations, expectations and problems. He adopts a non-judgmental approach and offers suggestions and guidance.

This is an example of which approach to performance appraisal?

A   Tell and sell approach
B   Tell and listen approach
C   Problem solving approach
D   360 degree approach   **(2 marks)**

(Total = 100 marks)

Answers

1 Business organisations and their stakeholders

1.1   C   **Rationale**: Collective goals or aims are a feature of organisations.

          Pitfalls: Watch out for closely related terminology like 'goals' and 'tactics'. You might have thought 'tactics' would fit here, but they are the lower level plans of functions: they may not be shared by the organisation as a whole.

          Ways in: If you didn't know the definition, you could have got to the answer by ruling out the other options. Stakeholders doesn't fit 'pursues'; profits are not the objective of all organisations; and tactics are at a lower level than goals.

1.2   C   **Rationale**: Synergy is the 2 + 2 = 5 factor, and is one of the key reasons for the formation of teams and organisations.

          Pitfalls: You need to read all the options carefully, especially if they look similar and all 'sound' plausible.

          Ways in: You should be able to define the other options, to confirm that they do not fit the definition given.

1.3   B   **Rationale**: In a limited company, the owners (shareholders) are separate from the managers of the concern (board of directors).

          Pitfalls: Some options look plausible because of the wording. 'Limited' doesn't mean 'only being allowed to trade up to' – but looks as if it might. The second half of the statement about partnerships is true – but this doesn't mean that the first half is also true.

          Ways in: You should have been able to rule out A (no company's turnover is limited), C (sole traders do have personal liability for debts: they do not have 'limited liability') and D (ordinary partnerships are different from limited companies).

1.4   D   **Rationale**: Such an organisation is part of the public sector. The voluntary sector comprises charities and other organisations whose members are volunteers. Private sector comprises non-governmental organisations, such as limited companies. The question specifically states that the organisation is run by central not local government.

          Pitfalls: Watch out for 'public' and 'private' sector terms – and be able to distinguish clearly between them.

          Pitfalls: Don't get sidetracked by the link between 'overseas markets' and 'geographical'.

1.5   B   **Rationale**: All these groups have a legitimate stake in the enterprise: the government, as a regulator; employees, as participants in the business; and environmental pressure group and local residents, because of potential impacts.

          Pitfalls: Don't forget external stakeholders!

1.6   C   **Rationale**: Primary stakeholders are those who have a contractual relationship with the organisation, including some internal and connected stakeholders. Secondary stakeholders are therefore external stakeholders.

1.7   B   **Examiner's comments**. The examiner commented that many students struggled with this question. Measures such as value for money or efficiency are often used in not-for-profit organisations such as local authorities. Students should not restrict their studies to the public sector perspective.

1.8   D   **Rationale**: A co-operative is a business which is owned by its workers or customers, who share the profits. Others features include open membership, democratic control, distribution of surplus in proportion to purchases and promotion of education.

2 The business environment

2.1 C **Rationale**: PEST stands for Political, Economic, Socio-cultural and Technological.

Pitfalls: SWOT (Strengths, Weaknesses, Opportunities, Threats) is a related exercise, as PEST data is fed into the O/T part of the business appraisal.

Ways in: You could eliminate as many distractors as you could identify: SMART (Specific, Measurable, Attainable, Relevant, Time-bounded) refers to objective-setting. WTO is the World Trade Organisation.

2.2 C **Rationale**: This would be interpreted as corruption. The other options are usually legitimate methods of influence. Although B may be questionable in some parts of the world, in others like the UK it is perfectly legitimate.

2.3 D **Rationale**: The statement defines demographics. Ergonomics is a study of the interaction of humans and their environments (used in design of office equipment and furniture, for example). Psychographics is the study of psychological factors (used in selection testing, for example).

Ways in: You could eliminate as many distractors as you could define in other ways.

2.4 C **Rationale**: Virtual organisation is the collaboration of geographically dispersed individuals and teams, specifically using the latest information and communication technology (ICT) enablers: the Internet, web-conferencing and so on.

2.5 B **Rationale**: Information technology has enabled managers or staff 'lower down' the hierarchy to make decisions previously made by middle management. This is known as delayering.

Pitfalls: You may have been tempted to think that this was downsizing. Downsizing, however, means reducing staff from all levels or layers in the business.

Ways in: It is 'layers' of middle management that have been removed. This may help to direct you to the answer 'delayering'.

2.6 A **Rationale**: This constitutes unfair selection for redundancy (on the basis of recent age discrimination legislation): redundancy is potentially fair grounds for dismissal as long as the basis of selection is fair. Options B and D are potentially fair grounds: there should be a reasonable attempt at performance or disciplinary management (warnings, training etc). You may have hesitated over C, but this is an example of 'substantial reasons' that would be considered by a tribunal.

Ways in: You could narrow the options by considering that there must be *some* way for companies to dismiss incompetent or deliberately obstructive employees.

2.7 C **Rationale**: Increasing diversity has an impact on HR policies in regard to equal opportunity and prevention of discrimination. Falling birthrates creates an aging workforce and skill shortages. All organisations need to take account of environmental regulation and consumerism. An increase in single-member households will impact on *some* organisations: notably, those which market goods and services to this segment (eg single-serve pack sizes), but the questions said 'most' organisations.

Pitfalls: You need to think through a range of compliance, marketing and skilling issues when appraising socio-cultural factors.

2.8 D **Rationale**: The other forces are bargaining power of suppliers and rivalry amongst current competitors in the industry.

Pitfalls: The five forces model is basic: you really need to learn the details...

2.9 C **Rationale**: Socio-economic groupings are often the basis on which markets are segmented, so that products/services and marketing messages can be targeted appropriately (to people with the right levels of income, aspiration, education and so on). You might have paused over Human Resources, because social class includes education factors, but the data cannot be used to predict skill availability.

2.10 A **Rationale**: Procurement, technology development, HR management and infrastructure are support activities. Inbound and outbound logistics, operations, marketing/sales and service are primary activities.

2.11 B **Rationale**: Technology is no longer regarded purely as a threat to job security: it can also support higher-level skilling, options for home-working, cleaner and safer work environments, better employee communications (eg through an intranet) and so on. Option A is true, because IT systems support lower-level decision making and direct communication between strategic apex and operational staff: replacing the role of middle management. Option C is true, because new technologies reduce product life cycles: products and processes can swiftly become obsolete. Option D should be obviously true: think of e-mail at one end of the scale, and 'virtual organisations' at the other.

2.12 B **Examiner's comments**: The examiners commented that only 31% of students chose the correct option. Steve, Sam, and Sunny all have support roles and the words 'administration' and 'information technology' should have immediately indicated a support role for Steve and Sam. Sunny's procurement role was not so clear cut but the responsibilities for dealing with the suppliers are sufficient to conclude that Sunny also has a support role.

2.13 B **Examiner's comments**: The examiner commented that only 20% of students chose the correct option. Options A and D are incorrect because there is no certainty that the job will be offered or accepted. Option C is incorrect because waiting a few weeks leaves the employee open to risks in those weeks.

2.14 C **Rationale**: Low switching costs means that it will be easy for customers to change from existing suppliers to a new supplier: this would facilitate entry to the market. The other options should clearly pose difficulties to a new entrant: not yet big enough to benefit from economies of scale (against competitors who are); high start-up costs; high degree of recognition of and loyalty to existing brands.

2.15 B Delegating

Rationale: Outsourcing (contracting some of the firm's activities to external providers) and delayering (removing levels of the organisation hierarchy) are strategies for downsizing (reducing the number of staff permanently or directly employed by the firm). Delegating is the process whereby a superior gives a subordinate part of his or her own authority to make decisions.

2.16 B **Rationale**: Option A may *reflect* a cultural trend (increasing expectation of quality of working life, say), but it is a compliance issue, as is option C. Option D is a demographic trend.

2.17 B **Rationale**: Lifestyle is generally considered a reflection of economic status and conditions, not a determinant of them. (For market segmentation purposes, for example, lifestyle factors are often measured in terms of attitudes, interests and opinions, rather than purely economic factors.)

3 The macro-economic environment

3.1 D **Rationale**: Exchange rates are a target of monetary policy: government policy on the money supply, the monetary system interest rates, exchange rates and the availability of credit. Fiscal policy is government policy on the three other options.

Pitfalls: This whole syllabus area is full of fine distinctions in terminology, which lend themselves to testing in a Multiple Choice and Objective Testing format.

Ways in: If you knew that there was a distinction between fiscal and monetary policy, you might have identified exchange rates as the only monetary issue.

3.2   C   **Rationale**: A budget surplus occurs when a government's income exceeds its expenditure: there is a negative PSNCR or PSDR. When a government's expenditure exceeds its income, so that it must borrow to make up the difference, there is a positive PSNCR and we say that the government is running a budget deficit.

              Ways in: If you recognised that a negative PSNC means no borrowing, you might have been able to start eliminating some options...

3.3   D   **Rationale**: The definition clearly distinguishes an indirect tax (eg sales tax) from a direct tax, which is paid direct by a person to the Revenue authority (eg income tax, corporation tax, capital gains tax and inheritance tax). Options A and B refer to the proportion of income taken by a tax.

3.4   C   **Rationale**: Increasing taxation lowers demand in the economy because people have less of their own money after tax for consumption or saving/investment. Increasing public expenditure should increase the level of consumer demand. Decreasing taxation has the opposite effect. Lowering interest rates should stimulate investment (by companies) and consumer expenditure, even if only after a time lag.

3.5   D   **Rationale**: An increase in the exchange rate makes a country's exports more expensive to overseas buyers, and imports cheaper: it therefore has the opposite of the first three effects. The lower cost of imports, however, is likely to reduce the rate of domestic inflation.

              Pitfalls: The permutations of increases/decreases in interest rate can be confusing: ensure that the logic makes sense to you!

              Ways in: You could group options B and C together (increased cost = reduce demand): since both cannot be the answer, and there is only one answer, neither of these options can be correct. This gets you quite a long way towards the solution... So if you don't know an answer, don't panic: logic can often help!

3.6   B   **Rationale**: Harmonisation of technical standards (eg for quality and safety) supports the free movement of labour, goods and services – and hence, free competition. (It is a feature of the European market, for example.) The other options are tariff (taxes and duties on goods entering the country) and non-tariff barriers to trade.

3.7   A   **Rationale**: Frictional unemployment occurs when there is difficulty in matching workers quickly with jobs. This means that frictional unemployment is temporary and short term and so statement 1 is true. A government can encourage labour mobility by offering individuals financial assistance with relocation expenses and by improving the flow of information on vacancies. This means that statement 2 is true.

3.8   A   **Rationale**: Government policy on taxation, public spending and public borrowing relates to fiscal policy. Government policy on interest rates and exchange rates are part of the monetary policy.

3.9   A   **Rationale**: Debts lose 'real' value with inflation: a company that owes a lot of money would effectively pay less (in real terms) over time. The other organisations would suffer because: inflation would make exports relatively expensive and imports relatively cheap; business might be lost due to price rises; and the cost of implementing price changes would be high.

3.10   D   **Rationale**: The four main objectives of macroeconomic policy relate to economic growth, stable inflation, unemployment and the balance of payments (balance between exports and imports).

3.11   D   **Rationale**: Recession is part of the business cycle: demand for output and jobs falls, and unemployment rises until recovery is well under way. Option A is an example of frictional unemployment; option B of seasonal unemployment; option C of technological unemployment.

              Pitfalls: It is easy to confuse cyclical with seasonal unemployment, or frictional unemployment that occurs on a seasonal basis (eg option A). You need to associate cyclical employment firmly with *business* cycles.

3.12   A   **Rationale**: It is particularly tempting to equate a trade surplus or deficit with a 'profit' or 'loss' for the country, but this is not the case.

3.13 A

3.14 B   **Rationale**: Potential growth is the rate at which the economy would grow if all resources were utilised: it is therefore determined by factors in the capacity of the economy (supply side), such as increases in the amount of resources available, or in the productivity or resources. Actual growth is determined both by growth in output (supply side) *and* aggregate demand (demand side). Options C and D were merely distractors.

4   Micro economic factors

4.1   B   In a free market economy, it is the interaction of supply and demand through the price mechanism that determines what should be produced and who should get it.

4.2   A   The supply curve for a perfectly competitive firm is its marginal cost curve above the average variable cost curve. The firm will not continue to produce if price is less than average variable cost.

4.3   D   Nothing. A minimum price (floor price) only leads to excess supply if it is set *higher* than the equilibrium price.

4.4   C   The other options relate to movements *along* the supply curve.

4.5   C   The effect of price being above the equilibrium (market clearing) price is that supply will extend and demand will contract.

4.6   D   A rise in the price of overseas holidays will lead to a movement along the demand curve rather than a shift in the demand curve.

4.7   B   Generally, if incomes fall, demand will fall.

4.8   C   Demand will transfer to the substitute.

4.9   D   Carpet underlay is a complement to carpet.

4.10   C   An increase in demand for cars will lead to an increase in demand for petrol, tyres and navigation systems. It will not increase the demand for holidays although people may use their cars to go on holiday.

4.11   B   This is a supply-side factor.

4.12   B   A reduction in income tax will increase real household income, and so demand for normal products will shift to the right – quantity demanded will be greater at any given price. Items A and D will cause a leftward shift in the demand curve. Item C would cause a movement to the right along the demand curve.

4.13   D   Coffee and tea are substitute products. Thus, a fall in the price of coffee will result in higher demand for coffee and lower demand for its substitute product, tea. The price of tea might therefore fall. Demand for drinking cups is probably insufficiently related to the consumption of coffee to make them a complementary product to coffee. Even so, lower coffee prices would be likely to raise the demand for drinking cups rather than reduce it.

4.14   D   The term 'inferior good' is a technical term in economics. An example of such a good might be small 'starter' homes.

4.15   D   It is assumed that cut flowers and flower vases are complementary goods. The rise in price of cut flowers will have an adverse effect on demand for flower vases, and the demand curve for flower vases will shift to the left. Given no change in supply conditions for vases, the new equilibrium price for vases will be lower.

4.16 B   As sea ferry tickets and hovercraft tickets are substitute goods, an increase in the price of hovercraft tickets will cause a shift to the right (increase in demand) for sea ferry tickets. Given no change in supply conditions, the consequence will be an increase in the number of sea ferry tickets sold, at a higher price than before.

4.17 A   A fall in the price of **sterling** would make London hotels cheaper for foreign tourists. A fall in the price of aeroplane tickets would make London cheaper to visit for foreign tourists. Events 2 and 3 would lead to a **rise** in demand for hotel rooms. In contrast, a fall in the value of the US dollar would make the UK more expensive to visit for US tourists and tourists from other countries where the US dollar is widely used, and demand for hotel rooms in London would fall.

4.18 C   A demand curve shifts to the left when demand for the good at any given price level is less than before. Changes 2 and 4 both have this effect, although Change 4 applies to normal goods, **not** to inferior goods. Change 1 causes a movement along the existing demand curve. Change 3 causes a shift to the **right** of the demand curve.

4.19 B   When rent controls are eased, the effect is similar to raising or removing minimum prices in the rented housing market. We should expect higher rents, more supply of housing, and a closing of the gap between demand for rented housing and supply of rented accommodation. Changes 2 and 3 should therefore occur. The reverse of Change 1 should happen, and homelessness should decrease. Given widespread homelessness, it is unlikely that the easing of rent controls will have any effect on demand for owner-occupied dwellings.

4.20 D   All of the above.

4.21 C   The income elasticity of demand measures the responsiveness of demand to changes in consumers' incomes. An 'inferior' good has a negative income elasticity: as incomes fall, more is bought.

4.22 B   A change in the price of a good will lead to a movement along the supply curve, not a shift in the curve itself.

4.23 C   As costs incurred in a producing sofas have fallen, producers will be prepared to produce more at any given price. A change in the price of sofas will lead to a movement along the supply curve. A decrease in the price of a substitute will lead to a decrease in the demand for sofas.

4.24 D   Percentage change in quantity = 50%. Percentage change in price = 25%.

4.25 A   Consumer surplus is the excess between what consumers are prepared to pay for a good or service and the prevailing market price they have to pay to purchase it.

4.26 B   To increase market share requires greater quantities of the firm's products to be both demanded and supplied. To sell more, a firm needs to lower price. For this to be profitable, demand must be elastic. To produce more, supply must also be elastic.

4.27 B   A rise in household incomes will lead to a shift in the demand curve, not the supply curve.

4.28 D   Assuming a normal good, a decrease in price results in a greater quantity being demanded. Given that demand is price elastic, the increase in quantity will be proportionally greater than the price fall.

4.29 D   Imagine you can buy a second car for $10,000 or buy a bike for $100 and they both give you the same extra utility. You wouldn't choose to buy the car as you're paying much more to achieve the same utility as you could get from buying the bike. If you get 10 times more utility for one thing compared to another you'd be prepared to pay 10 times more for it.

5 Business organisation, structure and strategy

5.1   D   **Rationale**: Line authority can easily be shown on the organisation chart.

Pitfalls: You may have hesitated if you didn't know the difference between functional authority (where an expert department has authority over the activities of other departments in the areas of its expertise eg the HR department setting recruitment policy for the sales and production departments) and line authority (direct authority flowing down the chain of command). However, you only needed to know the meaning of line authority to see that the statement was untrue.

Ways in: You may have paused to ask whether an organisation chart can improve internal communications, but it does in one key way: by highlighting the length and complexity of lines of communication between people who need to co-ordinate their work.

5.2   D   **Rationale**: This is the definition of span of control: all the others are distractors.

Pitfalls: All the distractors are plausible: note the need to think them through carefully. Option A is close to the correct definition – but if you think about it, the number of subordinate employees includes *all* those below the manager, whereas span of control is direct reports only.

5.3   B   **Rationale**: Support base is not one of Mintzberg's components of organisation structure: the other correct terms are middle line and support staff.

Pitfalls: The basic terminology of well-known models is must-learn material!

5.4   B   **Rationale**: While there may be elements of functional and geographical organisation (leading you to consider a hybrid structure), Y plc's situation suits divisionalisation: more or less autonomous product and regional businesses, with co-ordination from head office. 'Diversification' and 'acquisition' are good pointers to divisionalisation.

Pitfalls: Don't get sidetracked by the link between 'overseas markets' and 'geographical'.

5.5   C   **Rationale**: Matrix organisation is based on dual command: the classical principle of unity of command is 'one person, one boss'.

5.6   D   **Rationale**: Option A is a fact. Option B is true, because of informal 'short cuts' which are often developed and shared, by-passing health and safety rules and procedures. Option C is true, because the 'grapevine' encourages knowledge sharing and multi-directional communication. Option D is not true: managers can feed information into the grapevine and be part of their own informal networks.

5.7   C   **Rationale**: A centralised organisation is one in which authority is concentrated in one place. If all decisions are made in the same place then it will be easier for the decision-makers to see the 'bigger picture' and therefore understand the consequences of their decisions. Options A, B and D are advantages of decentralisation, where decisions are delegated.

Pitfalls: You may have hesitated over option D. The idea is that control and accountability are lessened as decisions are made further away.

5.8   A   **Rationale**: Statement (i) is true. Statement (ii) is not, because the informal organisation has its own agenda. Statement (iii) is not, because a strong informal organisation with its own agenda can undermine the formal organisation: create damaging rumours, safety/quality shortcuts, distractions from task goals etc.

6 Organisational culture and committees

6.1   A   **Rationale**: The role culture is a bureaucratic or mechanistic culture, as described in the scenario. Task culture is project-focused; existential culture is person-focused; and power culture is leader-focused.

Pitfalls: If you didn't know Harrison's model well, you might have confused 'focus on the task' (see in the scenario) with a task culture, or the strong central leadership with a 'power' culture.

6.2   D   **Rationale**: This is a problem with strong cultures (and ultra-cohesive groups).

Pitfalls: The other statements are plausible: you need to come up with counter-arguments to show that they are not always true. B is most plausible because it makes a limited claim that values 'can' replace rules: think of health and safety or financial controls, however, to disprove the claim.

Ways in: You could rule out two of the statements because they are dogmatic (so that just one counter-example would make them untrue).

6.3   C   **Rationale**: There are many spheres of culture: nation, ethnic group and social class are only three of them. 'Culture' applies to categories of people including genders, social classes and organisations.

6.4   B   **Rationale**: The fourth dimension in Hofstede's model is masculinity-femininity.

6.5   D   **Rationale**: Assumptions are foundational ideas that are no longer even consciously recognised or questioned by the culture, but which 'programme' its ways of thinking and behaving. Values and beliefs are the next level up: they are consciously held concepts which give meaning to the next level up again – observable factors such as rituals, artefacts and behaviour.

6.6   B   **Rationale**: This is just a case of learning who is associated with which theory and definition. For the FAB/F1 exam, the theorists' names are important.

6.7   A   **Examiner's comments**: The examiner commented that only 27%of students chose the correct answer. Make sure that you learn the distinctions between the cultural dimensions.

6.8   B   **Rationale**: R & D tends to be concerned with product research (not market research), and many organisations have internal R & D functions.

Pitfalls: Be aware of the difference between product and market research.

Ways in: If you were able to rule out statement (i), you were only left with two options to choose from – and you should be able to rule out statement (iv) if you know any organisations with an internal R & D department, leaving you with the correct option.

6.9   A   **Rationale**: Intangibility refers to the fact that there are no material or physical aspects to a service: physical elements help to reduce this effect, and make the provision concrete for the customer. Inseparability and perishability refer to the fact that services are created and consumed at the same time: they cannot be stored – and pose challenges to demand forecasting and scheduling. Variability refers to the fact that services are specific to the situation and cannot easily be standardised.

Ways in: What do physical elements *do* for a customer purchasing eg a train ride or legal advice? If you knew the meaning of the term 'intangible', the answer to this question would get you to the correct answer.

6.10   B   **Rationale**: A sales orientation assumes that customers must be persuaded to buy the products that the firm produces. A production orientation assumes that customer will buy whatever is produced: the focus of the firm is on meeting demand. A marketing orientation seeks to determine the needs, wants and values of customers and to produce what customers want to buy.

Pitfalls: Don't confuse selling and marketing!

6.11   B   **Rationale**: HRM is concerned with the most effective use of human resources. It deals with staffing levels, motivation, employee relations and employee services. It is the marketing function which manages an organisation's relationship with its customers, not HRM. Note that increasingly, HRM is undertaken by line managers as well or instead of HR departments.

6.12   D   **Rationale**: A standing committee is formed for a particular purpose on a permanent basis. Joint committees are formed to co-ordinate the activities of two or more committees: they need not be permanent. Task forces and ad hoc committees are specifically *not* permanent: they fulfil their allocated task and then wind up.

Pitfalls: The confusion of related terminology is often the target of testing.

6.13 A **Rationale**: HR and line departments generally provide details of salary/wage rates, time sheets etc – but the finance department generally administers payroll, so Josh is likely to be responsible.

6.14 A **Rationale**: Time, expense and compromise decisions are some of the disadvantages of a committee so Paul is correct. There are, however, many advantages to committees as well.

6.15 C **Rationale**: Diane and Joanne work at operational level as they are concerned with routine activities. Lesley is at an intermediate level and is managing resources. She is therefore part of tactical management. Tracey is concerned with direction setting for the business and is therefore part of strategic management.

6.16 B **Rationale**: Low masculinity (or femininity) is about high regard for values such as focus on relationships and quality of working life, and the acceptability of such values for both men and women: Mr Q's nurturing style would score on this dimension. His approach does not really say anything about power-distance (command-and-control v delegation-and-involvement). There are elements of uncertainty-avoidance in his attempt to minimise staff insecurity – but this would be high UA, not low UA.

Pitfalls: Don't confuse the masculine/feminine dimension with straightforward gender stereotypes!

6.17 C **Rationale**: Dependency increases stakeholder power and creates risks and constraints. A buyer would not necessarily want a supplier to be dependent on its business (for ethical reasons), any more than it would want to be dependent on a supplier (for bargaining and supply risk reasons). The other three are clearly desirable.

Pitfalls: You may have hesitated over information-sharing, because of intellectual property and confidentiality issues – but it is necessary for high-interest, high-power 'key players'.

6.18 A **Rationale**: Internal stakeholders include employees and management and so Janet is the only internal stakeholder. Customers and suppliers (like Mary at P Co) are connected stakeholders. Pressure groups such as D Group are external stakeholders.

7 Corporate governance and social responsibility

7.1 D **Rationale**: Statement (i) is incorrect, because there is no such 'guarantee'; statement (ii) because it is not necessarily so, and statement (iv) because other organisations (eg charities, government bodies) are often more concerned with social responsibility than businesses.

Ways in: It is always worth checking to see if logic helps. Words like 'guarantee' often signal an untrue statement, because they make such extreme claims. And if statement (i) is therefore incorrect, you've halved your options. It should then be obvious that (iv) is incorrect (if you think about a hospital, say).

7.2 B **Rationale**: Agency theory suggests that managers will look after the performance of the company if doing so serves their own interests: hence performance incentives and rewards. Stewardship theory views the managers as stewards of the assets of the firm. Stakeholder theory argues that managers have a duty of care to a range of organisational shareholders.

Ways in: You could have ruled out Options C and D as irrelevant, and then worked on the implications of stewardship and agency.

7.3 C **Rationale**: The objective of corporate governance is overall performance, enhanced by good supervision and management, within best practice guidelines. Business is to be conducted in a way that is both ethical and effective from the perspective of all stakeholders – not just shareholders.

7.4 B **Rationale**: Corporate governance includes the selection of senior officers (with influence over the future direction of the organisation), and relationships between the organisation and its key stakeholders. It is therefore regarded as being of strategic importance.

7.5   A   **Rationale:** This is a feature of poor corporate governance because it makes way for self-interested decision-making. The others may 'look' like negatives, but are in fact the opposites of three other features of poor corporate governance: lack of independent scrutiny; lack of supervision; and an emphasis on short-term profitability (which can cause pressure to conceal problems or manipulate accounts).

Ways in: You could have got to the answer with logic, with a sound grasp of corporate governance – but it would be worth learning the list of features of poor corporate governance, so you can recognise them in an exam question.

7.6   C   **Rationale:** These are some of the roles fulfilled by the board. The audit committee reviews financial statements, audit procedures, internal controls and risk management. The Public Oversight Board monitors and enforces legal and compliance standards. The nomination committee oversees the process for board appointments.

Pitfalls: You need to be able to distinguish clearly between all the various participants in the corporate governance system.

Ways in: Strategy formulation should have steered you towards the correct answer.

7.7   D   **Rationale:** Professional ethics concern the individual ethical sphere, not the wider sphere of Corporate Social Responsibility which operates at the level of the firm. All of the others are CSR principles: human rights as a component of ethical trading and investment; employee welfare as part of ethical employment; and support for local suppliers as an example of sustainability.

Pitfalls: The combinations were designed to test if your thinking was limited to internal organisational matters or commercial matters.

7.8   B   **Rationale:** Employment protection is just one example of an area which is subject to law. Corporate governance is an area which is subject to codes of best practice (and law in some countries). While 'ethics' in general is arguably not directly regulated, professional ethics is, due to the ethical codes and educational standards of professional bodies, which control their members. CSR is therefore the area subject to least regulation and most managerial discretion.

7.9   C   **Examiner's comments:** The examiner commented that only 47% of candidates answered this question correctly. Codes of practice are usually associated with a principles-based approach (rather than a rules-based approach) and so options A and B should have been easily eliminated. The words 'guidance' and 'should adopt' were the key words to lead to the correct option.

7.10 C   **Rationale:** Only Option C fulfils the requirement for full independence of the body that sets directors' remuneration (to avoid directors' awarding themselves unjustifiable rewards!). A nomination committee has the separate task of overseeing board appointments.

7.11 C   **Rationale:** This is the definition used by the Accounting Standards Board. Options B and D are other corporate governance reports that may be required (Option B being a requirements of the London Stock Exchange). Option A is just a distractor.

7.12 B   **Rationale:** 4 is incorrect and can actually be problematic for non-executive directors. Non-executive directors often have limited time to devote to the role as they are likely to have other time consuming commitments.

7.13 D   **Rationale:** 'Accommodation' here means adjusting to the demands of others (rather than being proactive). Option A describes a proactive strategy; Option B a defence strategy. Option C is a distractor, in case you were taking a wild guess and focused on 'accommodation' in the sense of housing for business facilities.

8   The role of accounting

8.1   B   **Rationale:** This is the main or overall aim of accounting.

8.2   B   **Rationale:** You should have a general feel for how long double entry bookkeeping has been around, even if you cannot remember the exact year.

8.3   D   **Rationale**: Non-commercial undertakings still prepare annual financial statements, for accountability to their trustees, members or funding bodies.

8.4   B   **Rationale**: The Management Accountant provides information for management: cost accounting, budgets and budgetary control and financial management of projects. The Financial Controller is responsible for routine accounting, accounting reports, cashiers' duties and cash control. A Treasurer would be responsible for treasury management: raising and investing funds and cash flow control. The Finance Director approves the budget.

8.5   B   **Rationale**: Time sheets are used to calculate hours worked and overtime, in order to calculate gross pay (before deductions). The system information for management (payroll analysis), information for employees (pay slips) and methods of payment (credit transfer forms), are all outputs.

       Pitfalls: It is worth sorting out the inputs, processing and outputs of any financial system.

8.6   A   **Rationale**: All the other aims relate to the control system relating to receivables and sales.

       Pitfalls: You have to get straight in your mind which transactions and controls relate to payables/purchases and which to receivables/sales.

       Ways in: Careful reading of the question should allow you to eliminate options B and D immediately (sales/supply, not purchases). You then have to think how credit notes work – but the fact that Option A mentions the 'purchase' ledger, and Option C the 'sales' ledger should lead you to the right answer.

8.7   C   **Rationale**: Option A refers to the income statement, not the statement of financial position. Options B and D are distractors, referring to audit reports.

       Pitfalls: If you were in a hurry, you might have selected option A immediately you saw the words 'true and fair'. Avoid such mistakes by reading through *all* question options carefully, keeping an open mind.

8.8   D   **Rationale**: An integrated package is expected to do everything, so it may have fewer facilities than specialised modules (especially as it also requires more computer memory). The other options are advantages of integration: ability to update multiple records from one data entry; ability to extract data from all relevant sources to compile specified reports; and less likelihood of discrepancies in different records.

8.9   B   **Rationale**: A suite is a set of several modules. A spreadsheet is a type of program, and a format for displaying and processing data: it is often used to integrate data from accounting modules for decision-support and management information systems. A database is a collection of data.

8.10   C   **Rationale**: The system does not by itself provide for data security: appropriate controls have to be designed and implemented by users. Computer files are as vulnerable to theft and wilful damage as manual files, and are perhaps even more vulnerable to corruption or loss of data through user error.

8.11   D   **Rationale**: Unfortunately: 'garbage in, garbage out!'...

8.12   B   **Examiner's comments**: The examiner commented that only 36% of students got this question correct. Mandatory reports to government and shareholders are required under national legislation. Codes of corporate governance are principles-based and voluntary in nature. International and local Accounting Standards do affect the content and presentation of accounts but it is national legislation which dictates the requirements for preparation and filing of accounts.

8.13   B   **Rationale**: 'Garbage in, garbage out'!

8.14   B   **Rationale**: Exception reporting focuses attention on those items where performance differs significantly from standard or budget.

       Pitfalls: The word 'exceptional' was placed in other options as a distractor!

8.15 C **Rationale**: Back-up storage, virus detection software and password protection are basic security requirements of any computer system, regardless of whether they are connected to the Internet. Because this system is not so connected, however, it cannot receive e-mail.

Pitfalls: Make sure you distinguish between intranet (internal network) and Internet (world wide network), and read questions carefully to see which is being discussed.

8.16 C **Rationale**: This is the definition of an Expert System. It is distinguished from a DSS by supporting decision-making at a higher and less structured level. Expert systems draw on a knowledge base to solve well-defined technical problems.

Pitfalls: 'Management', 'Expert' and 'Decision' were plausible distractors: make sure you can distinguish between the different types of system, and how they contribute to decision-making and problem solving.

8.17 D **Rationale**: Data is any kind of unprocessed information, and information is any kind of processed information.

8.18 D **Rationale**: The DBMS is the software that builds, manages and provides access to a database. Data storage is carried out in the database itself. The database administrator is a person (not a part of the system) who controls the system. EPOS is a form of data collection and input.

8.19 A **Rationale**: Data can be lost or corrupted as the result of deliberate actions such as fraud, sabotage, commercial espionage or malicious damage – as well as human error. The other statements are true: new staff pose a security risk because of the risk of human error (if they are inexperienced or untrained); it is impossible to prevent all threats (important to be realistic!); and smoke detectors are an example of protection from physical risks (in this case, fire).

Pitfalls: Don't forget physical security measures: you may have discounted Option D too quickly. Data security also involves protection against fire, flood, interruption of power source and so on.

8.20 B **Rationale**: OAS systems, with functions such as word processing, digital filing, email, schedulers and spreadsheets, are primarily designed to streamline administrative tasks: document management, communication, data management.

8.21 A **Rationale**: Managers need most information, at a significant level of detail, to enable them to make planning and control decisions. They have special access to information, because they can arrange to obtain the information they need through the accounting system. Shareholders and tax authorities are entitled to certain information, focused on particular areas of interest (mainly profits). Financial analysts may only have access to public information and reports.

8.22 C The audit committee of the board of directors

Rationale: In order to control the risks of fraud and error, the internal audit department should be separate from the finance department.

8.23 D **Rationale**: A quick phone call may be a more efficient way of obtaining or giving information than e-mail, for example. You may have hesitated over Option C because of often-stated warnings about 'garbage in, garbage out'. The risks of input error are the same – but computerised systems reduce the further risk of computation errors.

8.24 C **Rationale**: The purchasing or procurement function is responsible for authorising purchases (and suppliers) and approving. The other functions contribute, however: production, by requisitioning only needed items; goods inwards, by checking that what was purchased is what is in fact received; and accounts, by seeking proper documentary evidence and authorisation for payment.

8.25 B **Rationale**: This should be obvious from the context (debts represent goods bought on credit: hence, credit control) – but make sure that you could define the roles of all the other options, if you needed to!

9 Control, security and audit

9.1   B   **Rationale**: Options A, C and D were identified as aims of internal controls in the Turnbull report. However, the report also states that even a sound system of internal control reduces, but does not eliminate, the possibilities of poorly-judged decisions, human error, deliberate circumvention of controls and unforeseeable circumstances. Systems only provide reasonable (not absolute) assurance.

         Ways in: If you had to guess, you could probably see that option B is an exaggerated claim. Look out for options that say 'always' or 'never' or 'total', in a similar vein: these are much more likely to be untrue than true, in the complex world of business...

9.2   C   **Rationale**: Non-discretionary controls are as described: as opposed to discretionary controls which are subject to human choice. 'Mandated' is a similar idea, but mandated controls are required by law and imposed by external authorities (as opposed to voluntary controls, chosen by the organisation). Detect controls are controls designed to detect errors once they have happened. Administrative controls are to do with reporting responsibilities, communication channels and other means of implementing policies.

         Pitfalls: There is so much terminology in this area: fertile ground for exam questions. Be able to use distinctions within classifications (as in 'discretionary and non-discretionary', or 'prevent, detect, control') as well as across classifications, as in this question.

9.3   B   **Rationale**: Organisation in this context means identifying reporting lines, levels of authority and responsibility to ensure that everyone is aware of their control responsibilities. The full mnemonic stands for: Segregation of duties; Physical; Authorisation and approval; Management; Supervision; Organisation; Arithmetical and accounting; and Personnel.

9.4   D   **Rationale**: This is an internal control, rather than an internal check. Internal checks are more about dividing work (so that the work of one person can be independently proved by that of another) and using 'proof measures' to ensure the accuracy of records and calculations: options A, B and C are examples.

9.5   A   **Rationale**: Internal audit is *independent*, but is still part of the internal control system: it is a control which examines and evaluates the adequacy and efficacy of other controls. Internal auditors should report direct to the audit committee of the board of directors (in order to preserve independence). It is *external* audit which is for the benefit of shareholders: internal audit is a service to management.

         Ways in: Once you realised that the options were circling round different aspects of the definition of internal audit, and the difference between internal and external audit, you would be better able to sort out which statement was given to you 'straight' – and which were opposites of the true points.

9.6   C   **Rationale**: This should be straightforward if you think through what the potential threats involve. Lightning strike or electrical storms are a key cause of power supply failures and surges which may effect computer functions. Fire and accidental damage are also physical threats to data and equipment. Hacking is a non-physical threat involving unauthorised access to data (possibly resulting in data theft or destruction).

9.7   B   **Rationale**: System recovery procedures are set in place for activation in the event of breakdown, to get the system up and running again: this is a contingency control, because it plans for a 'worst case scenario'. Password access is an example of a *security* control: protecting data from unauthorised modification, disclosure or destruction of data. Audit trails (showing who has accessed a system and what they have done) and data validation (checking that input data is not incomplete or unreasonable) are examples of *integrity* controls: controls which maintain the completeness and correctness of data in the system.

         Pitfalls: There is a lot of vocabulary and procedure in this area: make sure that you could answer questions on a variety of different data security controls.

9.8   D   **Rationale**: It would be a limitation if controls *depended* on the method of data processing. The others are limitations, because: the costs of control must not outweigh the benefits; there is always potential for both human error and deliberate override of controls by management; and controls are designed to cope with routine transactions, not non-routine transactions.

9.9   B   **Rationale**: The primary responsibility of the external auditor is to report to shareholders on whether the client's financial statements are accurate and free from bias ('true and fair'). The other options are true.

9.10   B   **Rationale**: Substantive tests 'substantiate' the figures in the accounts. They are used to discover *whether* figures are correct or complete, not *why* they are incorrect or incomplete, or how the figures 'got there'. Option A is the aim of *compliance* tests.

9.11   C   **Rationale**: Correct controls are designed to enable the organisation to minimise the effect of errors: in this case, restoring data from the back-ups if the main data store is corrupted. Prevent controls are designed to prevent errors from happening in the first place, and detect controls are designed to detect errors once they have happened.

9.12   B   **Rationale**: Audit trails enable system administrators to maintain security, check transactions (in order to identify errors and fraud), recover lost transactions and monitor the use of network resources. Passwords are access controls and archives are long-term back-up storage: both are good system controls. Cookies are programmes that enable the personalisation and tracking of web browsing: not relevant here!

Pitfalls: There is lots of terminology in this area: get to grips with all the basic terms and procedures.

9.13   B   **Rationale**: A systems audit is based on the testing and evaluation of internal controls. A probity (or transaction) audit checks account entries to identify errors or omissions which may indicate fraud. A social audit measures the social responsibility or social impacts of the business.

Pitfalls: This is another area of distinctive clusters of terminology: make sure you can identify operational, systems and transactions audits – and the types of tests they use (compliance v substantive).

9.14   C   **Rationale**: This may suggest that internal audit work is not properly planned, reviewed or documented: a failure of due professional care. The other options show good status, scope and technical competence.

10   Identifying and preventing fraud

10.1   C   **Rationale**: Collusion is working with another party (eg customers or suppliers) to commit fraud. Misrepresentation is stating that something is so, when it is not, in order to mislead (eg overstating profits). Fictitious sales might involve generating false invoices or overcharging customers, in order to inflate revenue figures.

10.2   D   **Rationale**: Payslips can be deliberately miscalculated to pay extra amounts. Staff may collude with customers to under-record quantities of despatched goods on delivery notes so the customer pays less: conversely, employees may collude with suppliers to pay invoices for larger quantities than were actually delivered. Option (iv) may have made you hesitate: it seems such a positive, desirable thing! However, profits in excess of target may be siphoned off, with less scrutiny once targets have been met.

10.3   D   **Rationale**: One form of fraud is the intentional misrepresentation of the financial position of the business. Bad debt policy may be unenforced deliberately, in order to overstate profits.

10.4   B   **Rationale**: This is an important distinction in making sense of the three prerequisites for fraud: dishonesty (a willingness to act dishonestly), motivation (an incentive or reason to act dishonestly) and opportunity (an opening to act dishonestly). An unwillingness to act in these ways is a definition of honesty!

10.5 A   **Rationale**: Increased competition is a risk factor (because it may put pressure on managers to manipulate results) – but it is an *external* factor. The others are internal factors which increase risk because they disrupt supervision and control (options B and C) or introduce unknown factors (option D).

Pitfalls: Look carefully at question stems for qualifier key words such as 'internal' and 'external'.

10.6 C   **Rationale**: This may seem like normal behaviour in a 'workaholic' office culture, but failure to take full holiday entitlement may signal an employee trying to prevent a temporary replacement from uncovering a fraud. The other options are factors in *reducing* risk: lack of segregation enables fraud to go undetected; low staff morale is often a motive for fraud (in retaliation against the firm); and an autocratic management style may prevent questioning.

Pitfalls: Ensure that you know what 'segregation of duties' means: otherwise, it might look like a risk factor (because it sounds like allowing people to work independently and unsupervised, say).

10.7 C   **Rationale**: There is a reduction in working capital, which makes it more difficult for the company to operate effectively, potentially resulting in corporate collapse. The other effects should be obvious (remember, we are talking about removal of funds or assets and not overstatement of profits and/or net assets). Reputational damage refers to loss of shareholder and market confidence in the organisation's management when the fraud emerges.

10.8 B   **Rationale**: This should be clear from the context, because of the collusion with customers (if you remembered what collusion was). Physical security refers to keeping assets under lock and key: not to be dismissed as a fraud prevention measure! Sequential numbering works because it is easy to spot if documents are missing. Authorisation policies increase checks and accountabilities.

10.9 A   **Rationale**: The directors are responsible for the conduct of the business, the deterrence and detection of fraudulent (and other dishonest) conduct, and the reliable reporting of financial information. Not all organisations have a fraud officer. The responsibility of the external auditor is only to express an opinion on the financial statements, although audit procedures should have a reasonable expectation of detecting misstatements arising from fraud. The audit committee reviews the organisation's performance in fraud prevention, but also reports to the board.

10.10 C   **Rationale**: There are plenty of ways of securing access to data, using available software tools: password protection, encryption and so on. (Of course, the firm has to *use* them, but that is a separate issue!) Hackers are unauthorised people breaking into the system. Lack of managerial understanding creates loopholes in controls, and the ability to conceal fraud by technical staff. Integrated systems also help to conceal fraud, by ensuring that alterations to records are consistent: fewer discrepancies to trigger investigation.

10.11 C   **Rationale**: Investors will be making decisions (and taking risks) on inaccurate information. Suppliers will extend credit without knowing the true financial position of the company. (Staff and customers will eventually be effected if shortfalls in working capital threaten the business…)

10.12 D   **Rationale**: These are measures for fraud prevention and control. A fraud response plan specifically deals with investigating and dealing with the consequences of identified frauds. This includes taking immediate steps to secure the security of records that will be investigated (options A and C) and launching an investigation into the method and extent of fraud (option B).

10.13 C   **Rationale**: Limit controls limit opportunity for fraud: another example is limiting access to the computer network by means of passwords. Segregation of duties means ensuring that functions which *together* facilitate fraud are performed by *different* individuals: eg separating the cheque signing function from the authorisation of payments. Appropriate documentation involves recording, authorising and tracking transactions through purchase requisitions, orders, invoices and so on.

10.14 B   **Rationale**: Performance-based rewards increase pressures and motivation for managers to manipulate results.

Ways in: A good approach for these sorts of question is to work systematically through the options to eliminate those which are clearly true. That way, even if you are left with an option you are not sure about (because performance-related pay for managers is such a popular strategy, say), it is the best option you've got.

11 Leading and managing people

11.1 C **Rationale**: Position power is legitimate organisational authority, by virtue of a position in the organisation hierarchy: managers depend largely on it for their influence. Leaders are often required to exercise informal, interpersonal forms of influence, such as person power (charisma, inspiration) and expert power (valued knowledge). Physical power (intimidation) should be used by neither managers nor leaders!

Pitfalls: the classifications of power are a rich source of related terminology, and hence a potential source both of confusion – and of exam questions!

11.2 A **Rationale**: Frederick Taylor is associated with scientific management. The other writers are associated with the human relations school, focusing on the role of 'higher order' needs (such as challenge and interest in the work) in human motivation.

Ways in: You could halve your options by realising that Maslow and Herzberg belong to the same school: therefore the 'odd one out' must be one of the other two.

11.3 C **Rationale**: The 'country club' is low-task, high-people focus and 1.9 on Blake and Mouton's managerial grid. This describes Monica.Impoverished is 1.1 (both low), task management is 9.1 (all about the task), and dampened pendulum is 5.5 (swinging between the two extremes).

11.4 C **Rationale**: Psychologically distant managers (PDMs) maintain distance from their subordinates and they prefer formal procedures rather than informal ones, for example, a formal consultation method.

Ways in: Hopefully you were able to rule out the fourth statement and therefore option D. Psychologically close managers are closer to their subordinates. If you remembered that PDMs prefer formal procedures then you may have been able to work out that statements 1,2 and 3 were correct.

11.5 A **Rationale**: The essence of delegation is that the superior gives the subordinate part of his or her own authority. Power is not conferred by the organisation, so it cannot be delegated: it must be possessed. The most important thing to note is that responsibility and accountability are not delegated: the superior makes the subordinate responsible and accountable to him for the authority he has delegated, but he remains responsible and accountable for it to his own boss.

Pitfalls: It is easy to confuse these concepts, which is why they would make an excellent exam question.

11.6 C **Rationale**: Skilling was an important aspect of scientific management – but multi-skilled teamworking wasn't. Taylor's approach to job design (referred to in option A) was to break jobs down into single, simple tasks which were given to an individual as a whole (specialised, repetitive) job for an individual. The other options are key techniques (which, as a question in the Pilot Paper pointed out, are still prevalent in some work environments today...)

11.7 A **Rationale**: Option B is not a central concern of human relations: rather, this could apply to the scientific management school. Option C is a contribution of the contingency school. Option D has not yet been provided by any school of management or motivation theory: apart from anything else, business success depends on factors other than the productivity of the workers.

11.8 C **Rationale**: Democratic is a 'joins' style: decision is more or less by vote or consensus. Consultative means that the leader takes subordinate views into account, but still makes the decision. Autocratic is basically a 'tells' style and persuasive is a 'sells' style.

11.9 B **Rationale**: The monitor role involves scanning the environment and gathering information from a network of contacts. As spokesperson, the manager can then provide information on behalf of the department or organisation to interested parties. As disseminator, (s)he can also spread relevant information to team members. The role of leader means hiring, firing and training staff.

Pitfalls: Options B, C and D are all information roles, so the distinction between them is quite fine. However, questions have been set at this level of detail, so such models are worth learning.

11.10 D   **Rationale**: This is the key definition of the supervisory role: it is between non-managerial and managerial, acting as an information filter and overlap (since supervisors both do operational work and fulfil some managerial functions at a low level). Middle line and junior management are higher, since they are already managerial positions. Employee communications is a process, not a role, and is in any case much wider than managerial/non-managerial communication.

11.11 A   **Rationale**: A consultative style is the most popular among subordinates, although a 'sells' style is perceived to be most used by leaders – and a 'tells' style encourages the highest productivity in many circumstances.

11.12 B   **Rationale**: Responsibility is the duty to perform an action. Power is the ability to perform an action (and in particular, to influence others). Influence is a process by which a person can direct or modify the behaviour of another person.

           Pitfalls: These are fine distinctions in meaning – but they underpin the idea of management and leadership and are an excellent source of potential exam questions.

11.13 B   **Rationale**: Interpersonal roles are based on the manager's formal authority: they include the roles of figurehead, leader and liaison. Informational roles are based on the manager's position in internal and external information networks: they include monitor, spokesperson and disseminator. Decisional roles related to the work of the manager's department: entrepreneur, disturbance handler, resource allocator and negotiator.

11.14 C   **Rationale**: Contingency theories are based on the belief that there is no 'one best way' of leading but that effective leaders adapt their behaviour to changing variables. Adair's model sees the leadership process in a context made up of the task needs, individuals' needs and group needs.

11.15 B

> **Examiner's comments**. This question was not handled quite as well as some others. Students must ensure that they understand the main principles associated with the management theories in the study guide.

11.16 A   **Rationale**: This is a description of John Adair's action-centred leadership model. Contingency theory is more general: indeed, Adair's model is within the contingency school of thought. The managerial grid is based on two dimensions: concern for task and concern for people. Dispersed leadership (Heifetz) is the idea that individuals at all organisational levels can exert a 'leadership influence'.

11.17 B   **Rationale**: Planning is about determining objectives and how to reach them. Controlling is measuring and adjusting activities in line with plans. Commanding is instructing people to carry out plans.

           Ways in: even if you didn't recognise the description of organising, you could probably have eliminated the other options.

12   Recruitment and selection

12.1   C   **Rationale**: Screening means sorting through application forms received, in order to separate out candidates which are clearly ineligible for the vacancy, immediately worth short-listing and so on. It is selection because it is part of the process of measuring candidates against requirements, and selecting those who are most suitable. Recruitment is the process of defining requirements and reaching potential applicants: hence, options A, B and D.

12.2   B   **Rationale**: This is job description rather than job analysis, because a job description is the statement produced from a process of job analysis. This is job description rather than personnel specification, because it addresses the requirements of the *job*, rather than the qualities of the ideal job holder or person. Job advertisement is just a distractor.

           Pitfalls: The difference between job description and personnel specification has cropped up frequently in exams over the years. There is potential for confusion: remember that one describes the 'job', the other the 'person'...

12.3 C **Rationale**: 'Motivation' is a heading in an alternative method of person specification (the Five Point Pattern of Personality, by J Munro Fraser). Rodger's Seven Points are: physical make-up, attainments (qualifications), general intelligence, special aptitudes, interests, disposition (temperament) and circumstances.

12.4 B **Rationale**: The current trend is to devolve recruitment and selection (among other HRM activities) increasingly to line managers, who handle recruitment within their own departments.

12.5 D **Rationale**: All the other criticisms about the reliability of selection tests are valid – and yet tests are *still* more reliable than interviews at predicting performance in the job!

12.6 D **Rationale**: A leading question pushes the interviewee to give a certain answer. (In this case, it is obvious that the interviewer expects the interviewee to agree.) An open question requires self-expression; a closed question invites a one word either/or answer, and a problem-solving question presents candidates with a situation and asks them to say how they would deal with it.

Pitfalls: This is an easy aspect of interviewing technique to set questions on: make sure you can identify all types of questions.

12.7 C **Rationale**: This is a disadvantage because there may not be a clear interview strategy, and candidates may have trouble switching from one topic to another. Option A is an advantage, because it reduces individual bias, and saves time in sharing assessments (eg compared to a series of one-to-one interviews). Option B is an advantage, because a single interviewer may not be able to spot candidate weaknesses in technical areas. Option D is an advantage, because personal rapport may lead to favourable bias on the part of an interviewer.

12.8 A **Rationale**: These are all different types of bias and errors of judgement in interviewing. Option A is halo effect. Option B is contagious bias. Option C is stereotyping. Option D is projection.

Ways in: Stereotyping is probably the most recognisable of the options, so you could at least narrow your options by ruling out option C.

12.9 B **Rationale**: Proficiency tests focus on current ability to perform tasks. 'Standardised' is a desirable quality of any type of test, meaning that it is applicable to a representative sample of the population being tested. 'Sensitive' is another desirable quality meaning that the test can discriminate between different candidates.

12.10 C **Rationale**: Assessment centres are group assessments, usually used for higher-level positions, because of the time and costs involved in exploring candidates' personalities and skills in depth.

Pitfalls: Don't fall for the common trap of thinking that an assessment 'centre' is a place!

12.11 D **Rationale**: Two employer references provide necessary factual information and comparison of views (to minimise bias). The other options are untrue: option A because references are highly subjective and/or deliberately limited; option B because people can be more cautious or less honest in writing than on the telephone; option C because personal references are selected to be supportive (you can choose your friends in a way you can't choose your employers!)

12.12 D **Rationale**: Job descriptions can be narrow and restrictive, giving people a limited sense of what is their 'job' and what isn't. This can create demarcation lines which prevent people from flexibly switching tasks, or working effectively in multi-skilled teams. The other options are all potential uses of job descriptions, because they clearly state all the elements of a job: for calculating their value to the organisation (job evaluation), identifying gaps in job holders' ability (training needs analysis) and preparing selection criteria (recruitment).

12.13 C **Rationale**: A professional journal would not be read by the target audience, and the same could be said of the corporate website (although this would be a cost-effective way for the firm to promote itself generally as an employer). National newspapers will be too expensive, given that most of the audience will not be the firm's target group: low level positions are more likely to attract local applicants.

Pitfalls: If asked about choice of advertisement media, you need to think about cost and audience targeting together.

12.14 A **Rationale**: Succession planning develops managers in order to ensure managerial continuity over time – and internal promotion is a key way of grooming managers for higher positions. Induction time would be shorter, because an internal promotee is already familiar with the organisation's culture, structures, systems and personnel. Management will be familiar with an internal promotee and his or her performance so predicting job performance will be less risky. Innovation is *not* necessarily supported by internal promotion, because it does not bring 'new blood' into the organisation.

12.15 B **Rationale**: 'Maximum' information is not the point of interviews: squeezing as many questions as possible into the time allowed can restrict the flow of communication and put unnecessary pressure on the candidate, while a lengthy open-ended interview will be costly. The *relevance* of the information for selection is more important.

12.16 D **Rationale**: The key factors here are the urgency, and the fact that the consultants do not know the organisation: there is not enough time to give the consultants an adequate understanding of the complex recruitment needs. In option A, consultants would bring a 'fresh eye' and avoid bringing the same old types of people into the organisation. In option B, consultants would provide expertise and resources to handle large-scale recruitment, which the organisation lacks in-house. In option C, the organisation can be confident that use of consultants would not be resented and resisted.

Ways in: It helps if you have a checklist in your head of reasons to outsource recruitment: 'new blood', resources/expertise and internal support would certainly be on that list. 'Lead time to brief consultants on the needs of the organisation' would be on the list of reasons *not* to use consultants…

12.17 C **Rationale**: Attributes are simply 'characteristics' of any kind. Skills are learned behaviours, rather than capacities. Attainments are achievements or qualifications.

12.18 C **Rationale**: This should have been fairly straightforward. It would be quite difficult to write a job description or a person specification if a vacancy had not first been identified.

13 Diversity and equal opportunities

13.1 D **Rationale**: As well as compliance with relevant legislation, these are the main arguments for having an equal opportunities policy. It is good HR practice to attract and retain the best people for the job, regardless of race or gender.

13.2 C **Rationale**: The right to equal pay for work of equal value was established by the Equal Pay (Amendment) Regulations 1984. This does *not* imply that the woman has to be in the same job (option D). Job evaluation is recommended as a way of establishing relative values of jobs, but is not compulsory (option B). Equal Pay deals only with sexual discrimination – not race or other grounds.

13.3 D **Rationale**: Positive discrimination refers to actions being taken which give preference to a protected person, regardless of genuine suitability and qualification for the job. Statement 1 is not positive discrimination as the steps are only taken to encourage people to apply. It does not say that they will necessarily be accepted.

Diversity goes further than equal opportunities. The ways in which people meaningfully differ in the work place include not only race and ethnicity, age and gender but personality, preferred working style, individual needs and goals and so on.

13.4 C **Rationale**: Harassment is the use of threatening, intimidating, offensive or abusive language or behaviour focused on the race, religious belief, sex or sexual orientation of another person. This sounds like victimisation, but victimisation is a separate form of discrimination, involving penalising someone because they are involved in a claim of discrimination against an employer.

13.5 C **Rationale**: A business can better understand (and meet) the needs of market segments if it employs representatives of those segments: this is a business benefit, because it enhances customer loyalty, sales revenue, profitability etc. Option A is a legal/moral benefit (and addresses equal opportunities rather than diversity). Option B is a benefit to employees in a diverse organisation. Option D is not true of diversity, which requires significant management investment and less 'standardised' HR solutions.

13.6 B **Rationale**: The duty is to make 'reasonable' adjustments. The other statements are true.

13.7 A **Rationale**: Now that age discrimination legislation is in force, this would be direct discrimination (akin to saying 'blue-eyed, English-speaking people only need apply'). The other options may well be construed as *indirect* discrimination.

13.8 C **Rationale**: The organisation has laid itself open to a claim of indirect discrimination, because if the selection decision had been made on the basis of a question asked of a woman but *not* of men, it may have been construed as such. (This rules out options D and A.) The claim would not succeed (ruling out option B) because the organisation would be able to justify the apparently discriminatory conditions on non-discriminatory (job-relevant) grounds.

Pitfalls: You need to get to grips with the basics of how this works, and recognise examples when you see them.

13.9 C **Rationale**: Equal opportunity is a narrower concept based on eradicating discrimination based on the crude dimensions of individual difference. The other options are just distractors.

13.10 A **Rationale**: Positive discrimination (treating a minority group 'unfairly' well) is not permitted, except in relation to training provision. 'Quotas' are positive discrimination, because selection decisions cannot be justified on non-discriminatory grounds: 'targets' (as in option D) are 'positive action' – because they lead organisations to encourage under-represented groups to apply for jobs, and make non-discrimination a performance measure for selectors.

14 Individuals, groups and teams

14.1 C **Rationale**: Members of an effectively functioning group will take an active interest (as opposed to option C) in decisions affecting their work. Option A is healthy, particularly in avoiding problems that occur when groups seek consensus at all costs (eg 'group think'). Option B is healthy, as it unites and stimulates the group. Option D can be a sign that the group is supporting the performance of its members – not just that they are focusing on their own performance at the expense of the group.

Pitfalls: If you were trying to go by 'common sense' instead of knowledge, you might think that intra-team disagreement and inter-team competition were negatives: not so. The examiner does not set 'trick' questions, but questions can be designed to separate those who have studied from those who are guessing!

14.2 C **Rationale**: Personality is a relatively stable and distinctive concept: it is very difficult (if not impossible) to change personality, and the attempt has radical effects! The other options are constructive approaches to handling personality clashes in a team.

14.3 B **Rationale**: This is typical of 'storming' behaviour. Forming would be more tentative: just getting to know one another. Norming would be further along in the process of settling into shared values and behaviours. Performing would be still further along in performing the task.

Pitfalls: Don't assume that 'storming' is all about conflict! If you did this, you might have mistaken this description for norming, say.

Ways in: Underline some key words in the micro-scenario: 'debating', 'factions', 'disagree'...

14.4 C **Rationale**: This is the definition of attitudes. Personality traits are relatively stable, enduring qualities of an individual's personality (eg 'impulsiveness'). Perceptions are how people 'see' things, according to how the brain selects and organises information. Emotional intelligence is a concept popularised by Daniel Goleman to describe awareness of, and ability to manage, one's own emotions and those of others. None of these concepts is explicitly mentioned in the syllabus – but you are required to know something about the 'characteristics of individual behaviour', so it is worth getting to grips with some of the basics.

Ways in: Perceptions are about thinking, emotions are about feeling – and the question asked for something that combines thinking, feeling and intention. So you could probably rule out B and D.

14.5 C **Rationale**: Teams are not the best vehicle for crisis decision-making, because group decision-making takes longer, and decisions may protect the team at the expense of the right (possible tough) solution. Teams are, however, great for decision-making where the hearing of different viewpoints is beneficial. They are also great for ideas generation (think of group brainstorming) and coordination (teams are often cross-functional). You might have hesitated over option D, but it is important to realise that distance is now no obstacle to team working (think of virtual teams, connected by IT and communications links).

Pitfalls: Don't forget 'virtual' teams in your thinking.

14.6 B **Rationale**: Blocking (or difficulty stating) is where members put obstacles in the way of proposals: this may be a positive contribution in circumstances where the proposals are risky or unrealistic – but it is probably contributing to the problem here. Bringing-in is encouraging the contribution of others; summarising, drawing together passages of discussion; testing understanding, checking whether points have been understood. They are generally supportive behaviours, which could be used to get the team back into constructive discussion.

14.7 B **Rationale**: 'Compatibility' is not the same as 'homogeneity': teams need diversity, in order to have a mix and balance of contribution and roles. The other three options correspond to team identity, team solidarity and shared objective: the three key tools of team building.

14.8 B **Examiner's comments**: The examiner commented that only 33% of the students chose the correct answer. They key words in the question were 'keen eye for detail', 'always meets deadlines' and 'reluctant to involve others'. These phrases are typical characteristics of a completer-finisher.

14.9 D **Rationale**: The definition of a group is, basically, 'any collection of people who *perceive* themselves to be a group' (Handy). Identity means that there are acknowledged boundaries to a group, which define who is 'in' and who is 'out', 'us' and 'them'. Groups *may* have a defined leader and purpose, but not always. Conformity can be an attribute of groups or crowds.

Pitfalls: Note that this wasn't a question about the difference between a group and a team – although this too would make a good exam question…

14.10 A **Rationale**: This should be straightforward if you have understood the Belbin model. A healthy team has a mix and balance of roles. However, members can adopt more than one role, or switch roles as required: there need not be nine members with fixed roles. Belbin argues that it is the *process* roles (how people behaviour, contribute and interact with others), rather than the functional roles (technical skills and operational knowledge) that impact on team functioning – although functional roles are still important for getting the task done!

14.11 D **Rationale**: Adjourning is where the group sees itself as having fulfilled its purpose, and there is a process of disconnecting from the task and group – because there will have to be a renegotiation of aims and roles for the new task. Mourning is a related process, but refers to groups which are going to disband altogether. Dorming is where a group grows complacent about performance. Norming is a much earlier stage in the cycle, where the group reaches agreement about work methods, roles and behaviours.

Pitfalls: Dorming, mourning and adjourning are all late stages of group development, and can be confused if you are not clear about them. Although 'forming, storming, norming and performing' is better known, these additional stages are part of Tuckman's model.

14.12 C **Rationale**: Competition with other groups enhances solidarity, and competition within a group destroys it, so options A and B are the opposite of solidarity-enhancing. Option D would lead to 'group think': inability to confront problems, lack of criticism of poor decisions, false consensus. It may create high solidarity, but not healthy solidarity.

14.13 C **Rationale**: A role may be seen as a part you play: people sometimes refer to wearing 'different hats' in different situations or with different groups of people.

14.14 B **Rationale**: A multi-skilled team is one which brings together versatile individuals who can perform any of the group's tasks. Multi-disciplinary (or multi-functional) teams bring together individuals with *different* skills and specialisms, so that their skills can be pooled or exchanged. Self-managed teams are given discretion to plan their own task sharing and work methods, within defined task objectives: there is no suggestion that this is the case here. A virtual team is a geographically dispersed team, connected by information and communication technology (ICT) links.

14.15 D **Rationale**: The Shaper is the 'dynamo' of the team: one of the forms of leadership in Belbin's model. The Plant is the ideas person and creative problem-solver. The Co-ordinator is the chairperson, clarifying goals, delegating, promoting decision-making. The Implementer is the person who turns ideas into practical actions.

Pitfalls: There are several 'leader' roles in Belbin's model: you need to distinguish between them. The Plant is an ideas leader; Resource investigator an entrepreneur; Co-ordinator a task organiser; and the Shaper an interpersonal leader...

15 Motivating individuals and groups

15.1 D **Rationale**: Intrinsic rewards are 'part of' the work itself: extrinsic rewards are 'external' to the work itself.

Pitfalls: Potential confusion between intrinsic and extrinsic: a classic exam test!

15.2 C **Rationale**: Affiliation is actually a category in another need model by David McClelland. The other options are Maslow's (although freedom of inquiry and expression overarches the hierarchy itself).

15.3 B **Rationale**: In Herzberg's theory, only training is a 'motivator factor'. The others are all 'hygiene' factors: if they are inadequate, employees will be dissatisfied, but even if they are got right, they will not provide lasting satisfaction or motivation. Herzberg argued that satisfaction comes only from the job.

Pitfalls: Herzberg is frequently examined, and examiners are frustrated to see students get the basics of the theory wrong! Make sure you can sort the motivator factors from the hygiene factors.

15.4 A **Rationale**: Goals are things people choose to pursue: each individual will have their own goals, which may vary with time, circumstances and other factors. The idea of innate (in-born, instinctive) needs and drives is that they are biological or psychological imperatives, common to all people. (This is what makes it possible to have need theories with discussion of only a few innate needs.) Satisfaction arises when a goal is achieved.

15.5 C **Rationale**: Willy's expectancy (expectation that by working hard he will be given the team leadership) is high, but valence (importance to Willy of becoming a team leader) is neutral, because he has both positive and negative feelings about it. Since Motivation = E x V, if V is 0, motivation is also 0:

Pitfalls: Make sure you get valence and expectancy the right way round, and that you recognise why Willy's valence is 0.

Ways in: Work through the equation, calculating your own values for V and E...

15.6 A **Rationale**: Herzberg used the other three terms to describe the same set of factors: the ones that maintain morale but do not positively motivate (maintenance); prevent dissatisfaction but do not promote satisfaction, in the same way that hygiene prevents ill-health but does not promote well-being (hygiene); and that relate to the environment of work rather than to the work itself (environmental). The opposite set of factors is 'motivator' factors in the work itself, which – according to Herzberg – positively create satisfaction and motivation to superior performance.

Pitfalls: An exam question may refer to hygiene factors by any one of its three names, so it is worth using this question to check that you know them all!

15.7 C **Rationale**: Autonomy is a degree of freedom or discretion in the job: the removal of restrictive controls.

Ways in: You may have spotted that all the core dimensions are all intrinsic to the job itself: they are all what Herzberg would call 'motivator' factors. You could then eliminate some of the options that are clearly extrinsic to the job, or 'hygiene' factors...

15.8 C **Rationale**: Participation will only work if the individual has the ability and information to participate effectively (the principle of 'capacity'): otherwise, they will feel frustrated and under pressure. You may have hesitated over option D, but this is necessary for people to take participation seriously (the principle of 'consistency').

15.9 A **Rationale**: Theory X is the managerial assumption that most people dislike work and responsibility and will avoid them if possible they have to be coerced and controlled to work adequately – hence the kinds of management measures described. Theory Y is the managerial assumption that people can be motivated to accept challenge and responsibility and contribute willingly to the firm – resulting in a quite different management style! You should have known that there are no theories W or Z!

Pitfalls: You really do need to know which way round X and Y are! (If it helps, think of X as a 'cross' against workers' names...)

15.10 C **Rationale**: Options A, B and D are essential for an individual to work out how much effort will be required, and whether it will be worth it for the rewards expected (due to consistency) to be available. However, 'immediacy' is not necessarily required: people may have a high tolerance for 'delayed gratification', and be willing to wait for rewards as long as they have a reasonable expectation that they will eventually accrue. (As a student, for example, you may be working sacrificially hard now, in order to gain qualifications that will benefit your career in several years' time.)

15.11 D **Rationale**: Team members may work for individual rewards, rather than contributing to the group, especially since there is a problem offering rewards for less measurable criteria such as team-work. Option A is clearly a benefit. Option B is a benefit of PRP because it relates rewards directly to business objectives. You may have hesitated over option C but this is a benefit because PRP is a way of rewarding employees when there is no other way to do so (eg because they have reached the top of the salary/wage range their position is eligible for).

15.12 C **Rationale**: Job enrichment cannot offer management a cheap way of motivating employees: even those who want enriched jobs will expected to be rewarded with more than job satisfaction. The other options have been found in practice to be benefits of job enrichment.

15.13 B **Rationale**: According to Maslow, self-actualisation is the final 'need' to be satisfied. It is the fulfilment of personal potential. Maslow claims that this can rarely be satisfied.

Ways in: It might be worth memorising the triangular diagram and perhaps adding pictures to help you remember.

Pitfalls: You may have hesitated over option A but this was just a fictitious distracter. Esteem needs and physiological needs are lower down the hierachy.

15.14 B **Rationale**: Job evaluation focuses on job content, to measure the relative value of jobs, compared to each other, *not* their worth in money terms. Actual pay levels are set with reference to the other options, among others.

15.15 A   **Rationale**: Option A is valence (V). Option C refers to 'expectancy' (E). Option B is 'force of motivation (F): the product of valence and expectancy. Hence the equation: $F = V \times E$. The final option is a pure distractor.

15.16 C   **Rationale**: Eva's new tasks are of the same skill level and responsibility as her original task, so her job has been horizontally enlarged rather than vertically enlarged (which would be job enrichment). If she had gone from just packing one shift, to just stamping on the next shift (and so on), this would have been job rotation. Option B is an irrelevant distractor: job evaluation is a method of measuring the value of jobs for salary/wage setting and nothing to do with job design.

      Pitfalls: Any area like this where students frequently confuse similar terminology is ripe for examining. Read, think and check your answers carefully, to avoid careless errors!

15.17 B   **Rationale**: Micro-division of labour (or job simplification) is breaking down jobs into their smallest possible components, and having one person carry out one component. Division of labour (option C) is specialisation, but not to this extent. Job enlargement implies greater task variety, and empowerment, greater task significance and responsibility.

16   Training and development

16.1 C   **Rationale**: The Theorist seeks to understand basic principles and to take an intellectual, 'hands off' approach prior to trying things. Pragmatists and Activists are the opposite. You may have hesitated over option A, but Reflectors learn by thinking things through, rather than necessarily by applying theoretical concepts.

      Pitfalls: This is an area ripe for exam questions, because of the clarity of the style classifications. Make sure you can identify the label to go with a description and vice versa.

      Ways in: You could probably rule out Activist and Pragmatist quite quickly, because of Sara's dislike of 'hands on' methods.

16.2 C   **Rationale**: The scientific approach to problem-solving *is* a characteristic of learning organisation, but this involves experimentation and learning by testing ideas and making mistakes. Learning organisations have a high tolerance for risk, and regard errors as learning opportunities.

      Ways in: If you don't recognise the concept or model, don't give up and guess: think through the options and how they relate to each other. A question phrased 'which is *not...?*' suggests that you are looking for the 'odd one out'. If you look at the options, you should find three that are compatible with each other – leaving one that isn't.

16.3 D   **Rationale**: This is a positive and realistic view of the benefits and limitations of training: not *all* performance problems are amenable to training, and may need other sorts of intervention (discipline, counselling, equipment repair, job re-design, motivation and so on). Option A would fail to involve trainees and line managers, who are key stakeholders in training. Option B would limit training provision, ignoring its significant benefits. Option C would fail to design training programmes appropriately for specific training needs and learner style preferences.

16.4 B   **Rationale**: Conditioning may have sounded familiar if you only read as far as 'modification of behaviour', but it involves specific repetition-and-reward techniques. Education is the gradual acquisition of knowledge, by learning and instruction, often leading to qualifications. Development is a wider experience of the growth or realisation of a person's ability and potential through a wide range of learning experiences.

      Pitfalls: This kind of related terminology lends itself to exam questions. Training, education and development all involve 'learning', but the learning experiences are of different types, and with different overall aims.

16.5 B   **Rationale**: The learning cycle is experiential learning or 'learning by doing'. 'Action learning' sounds similar, but is actually a specific learning method by which managers are brought together as a problem-solving group to discuss real work issues. Programmed learning is highly structured learning, which doesn't apply here. Reflection is a way of thinking about what you have learnt.

16.6 C   **Rationale**: 'Employability' refers to an individual's having a portfolio of skills and experience that are valuable in the labour market, thus enhancing his or her mobility (and ability to get a job outside the present employer). This is a double-edged sword for the organisation: it is socially responsible and fosters employee satisfaction but may also cause a skill drain to other organisations. You should be able to see how training contributes to the other options, and why they are benefits for the organisation.

Pitfalls: Look out for qualifier keywords like 'for an organisation' (that is, *not* 'for the individual'). Think carefully through 'which is the exception?' questions, too. Logically, an option may be an exception for more than one reason: in this case, because it isn't a benefit (but a drawback) *or* because it isn't a benefit to the *organisation* (but a benefit to the individual). In a well designed question, you should get the same answer either way!

16.7 C   **Rationale**: Day release is 'off-the-job', because the learning comes from the employee's attending a college or training centre one day per week. The other methods are all 'on the job'.

Pitfalls: Note the variety of 'on the job' methods: don't forget to include job rotation (which you might otherwise connect with job design and Herzberg) and temporary promotion (which you might not think of as training).

16.8 D   **Rationale**: On-the-job approaches support 'transfer of learning': skills are learned in the actual context in which they will be applied – so application is seamless. Options A and B are advantages of *off*-the-job training: the learners don't have the distraction of other work duties, and errors while learning are less likely to have real consequences. You may have hesitated over option C, but there is a risk that by learning on the job, people will pick up 'bad habits' and short-cuts – rather than best practice.

16.9 C   **Rationale**: Level 1 measures how employees rated the training. Level 2 measures how much they learned: what they know or can do that they didn't do before. However, for a manager concerned with departmental productivity, the important thing is whether the trainees *applied* what they learned effectively to the job: Level 3. Level 5 is the impact of training on the wider 'good' of the organisation and its stakeholders: this kind of information is usually only available (and worth the cost of gathering and analysing it) at senior management level.

16.10 D   **Rationale**: Option A relates specifically to management effectiveness and succession; option B to planning opportunities for new challenges and learning through career moves (whether vertical or lateral); and option C to a structured programme of self-managed learning required by professional bodies.

16.11 A   **Rationale**: A Pragmatist likes to learn in 'hands-on' ways that have a direct link to real, practical problems – so on-the-job practice is ideal. Option B would suit an Activist – a similar style, enjoying practical, active, participative learning, but without the need to see a work-related 'payoff'. Option C would suit a Reflector, since a journal offers opportunity for learning through reflection. And option D would suit a Theorist, with a preference for structured intellectual study.

Pitfalls: The pairs of 'hands off' and 'hands on' styles are quite similar: don't confuse them. It may help to relate each style to a different stage of Kolb's learning cycle, to make them more distinct. The Pragmatist focuses on the job; the Reflector reflects on what happened; the Theorist seeks to understand it; and the Activist plans to try something new.

16.12 C   **Rationale**: Employee satisfaction would not be regarded as a quantifiable benefit – unless it could be correlated directly with figures such as reduced absenteeism and labour turnover (although it would be difficult to relate this specifically to training, as opposed to other effects).

Pitfalls: Watch out for qualifier keywords in the question like 'quantitative' or 'qualitative' (benefits, characteristics). Examiners don't try to trick you – but they do like you to read questions carefully!

16.13 A   **Rationale**: It is important to separate development, training and education in your mind for this syllabus. Development is the growth of a person's potential. Training is a planned learning event. Education is knowledge that is acquired gradually by learning or instruction.

16.14 C   **Rationale**: A formal training needs analysis involves systematic study (at the level of the individual, job or department) of the required level of competence, the present/actual level of competence and any gap between them. The other options are all ways in which learning needs may 'emerge' in the course of work: option A through monitoring developments in your field; option B as a 'critical incident' and option D as on-going performance feedback.

16.15 A   **Rationale**: It is the networked aspect that makes e-learning different from CBT (using stand-alone computers). Blended learning involves learning using a combination of different methods and technologies: this would be the correct option if the learning support was available from face-to-face tuition, say.

            Pitfalls: Learning technologies is fertile territory for exam questions, because there are so many closely-related methods and terms (coaching, mentoring etc).

            Ways in: Just about anything with an 'e-' in front of it, these days, is about the Internet – not stand-along computers, so you should be able to rule out option B.

16.16 A   **Rationale**: This is Kolb's learning cycle which is a 'learning by doing' approach. It puts the learner in an active problem-solving role and encourages them to formulate and commit themselves to their own learning objectives.

            Ways in: Simplified, this learning by doing approach involves:

            Act   →   Analyse action   →   Suggest principles →   Apply principles→   Act ... and so on→

17   Performance appraisal

17.1 A   **Rationale**: Job evaluation is a method of measuring the value of a job, *not* the performance of the person holding the job. The other three options are key applications of performance appraisal. (Succession planning is a form of promotion or potential review, aimed at identifying future managers.)

            Pitfalls: This is a common source of confusion (akin to the difference between job descriptions and person specifications in recruitment).

17.2 D   **Rationale**: Overall assessment is narrative comment without the guidance on how the terms should be applied. Grading uses rating scales (definitions of performance on each characteristic from 1-5, say). Behavioural incident methods compare specific behaviours against typical behaviour in each job.

17.3 B   **Rationale**: Achievable (which is part of the SMART objectives framework) is different from 'easily achievable': one of the key points of performance measures is that they should be motivational, which means that they should be at least a little bit challenging.

17.4 B   **Rationale**: This manager tells in the first part and listens in the second part of the interview, taking on a dual role as critic and counsellor – and not assuming that all performance problems are the fault of the employee himself. Tell and sell would be more one-sided ('selling' simply being gaining acceptance of the evaluation and improvement plan). Problem-solving is even more of a collaborative, proactive process, with the manager in the role of coach. Sell and listen is not an appropriate method.

17.5 D   **Rationale**: 360-degree is, by definition, a 'rounded' view of an individual's performance from the appraisee, colleagues, superiors, subordinates and relevant business contacts. Self appraisal is likely to be biased by self-perception; peer appraisal by team relationships; and upward appraisal by subordinates' fear of reprisals.

17.6 C   **Rationale**: This is the definition of performance management. It differs from performance appraisal in its emphasis on collaboration, objective-setting and on-going management.

17.7 D   **Rationale**: These are all valid criteria.

17.8　A　**Rationale**: Multi-source feedback is another term for 360-degree feedback or appraisal. (360-degree management was a distractor.) Management by objectives and performance management are both approaches to collaborative objective-setting, on-going development and periodic review.

17.9　D　**Rationale**: This is a double edged sword: a link between assessment and reward may motivate employees to take appraisal seriously, but can also make it threatening if they fear that they haven't done well. Moreover, there are other factors in setting rewards – and if there isn't a real connection between a positive appraisal and a meaningful reward, the 'implication' that there is will only undermine the appraisal system. The other options are clearly positive.

17.10　C　**Rationale**: Options A, B and D were identified as barriers to effective appraisal by Lockett: 'appraisal as unfinished business' (distracting from future-focused improvement planning); 'appraisal as bureaucracy' (a mere form-filling exercise); and 'appraisal as an annual event' (where on-going performance management is required). Lockett also identified 'appraisal as confrontation' as a barrier, but this is not what is implied by Option C, which reflects a genuine, job-relevant, problem-solving approach.

17.11　C　**Rationale**: Although appraisals can be used to measure the extent to which an employee is deserving of a bonus, it cannot be used to measure the effectiveness of the appraisal scheme itself. Funds may not be available for bonuses but this does not mean that the appraisal system is ineffective. Appraisals must be carried out with serious intent and managers must be committed to the system. The system should be fair and reasonably objective.

17.12　C　**Rationale**: This is an advantage because it gives the individual a greater sense of meaning and contribution to the organisation. It is also an advantage to the organisation – as are all the other options. You may have hesitated over Option A: this would certainly be an advantage to appraisees identified for promotion – but not everyone.

17.13　D　**Rationale**: This involves setting specific targets and standards of performance, and measuring performance against them. Behavioural incident focuses on job behaviours; rating scales are the same as grading; and guided assessment is narrative comment on defined characteristics.

18 Personal effectiveness and communication

18.1　D　**Rationale**: The communication here is both upwards and 'sideways'.

Pitfalls: Lateral is the same as horizontal: don't get sidetracked!

18.2　D　**Rationale**: Personal development planning is something the individual does for his or her own improvement and learning, although a coach, mentor or counsellor may facilitate this process. Options A, B and C are all types of 'developmental relationships': a coach helps a trainee for a brief period to work on job-relevant skills; a mentor helps a less experienced person over the long term to work on more general personal development issues; and a counsellor helps an individual to work through emotional or social issues or problems.

Pitfalls: These are distinct roles: make sure you can identify them correctly.

18.3　C　**Rationale**: An assertive style of communication will help in time management, because it enables you to say 'no' (appropriately) to interruptions and unscheduled demands. The other options are problems: options A and B are invitations to waste time in non-essential communication. Option D may look organised and decisive – but e-mails arrive so frequently, they would de-rail your entire schedule if you let them: better to batch them and deal with them at certain times.

18.4　C　**Rationale**: The wheel has a central figure who acts as a hub for all messages between members. The circle involves a message going from one person to another. The 'Y' involves a message going from person to person up a chain, until it reaches someone who is in contact with more than one person. And all-channel involves everyone sending messages to everyone else.

Ways in: If you can visualise the situation, it helps: you could then eliminate the circle and all-channel, at least.

18.5 D   **Rationale**: A mobile phone enables both colleagues and customers to reach you when you are out of the office. It also enables you to call the office eg to check inventory availability of items, place immediate orders and so on. (If you had a laptop, this would be even better: you could have direct connection with office systems.) Options A, B and C all involve linked computer systems, so are not relevant.

18.6 A   **Rationale**: Security is a key vulnerability of e-mail: there is no guarantee of privacy (and a risk of accidentally sending the message to the wrong person). The other options are significant strengths, however. If you hesitated over D, think about how e-mail can be used for memos/reports/letters, and how many formats (visual, audio) can be 'attached' to e-mail messages.

18.7 B   **Rationale**: Counselling is facilitating others through the process of defining and exploring their own issues and coming up with their own solutions: this is relatively non-directive. Advising is a relatively directive role: offering information and recommendations on the best course of action to take. Counselling is often *not* directly task-related: it is often about helping employees to formulate learning goals or to cope with work (or non-work) problems.

           Ways in: You should have immediately realised that non-advisory is not an option.

18.8 C   **Rationale**: The grapevine is a 'rumour mill': information is often inaccurate and exaggerated. Communication is, however, fast, selective (in that information is not randomly passed on to everyone) and up-to-date (information is often more current than in the formal system).

18.9 D   **Rationale**: Exception reporting may improve the quality of upward communication (making it more selective), but it does not encourage it: if anything, it may create a culture in which staff don't 'bother' their superiors with information. The other options are all ways of encouraging upward flow of information and ideas – which otherwise tends to be rare in organisations.

18.10 D   **Rationale**: The sender encodes the message and transmits it through a medium to the receiver who decodes it into information. The answer cannot be A since you need to have a message to feedback on before you provide the feedback.

           Ways in: It might help you to picture the radio signal diagram in your mind.

18.11 C   **Rationale**: Notice boards are unsuitable for upward communication, and organisation manuals and team briefings are for downward communication.

           Pitfalls: You needed to be aware of the nature of a team briefing, which is for information and instructions to be given (downward) to a team.

18.12 C   **Rationale**: Noise is the *other* main type of communication problem: interferences in the environment in which communication takes place, affecting the clarity, accuracy or arrival of the message. Redundancy is a *positive* principle in this context: you can use more than one form of communication, so that if one message does not get through (perhaps because of noise or distortion), another may. Feedback is an essential part of the communication cycle: it is the response which indicates to the sender whether the message has been correctly received.

18.13 D   **Rationale**: The wheel was the fastest and the Y was the second fasted in Leavitt's experiment. The chain was the slowest. The reason was the fact that messages came through and were distributed from a central source.

18.14 A

           Examiner's comments. The examiner commented that around 50% of students got this question wrong and highlighted the point that students must clearly understand the key definitions within the syllabus. For example, coaching is not one-way so option B could immediately be eliminated. It is important to look for key words (clues) to the right answer.

18.15 B   **Rationale**: Research shows that people pay *more* attention to non-verbal cues in interpreting what someone means than they do to the words themselves. The other statements are true.

           Pitfalls: You may have wrongly selected option C if you associated non-verbal communication too narrowly as 'body language': be aware of the full range of non-verbal signals that can be given or received.

18.16 B   **Rationale**: SMART is 'Specific, Measurable, Attainable, Relevant and Time-bounded', although versions differ. Options A and C are both very plausible – and also qualities of effective goals – but you wouldn't want to replace 'measurable', which is essential (otherwise, how will you know when you've reached your goal?).

19 Ethical considerations

19.1   C   **Rationale**: 'Fiduciary' means 'of trust'. Although this is a terminology question, it addresses the important point that all managers (and organisations) are accountable to some external entity and purpose.

19.2   A   **Rationale**: Utilitarianism is based on 'usefulness': the greatest good of the greatest number. Deontology is an alternative approach based on absolute moral principles (or categorical imperatives): what is morally 'right' in a situation. Virtue ethics is a belief in pursuing positive moral qualities, which flow out into behaviour. CSR is an entirely different concept, to do with the obligations of an organisation towards its secondary stakeholders.

19.3   D   **Rationale**: Grease money refers to payments for benefits to which the company is legally entitled – just to 'oil the wheels'. Bribery is payment for benefits to which the company is *not* legally entitled – to 'bend the rules'! In either case, this is unethical (and in some situations, illegal) – regardless of the legitimacy of the claim or the purposes to which the payment is (supposedly) put.

           Pitfalls: Know the difference between extortion, bribery, grease money, gifts and hospitality.

19.4   B   **Rationale**: The emphasis on managerial responsibility is a feature of the integrity or values-based approach to ethics management. A concern for the law alone is a compliance based approach. Options C and D are examples of responsibilities.

19.5   D   **Rationale**: Options A and C are irrelevant, and option B is incorrect, since whistle-blowing gives some protection to employees from being in breach of confidentiality.

19.6   D   **Rationale**: These are all potential ethical issues. Materials used impacts on product safety and eco-friendliness (eg for recycling). Quality is a safety and customer satisfaction issues. Advertising poses issues of truth and non-manipulation. You may have hesitated over supplier labour practices, but this is a key area of ethical sourcing. It can cause significant damage to corporate reputations. Packaging raises issues of safety/perishability, eco-friendliness and truthful product labelling.

19.7   C   **Rationale**: Accountability and social responsibility are classed as professional qualities, not personal qualities. Ambition is a personal quality – but is not considered essential in a professional ethics context: it can even pose ethical dilemmas...

           Pitfalls: You need to read the question stems carefully to pick up fine distinctions such as 'personal' and 'professional'.

19.8   D   **Rationale**: Independence in appearance means avoiding situations that could cause a reasonable observer to question your objectivity. In the scenario, this is a risk – while independence of mind (free from actual partiality) isn't. The pure distractors were plausible because of the possibility of raising questions (scepticism) with your superiors (accountability) – but irrelevant.

19.9   D   **Rationale**: Employability training helps employees to get other employment but it is not an ethical objective.

19.10 C   **Rationale**: The saying is: 'the law is a floor'. By meeting non-legal regulations (including the rules of your workplace) you should meet a higher standard of behaviour than the legal requirements. Ethical behaviour is a higher moral standard, based on society's expectations and principles.

20 Mixed Bank 1

20.1 C The correct answer is isolated from its external environment.

The difference between an open and a closed system is very basic, and depends on the relationship the system has with its environment. A system being closed to protect from unauthorised access merely refers to the system's security arrangements. Incapability of further technical enhancement refers to a stage in the system's life cycle.

It is true that a system could be described as 'closed' if it has been shut down but not in the context of systems theory.

20.2 B The correct answers are: Managers are responsible for coordinating tasks; insistence on loyalty to the organisation; hierarchical structure of control in an impersonal organisation.

In contrast, Homer would recognise the other feature as typical of an organic system of management.

20.3 C The correct answer is: To record financial information.

This is its basic, original role and is still the best way to describe its part in the modern business organisation.

20.4 D The correct answer is: Improves the motivation of junior managers

While the other options may arise in a decentralised organisation, they are not necessarily features that are specifically associated with decentralisation.

20.5 C The correct answer: There is little similarity between team members' work.

Where there is little similarity in work, subordinates will not be able to help each other, and will rely more heavily on their managers.

Where the work is routine, or the team very experienced, team members will require less support so a wider span may be appropriate. the wider the geographical dispersion, the narrower the span.

20.6 D The correct answer is: Independence of the non-executive directors.

This will be examined in the internal position audit of the company rather then the environmental analysis which looks at matters external to the company.

20.7 C The correct answer is: Managing the prompt payment of suppliers.

The purchasing manager will be concerned with all aspects of supplier management (eg discussing prices, discounts, delivery lead times, specifications, chasing late deliveries, sanctioning payments).

20.8 C The correct answers are: Committees and reports slow down the decision-making process. Innovation is difficult; over prescriptive rules produce a simplistic approach to problems.

The other statement describes the adhocracy, which is complex and disorderly and does not rely on standardisation to co-ordinate its activities. It also relies on the expertise of its members, but not through standardised skills.

20.9 C The correct answers are: It may introduce bugs that do not exist in the standard version. It may delay delivery of the software.

Customisation should not stop the company from being able to buy 'add-ons' to the basic package. In fact they are sometimes used to give the package more flexibility to suit particular needs. Dependence on the supplier for maintenance is also a disadvantage of ready-made packages.

20.10 A The correct answer is: Professional body.

External stakeholder groups – the government, local authorities, pressure groups, the community at large, professional bodies – are likely to have quite diverse objectives.

20.11 A The correct answer is: Dual authority.

Dual authority may lead to conflict between the managers involved.

The advantages of such a structure are:

– greater flexibility
– improved communication
– motivating employees

20.12 A The correct answer is: The board of directors.

As with all company-specific matters it is the directors who are primarily responsible for the implementation of procedures, which follow best practice with regard to the current corporate governance advice in the Combined Code.

20.13 B The correct answer is: Shareholders are accountable to auditors.

All the other statements are true. Both directors and auditors are agents of the shareholders and their primary duties relate to them.

20.14 B The correct answer is: To examine and express an opinion on the company's periodic financial statements.

This is a Companies Act requirement. All the other responses are specific director responsibilities.

20.15 B An audit trail shows who has accessed a system and the operations performed.

20.16 B The correct answers are: Authoritative, Accurate, Relevant.

It should be **accurate** – in the sense of correct for the purpose. Inaccurate information is of little use for strategic, tactical or operational purposes. **Authoritative** means that the source of the information should be reliable. It must also be **relevant to** the user's needs. Information that is not needed for a decision should be omitted, no matter how 'interesting' it might be. If the information is **comprehensive**, it may be more wide ranging than it needs to be. It needs to be complete ie include everything that is needed.

20.17 A The correct answer is: External auditors need to assess the work of internal audit first.

Although some of the procedures that internal audit undertake are very similar to those undertaken by the external auditors, the whole basis and reasoning of their work is fundamentally different.

20.18 D The correct answer is: Hardware purchase costs; installation costs; software purchase costs.

Capital costs, which are capitalised and then depreciated, include installation, hardware purchase and software purchase costs. The remaining costs are revenue items which are expensed as incurred.

20.19 C The correct answer is: Shareholders.

It is very important that external auditors are independent of the company's management.

20.20 A The correct answer is: Banked, complete, prevented.

In any business controls over cash receipts are fundamental if the company is to keep a healthy cash position.

20.21 C The correct answer is: Dishonesty, motivation and opportunity.

If one or more of them can be eliminated, the risk of fraud is reduced.

20.22 B The correct answer is: A higher than normal risk audit.

The instances given are all examples of inherent risk or control risks and therefore they would be indicative of higher risk audit.

Certain of the factors combined, such as a poor internal control environment coupled with a dominant chief executive, might raise the auditors' suspicions of fraud, but not necessarily. However, they would all increase the overall risk of the audit.

20.23 D   The correct answer is: information about personnel from the payroll system. Value of sales from the accounting records. Information on decisions taken from the minutes of a meeting.

Data and information captured from internal sources come from transaction systems, such as the payroll system and the sales ledger, or is communicated formally or informally, as in a decision taken at a meeting.

Although the type of information is circulated within the organisation, it is captured from outside. For example, the source of the market information is the market itself, which is clearly external to the organisation.

21 Mixed Bank 2

21.1 B   The correct answers are: Controlling, Co-ordinating, Commanding

Fayol wrote that to manage is to forecast and plan, to organise, to command, to co-ordinate and to control. Commanding is the exercise of centralised authority and leadership. Co-ordinating involves harmonising the activities of all groups towards the common objective. Controlling is measuring performance and accounting for deviations from plans. Writers after *Fayol* substituted functions such as motivating and consulting for commanding.

21.2 B   The correct answer is: Organisational design will be determined by a number of factors all of which dependent on the others.

These factors include elements such as the company's objectives, the environment, the staff, the culture, the management style, the tasks carried out, the structure and the technology used.

21.3 C   The correct answer is: Planning and control.

The five categories are setting objectives, organising the work, motivation, the job of measurement and developing people. Planning and control are included within setting objectives and measurement. *Drucker* gave more emphasis to the 'human resource' aspects of management than writers on classical management theory such as *Fayol*.

21.4 D   The correct answer is: Position power.

Position power or legitimate power is conferred by the authority linked to a formal position within the organisation structure.

21.5 B   The correct answer is: Benevolent authoritative, participative, exploitative authoritative, democratic.

These are *Likert's* four management styles.

21.6 D   The correct answer is: Storming.

This is the storming stage, as identified by *Tuckman*. During this stage, conflict can be quite open. Objectives and procedures are challenged and risks are taken. However, there is a considerable amount of enthusiasm within the group and new ideas emerge. So too do political conflicts, as leadership of the group becomes an issue. This appears to be the situation described in the question.

21.7 D   The correct answers are: Membership is voluntary; Tasks are not assigned by management; Communication is open and informal.

An organisation can be described as a collection of groups both formal and informal.

It is important not to underestimate the importance of groups within an organisation. *Elton Mayo* first established this point through the Hawthorne Experiments.

It is also important to remember that there are alliances and power structures that exist within an organisation, other than those documented in an organisational chart.

21.8 D The correct answer is: Shaper.

All of *Belbin's* roles are important to the effective functioning of a team.

You should familiarise yourself with all eight roles.

- – Plant
- – Shaper
- – Resource investigator
- – Monitor evaluator
- – Company worker
- – Completer finisher
- – Team worker
- – Chairman

21.9 C The correct answers are: Shaper, Plant, Finisher.

The shaper is a leader role, where the role holder spurs the team to action. The plant provides the creative thinking in the team, while the finisher's actions are directed to the completion of the task.

Attacking is a type of group behaviour identified by *Rackham & Morgan*.

21.10 D The correct answer is: All four.

A team is a number of people with complementary skills who are committed to a common purpose for which they hold themselves basically accountable. This is a control mechanism which improves work organisation by using knowledge from a broad range of perspectives to evaluate decision options.

21.11 A The correct answer is: Forming, norming, storming, performing.

Forming is the stage where the team comes together. Storming happens next; the group re-assesses its targets and (hopefully) trust between group members develops. Norming is a period of settling down, when the group established norms and procedures for doing their work. Performing then occurs; the team sets to work to execute its task and the difficulties of development no longer hinder it.

21.12 A The correct answer is: *Herzberg.*

Herzberg found that people's behaviour in the workplace was affected by more than their physical and social needs; the content of the work itself had an effect on motivation and performance.

21.13 C The correct answers are: Define the problem carefully; Try to develop options that would result in mutual gain. Look for a wide variety of possible solutions.

Bruce's course would have covered many approaches to resolving problems. The negotiation techniques you should have identified include trying to develop options that would result in mutual gain; defining the problems carefully and looking for a wide variety of possible solutions. Evaluating progress towards objectives and creating a trusting supportive atmosphere in the group will enhance the project team's performance but would not be considered negotiation techniques.

21.14 C The correct answers are: Usually unstructured so can discuss a wide range of topics; Requires little or no planning. Gives a real impression of feelings.

The feature is an advantage associated with other types of communication. Complex ideas that require deeper consideration are probably best communicated in written form, or perhaps in a presentation. Holding a meeting is the main communication technique for allowing multiple options to be expressed. However, an effective chairperson is needed if all sides are to be heard.

21.15 D The correct answers are: Agree goals in advance and prepare a focused agenda and ensure people stick to it.

Ensuring meeting goals are agreed before the meeting and producing an agenda based around achieving the agreed goals should ensure attendees are fully aware of the meeting purpose.

21.16 B   The correct answers are: Colloquialisms, Jargon, Double meanings.

Colloquialisms should only be used in informal conversation and jargon should be avoided, although it may be used where it is an excellent form of shorthand and unique to the particular organisation, provided it remains comprehensible and is understood by all parties. Acronyms can be used freely as long as they are explained.

21.17 D   The correct answers are: Lack of privacy – can be forwarded on without your knowledge. People may not check their email regularly. Requires some computer literacy to use effectively.

Complex images can be included as an attachment to an email and there is no limitation on their transmission.

21.18 A   The correct answer is: The sequence is 5, 2, 6, 1, 4, 3.

The sequence of items on an agenda is apologies for absence, approving the minutes of the previous meeting, matters arising out of the minutes, the main items of business on the agenda (subjects for discussion), any other business (items not on the agenda) and finally deciding the date of the next meeting.

21.19 A   The correct answers are: Peers; Self-appraisal; Customers.

Peers or co-workers could be members of a team or people receiving or providing services.

Customers can be a useful source, especially for sales staff. Knowing what customers think of you helps to improve your technique.

When individuals carry out their own self-evaluation, it is a major input to the appraisal process because they can identify the areas of competence that are relevant to the job and their own relative strengths.

21.20 C   The correct answer is: Upward.

There is a current trend towards this more progressive appraisal system where subordinates appraise their superiors.

Potential problems with this method may include:

–   Fear of reprisal
–   Vindictiveness
–   Unwillingness of superior to respond to feedback

21.21 B   The correct answer is: Deal with grievances.

Grievances should be dealt with by a formal mechanism separate from the appraisal process. If a grievance arises during appraisal it should be dealt with using the normal grievance procedure.

21.22 A   The correct answer is: Accounts payable clerk.

It is unlikely that the accounts payable clerk will be asked. The others will all come in contact with the sales manager and therefore potentially could be asked to assist with completing the appraisal forms required by 360 degree feedback process.

21.23 B   The correct answer is: Enabling accounting.

Enabling accounting is a made up term here, and sounds like a rather dubious practice for a business. Accounting should be a well-controlled and regulated process.

The other options are all characteristics of a learning organisation.

21.24 C   The correct answers are: Fear of reprisals; Employee point scoring; Lack of authority.

The advantages of upward appraisal are that the subordinates feel more involved, managers receive objective feedback and can therefore improve their performance.

22 Mixed Bank 3

22.1 B   PEST

22.2 B   Designing systems and standardising work.

22.3 A   The number of employees reporting to one manager.

22.4 A   The directors of the company.

22.5 D   Arithmetic, physical.

22.6 B   Sales invoicing and payroll.

22.7 C   Hersey and Blanchard.

22.8 B   All team members have different skills and specialisms which they pool.

22.9 D   Maslow and Herzberg.

22.10 D   Mentoring and secondment.

22.11 D   Diagonal.

22.12 B   Prefers to think things through first.

22.13 C   **Rationale**: Collective goals or aims are a feature of organisations.

22.14 C   The others are distractors! Make sure you do know these technical terms as the examiner could set a similar question to trip you up.

22.15 D   All of these are examples of weaknesses in financial controls. There are other instances too which you will find in the Chapter.

22.16 B   **Rationale**: The **Management Accountant** provides information for management: cost accounting, budgets and budgetary control and financial management of projects.

22.17 C   **Rationale**: The **purchasing or procurement function** is responsible for authorising purchases (and suppliers) and approving.

22.18 C

22.19 C

22.20 B   **Rationale**: A suite is a set of several modules. A spreadsheet is a type of program, and a format for displaying and processing data: it is often used to integrate data from accounting modules for decision-support and management information systems. An algorithm is a set of rules followed in calculations, especially by a computer.

22.21 B   (or 'position' power).

22.22 D   **Rationale**: The definition of a group is, basically, 'any collection of people who perceive themselves to be a group' (Handy). **Identity** means that there are acknowledged boundaries to a group, which define who is 'in' and who is 'out', 'us' and 'them'.

22.23 B   Specialist.

22.24 D

23 Mixed bank 4

23.1   C   Output control. Ouchi assumed that output control was part of market control, where it is possible to price output of a system effectively and where there is external competition as a reference.

23.2   D   Five pop fans. They are a random collection of people. They have no common purpose, or common leader and they do not see themselves as having a common identity.

23.3   B   Passive acceptance of work decisions. Members of an effectively functioning group will take an active interest in decisions affecting their work, rather than passively accepting them.

23.4   A   Position power. A header is someone who does not have to rely on position power alone.

23.5   A   These suggests a lack of trust by the manager toward staff. The other reasons are likely to lead to reduced delegation in themselves.

23.6   C   Evaluating progress towards objectives will enhance team performance but would not be considered a negotiation technique.

23.7   D   Allocating scarce resources. This could be concerned with people as a resource but is not people-centered.

23.8   C   To take reasonable care of themselves. Although there is an employer duty of care towards employees, this does not cover employee negligence or stupidity.

23.9   A   These are groups outside the organisation's boundary, in its environment. The others are within the boundary and belong to the organisation system.

23.10 A   Suspension without pay or demotion. Dismissal is a course of action an employer can take although not provided for specifically in the employee's contract of employment.

23.11 D   Task. The matrix structure requires a culture that reacts quickly to change and focuses on particular projects or tasks as dictated by the needs of the business. A task culture will suit this best as it focuses an achievement of the task above all else, and is very flexible and reactive to changes in the environment.

23.12 B   This quote is variously attributed to Schein and Handy. An organisation's culture is exclusive, shared and gives its participants a sense of community.

23.13 C   The others are internal stakeholders.

23.14 A   B is 'operating core', C is 'middle line', D is 'techno-structure'.

23.15 D

23.16 D   Teeming and lading is the theft of cheque receipts. Setting subsequent receipts against the outstanding debt conceals the theft.

23.17 B   All three are essential: dishonesty, opportunity and motivation.

23.18 A

23.19 B

23.20 D   The worst of both worlds.

23.21 C   The shaper thrives on pressure.

23.22 A

23.23 B   There are drawbacks to linking appraisal to salary review, not least that there may not be enough money to reward the employee for his performance.

23.24 C   Salary and hours of work will be in the employment contract.

24 Mixed bank 5

24.1 D   In fact it may be more difficult to see where a mistake has been made.

24.2 A   The other areas are dealt with by a combination of best practice, codes and some legislation.

24.3 C   Strengths and weaknesses are internal.

24.4 C   1 and 3 are the responsibility of the internal auditor, and ultimately of management.

24.5 B

24.6 A

24.7 A

24.8 B   Coercion means compelling someone to do something.

24.9 B   2 and 3 will generally be carried out by higher levels of management.

24.10 C   Lateral communication is between those of equal rank.

24.11 D

24.12 D   This may also be worded as: have an experience, review the experience, conclude from the experience and plan the next steps.

24.13 C   **Rationale**: The scalar chain is the downward flow of delegated authority in an organisation and the need for reports to flow back 'up': it is often a source of slow communication and rigidity (eg in bureaucracies). Horizontal structure allows the flow of information and decisions across functional (vertical) boundaries: it is a key approach to flexibility – including project teams (which are also cross-functional). The 'Shamrock' is a form of numerical flexibility, where a firm has a core staff and a various peripheral 'leaves' which it can draw on as the demand for labour fluctuates.

Ways in: You could narrow your options by ruling out project teams: otherwise, you simply needed to know your terminology well.

24.14 C   **Rationale**: Minute-taking is one of the roles of the secretary, who essentially provides administrative support to the committee. A is the role of the chair, while B and D may be imposed on the committee by the authorities to which it reports.

24.15 A   **Rationale**: Apollo is associated with role culture; Athena with task culture; Dionysus with person culture.

Pitfalls: Since the syllabus specifically mentions Handy (not Harrison), it would be worth learning the 'god' labels.

Ways in: You might be aware that Zeus was 'king' of the gods in Greek mythology: this might help with the association to the power culture of the leader.

24.16 D   **Rationale**: The founder influences culture through founding values; history/experience through creating expectations and stories; recruitment and selection by choosing people who will 'fit' (or change) the culture; industry by having its own culture; and labour turnover by allowing people who don't 'fit in' to 'get out'.

Pitfalls: You may immediately have ruled labour turnover out as an irrelevance. Key point in answering MCQ questions: don't rule out *any* option at first glance!

24.17 D   **Rationale**: Boundaries are the rules that restrict management's freedom of action: they include legislation, regulation and contractual agreements. Responsibilities are obligations which a company voluntarily undertakes. The primary economic objective relates to optimal resource-conversion (eg profitability). Non-economic, social objectives modify management behaviour in line with stakeholder expectations.

Pitfalls: Environmental protection may be a non-economic, social objective. The point about the *regulations*, however, is that they are not negotiable!

24.18 B **Rationale**: A framework approach sets out principles and guidelines, rather than detailed rules to cover every specific situation. This leads to listed advantages – but not to consistent application, since there is a high degree of discretion in applying guidelines to different cases.

24.19 A **Rationale**: The principle of due care is that, having accepted an assignment, you have an obligation to carry it out to the best of your ability, in the client's best interests, and within reasonable timescales, with proper regard for the standards expected of you as a professional. In this scenario, any answer you give on the spot would risk being incomplete, inaccurate or out-of-date, with potentially serious consequences, if the client relies and acts on your reply. Integrity is honesty, fair dealing and truthfulness; professional behaviour is upholding the reputation of your profession; and confidentiality is not using or disclosing information given to you by employers or clients in the course of your work. (None of these issues applies directly here.)

24.20 B **Rationale**: This is a major problem for non-executive directors, because they are likely to have other commitments. You should have had to think through the other options, however. Some of the *advantages* of non-executive directors are that they offer a comfort factor for third parties such as investors and suppliers; they have a wider perspective and (hopefully) no vested interest; and they have a combination of knowledge/expertise and detachment.

24.21 B **Rationale**: Using local suppliers is part of the government's sustainability strategy, as it develops and preserves local business, employment and communities. Minimising energy consumption conserves resources. The other two options are not directly related to sustainability goals.

24.22 B

> **Examiner's comments**. The examiner noted that almost 50% of students selected the wrong answer. The key words in the question were 'arises from a permanent reduction in demand'. This would rule out cyclical and seasonal as these both imply peaks and troughs, not 'permanent reduction'. The examiner advised that students read the questions carefully and look for key words in the statement or question. The key words will help students choose the right option and steer them away from incorrect ones.

24.23 D **Rationale**: These are three of the ways that government can directly affect the economic structure, according to Porter. Demand is affected as the government is a major customer. Governments can affect capacity expansion, for example, by using taxation policies to encourage investment in equipment. Government can introduce regulations and controls within an industry which may affect growth and profits and may therefore affect competition.

24.24 A

> **Examiner's comments**. The examiner commented that only 36% of students got this question correct. The examiner stated that it is important for students to be realistic about what the external auditing function can achieve. (In other words, common sense should help to answer this type of question.)

25 Mixed bank 6

25.1 D **Rationale:** The shareholders are the owners, as they provide the capital for the business.

Pitfalls: Read the options carefully. Shareholders are not the same as stakeholders (individuals or groups who have an interest or stake in the business). Don't be distracted by the distinction between 'executive' and 'non-executive' directors: they are still directors (people appointed by shareholders to run the company).

25.2 A **Rationale:** This is the definition of the 'technostructure' in Mintzberg's components of structure. D defines the 'strategic apex' component of the model.

Pitfalls: Options B and C are distractors, in case you related 'techno-…' to technology or the people who are assumed to work with it. Get to grips with definitions of key models!

25.3 C **Rationale:** Secure continuity of supply *and* quality are Z's priorities. Long-term partnership helps secure both (i), while having a small number of suppliers avoids the risk of supplier failure (ii).

Ways in: If you highlighted the issues in the micro-scenario, you should be able to consider the consequences of each of the strategies listed: options (iii) and (iv) should stand out as posing risks to quality and supply.

25.4 B **Rationale:** This is the definition of tactical management, carried out by middle management. Strategic management is at a higher level of establishing corporate direction and policy: carried out by senior management. Operational management is at a lower level of implementing the tactical plans: carried out by supervisors and operatives.

Pitfalls: You may have been sidetracked by the word 'innovating', if you associated it with strategic innovation. However, in this context, innovating simply means finding new ways to achieve business goals.

Ways in: If you distinguished carefully between 'means' and 'ends' you could rule out strategy (which is concerned with ends).

25.5 A **Rationale:** Strategic management is a process which may or may not be carried out in a given organisation. Executive directorship and internal controls are elements of corporate governance.

25.6 C **Rationale:** This is the definition of a progressive tax (such as income tax in general). Option A is a 'regressive' tax (such as road tax) which is the same for all people. Option B is a 'proportional tax' (such as Schedule E income tax within a limited range of income). Option D is the definition of an 'ad valorem' tax.

Pitfalls: Related clusters of terminology are always attractive to examiners, because of potential confusions. (Direct and indirect tax is another example.)

Ways in: If in doubt, think through the key words: they may throw up some ideas. 'Progressive': 'as it progresses', 'going forward': this might help you lean in the direction of option C.

25.7 D **Rationale:** The first three are circumstances defined as redundancy. Dismissal on the grounds of pregnancy is automatically considered to be unfair dismissal.

25.8 D **Rationale:** This should be straightforward if you work through the options.

Ways in: Start with the obvious combinations: 'loans' matches financiers, 'social' matches public. After that, the distinctions are finer – but the options are fewer!

25.9 C **Rationale:** Researchers may connect to this network via the Internet (world wide web), and the university may have an intranet for its own lecturers and students. An extranet, however, is an intranet that is accessible to authorised 'outsiders', using a valid username and password.

Pitfalls: Easy terminology confusion: don't make this mistake!

25.10 C **Rationale:** Ethics are 'moral principles': all the other options set behavioural guidelines of a different sort.

25.11 B **Rationale:** Motivation is the incentive to behave dishonestly: one part of this equation is the risks, and whether they are worth the rewards – so strong disciplinary penalties for fraud are a disincentive. Opportunity is having an opening for fraud: internal checks and controls (such as segregation of duties and authorisations) limit those openings. Dishonesty is a predisposition or tendency to behave unethically: it needs to be spotted early – ideally before a person joins the organisation!

25.12 D **Rationale:** The database concept encourages management to regard data as an organisational resource, which needs to be properly managed. However, there are problems of data security and privacy, due to the potential for unauthorised access and sharing. If the organisation develops its own system from scratch, initial development costs will be high.

25.13 B **Rationale:** The studies were carried out at the Hawthorne Plant of Western Electric. The Ashridge studies are a study in leadership styles (tells, sells, consults, joins). Hofstede's model describes dimensions of difference in national cultures.

147

25.14 A **Rationale:** Political, Economic, Socio-cultural and Technological (PEST) factors are the external factors which may impact on the organisation. SWOT (strengths, weaknesses, opportunities and threats) incorporate data from the environmental scan, by analysing PEST factors that present opportunities and threats: however, the name given to this process is corporate appraisal. Option C would be called competitive intelligence. Option D is a distractor based on the potential confusion with the 'natural environment'.

25.15 C **Rationale:** IASs are standards for financial reporting: the preparation of financial statements and accounts. They are used as bases and benchmarks for companies and national standard-setting systems.

25.16 B **Rationale:** Local nature appreciation groups would have high interest (due to potential environmental impacts) but relatively low power: because of their high interest, though, they might be able to band together or lobby to increase their power. So a 'keep informed' strategy is appropriate to segment B.

25.17 D **Rationale:** Fraud response relates specifically to investigation and damage minimisation (not prevention), including: actions that will be taken to protect the security of records that will be required for identification; protection of vulnerable assets; investigation procedures; and crisis management. Implementing this plan would be the responsibility of a fraud officer.

25.18 B **Rationale:** A growing economy is more easily able to provide welfare services without creating a heavy tax burden on the community. Growth has potential adverse effects for employment, where some sections of the population are unable to adapt to demands for new skills. It also has potential adverse effects for the environment, in terms of resource usage, pollution, emissions etc.

25.19 B **Rationale:** Options (i) and (iv) are managerial attributes.

Ways in: These observations are not exclusive to Bennis: other writers have focused on the same elements, so you didn't need to know Bennis' work (although it is mentioned in the syllabus) to get to an answer here.

25.20 D **Rationale:** Deterrence is an approach which seeks to minimise threats due to deliberate action, by creating penalties to 'put people off' attempting the action. Correction is an approach to ensure that vulnerabilities are dealt with when found. Detection is an approach to identifying vulnerabilities and attacks (eg keeping a log of patient records accessed or removed). Threat avoidance means eliminating a threat (eg by changing the system so no unauthorised access is possible).

25.21 C Rationale: This should be straightforward if you think systematically through the process.

25.22 C **Rationale:** In the PEST model, social factors include demographics: the study of population structures and characteristics. Birth and mortality rates affect population numbers, distribution (if they are unequal in different areas) and age structure (lower birth and mortality rates creates an ageing population).

25.23 B **Rationale:** Interdependence of team members is important, because no-one feels they could earn higher rewards on their own: everyone's contribution is necessary, and everyone 'pulls their weight'.

26 Mixed bank 7

26.1 C **Rationale:** Non-statutory deductions (such as pension contributions) should be authorised, to prevent money being 'siphoned' off via non-existent deductions. However, statutory deductions are non-discretionary: they cannot *not* be authorised!

26.2 C **Rationale:** The production mixer has expert power, because he has knowledge that is recognised and valued by the rest of the staff. The shop-floor staff exercise negative power: the power to disrupt operations. Neither have position power (organisational authority), nor (as far as we know) personal power, or charisma.

Pitfalls: Don't confuse 'personal power' with 'the power of an individual': personal power means charismatic leadership qualities or the ability to inspire followership.

Ways in: You should be able to narrow the options by recognising negative power.

26.3 D   **Rationale:** In Belbin's model, the Plant is the ideas person; the Monitor-Evaluator the discerning critic; and the Team worker the diplomatic relationship-builder.

      Pitfalls: Belbin's model lends itself to exam questions about the different roles, so you really do need to be able to identify and describe each. Not all the role labels are descriptive enough for you to be able to guess...

26.4 C   **Rationale:** There are several risks associated with outsourcing: being locked in to an unsatisfactory relationship; losing in-house assets and knowledge; sharing confidential information; and 'reputational' risk (if the supplier gives poor service, or is found to be unethical in its practices, say). The other statements are untrue: an organisation should *not* outsource its 'core competences' (areas of unique and non-replicable competitive advantage); outsourcing often creates economies of scale (taking advantage of the larger dedicated resources of the contractor); and outsourcing still incurs significant costs, including internal costs of managing the relationship.

26.5 B   **Rationale:** Process theories explore the process by which individuals come to value, select and explore goals: in other words, *how* people become motivated. Content theories (including Maslow's hierarchy of needs and Herzberg's two-factor theory) explore the needs that motivate people to act in certain ways: in other words, *what* motivates people.

      Pitfalls: This is a frequent source of exam questions on motivation: please make sure you get content and process the right way round!

26.6 B   **Rationale:** Reporting by exception means only reporting to managers when there is a deviation from plan. Options A and C would increase information flow. Option D would not address the problem: information overload is about excessive complexity as well as volume!

26.7 A   **Rationale:** This is straightforward, if you recall the managerial grid. It does not represent a continuum (option C) because it assumes that the two things are compatible: they can both be high or low at the same time. The grid can be used in appraisal, to focus attention on the manager's approach, but does not indicate 'success' or effectiveness (option B).

      Pitfalls: Option D is a pure distractor based on potential confusion between 'grid' and 'matrix'. Remember, questions aren't designed to trick you, but they are designed to test your knowledge – not your ability to guess plausibly!

26.8 D   **Rationale:** Closed questions pin the candidate down to either/or options. Probing questions push for an answer where a candidate is being vague. Open questions wouldn't work here, because they give the candidate space to answer in any way (s)he wishes. You may have hesitated over leading questions, but these would encourage the candidate to give a *particular* reply, suggested by the interviewer – not to pin down what the *candidate* meant.

      Pitfalls: This is classic objective-testing question territory: make sure you can identify all types of question by name and from examples.

26.9 C   **Rationale:** An instrumental orientation accounts for why some people take jobs offering high monetary rewards rather than intrinsic interest or job satisfaction (up to a certain point). Option B is a form of job design which more or less assumes the *opposite*: that people seek intrinsic satisfactions in work itself. Option D is an approach to motivation based on the assumption (not always accurate) that workers have an instrumental orientation to work. Option A is irrelevant, relating to McGregor's Theory X and Theory Y.

      Pitfalls: Be ready to think through questions that address more than one area of the syllabus.

26.10 A   **Rationale:** 'Tell and listen' is one of Maier's three approaches to appraisal interviewing: 'tell and sell' and 'problem-solving' are the other two approaches.

26.11 A   **Rationale:** You can take advantage of personal work patterns, which include times of high energy and focus as well as low. The other options all expose you to the demands of other people, which may be harder to manage.

26.12 B   **Rationale:** Esteem needs are for recognition and respect from others. Option A would be self-actualisation and option D would be a social need.

       Pitfalls: Worth learning the hierarchy of needs in order of priority: a question may test your understanding that once a level of need is satisfied, you move up to the next level.

26.13 C   **Rationale:** This is the definition of dorming. Forming is a 'getting to know each other' stage; norming the development of agreed ways of behaving; and storming a stage of conflict and testing.

26.14 D   **Rationale:** This should be straightforward, if you work through the options carefully. A person specification is prepared *from* a job description. Testing follows interviewing, as a more rigorous form of selection. Reference checking comes last, as it only applies to candidates who are potentially going to be offered a job.

26.15 B   **Rationale:** A coach is often the trainee's immediate superior: indeed, coaching is accepted as a style of management/leadership. A mentor is *not* usually the immediate superior of the protégé, so that there can be open, confidential discussion of work and non-work issues.

26.16 B   **Rationale:** Cognitive psychology argues that the human mind uses feedback information on the results of past behaviour to make rational decisions about whether to maintain successful behaviours or modify unsuccessful behaviours, according to the outcomes we want. Behaviourist psychology focuses on the relationship between stimuli and responses: we are 'conditioned' to respond in ways that are repeatedly positively reinforced (rewarded) and to avoid behaviours that are repeatedly negatively reinforced (punished). Option C is not a learning theory, and option D is a particular learning model (by Honey & Mumford) not relevant here.

       Ways in: Contingency theory should be familiar from organisation and management topics: you could rule that out. If you also knew that 'cognitive' means 'thinking', you could probably go a step further...

26.17 B   **Rationale:** The third element in the auditor's independence is the responsibility structure – which does *not* mean freedom from accountability (option D). The internal auditor is accountable to the highest executive level in the organisation (preferably the audit committee of the board of directors). Option B is the opposite of independence: internal auditors should not install new procedures or systems, or engage in activities, which they will later have to appraise – as this might (or might be seen to) compromise their independence.

26.18 C   **Rationale:** Cultural change is a good reason to seek 'new blood' in management, rather than promote people who are used to thinking in familiar ways. Options A and D argue for internal promotion as a matter of policy and staff retention (option A) and as a way of preserving culture (option D). You may have hesitated over option B, but note that the vacancy is not immediate: organisations often plan ahead to develop people for promotion (succession planning).

26.19 A   **Rationale:** Off-the-job training allows people to make mistakes in learning, without the costs and consequences of making the same mistakes on the job. However, formal courses may *not* always be directly relevant to the circumstances of the job and workplace (option B), and it may not be easy to 'transfer learning' from the classroom to the job, for various reasons (option C). Meanwhile, formal courses take people away from work (option D). You could think of options B, C and D as advantages of on-the-job training.

       Pitfalls: Make sure you get 'off-the-job' and 'on the job' the right way round as you read the question – and as you think through the options.

26.20 C   **Rationale:** Remember that direct discrimination is less favourable treatment of a protected group. Indirect discrimination is when requirements cannot be justified on non-discriminatory grounds.

26.21 B   **Rationale:** This is likely to be a sensitive issue. How do you identify job applicants' ethnic origins without potentially causing offence or suspicion? How do you apply particular performance monitoring to ethnic minority staff without seeming to discriminate? All the other options are much more straightforward!

26.22 D **Rationale:** The first three options are internal checks to an internal control system. External auditors will need to check that directors and management act on any internal audit recommendations.

26.23 B **Rationale:** The lowest level is how trainees feel about the training: this is an inexact measure of results. Level 2 is trainee learning, measuring what the trainees have learned (what they know or can do at the end of the course, compared to pre-training tests): the likely focus of trainers. Level 3 is changes in job behaviour, which measures whether learning has been *applied* successfully to the job: the likely focus of departmental managers. Level 4 is whether these changes result in measurable performance gains for the organisation: the likely focus of senior management's cost-benefit analysis of training. Level 5 (which many organisations never reach) is evaluating impacts on 'wider' goals such as greater social responsibility.

Pitfalls: Try to understand the logic of the levels, and what they measure – otherwise, it is easy to mix them up!

Ways in: You should be able to allocate trainee reactions to the lowest, and 'ultimate value' to the highest spots, which narrows the remaining options.

26.24 C **Rationale:** Physical access controls are basically 'lock and key' systems – basic though that may sound! Card entry and PIN systems are ways of identifying yourself (by swipe card and keypad entry respectively) in order to gain authorised entry to an area or storage device. Logical access systems are non-physical access controls, involving password-protected access to data in the system. Back-ups are not access controls at all: they are integrity and/or contingency controls.

26.25 B **Rationale:** Connected stakeholders include shareholders, customers, suppliers and financiers. Don't confuse this with internal stakeholders which include employees and management.

27 Mixed bank 8

27.1 B The span of control refers to the number of subordinates immediately reporting to a superior official. Delayering would mean that more subordinates would report to one of the superior officials so the span of control is widened. The scalar chain is concerned with the chain of command and the number of levels of management.

27.2 B According to the Chartered Institute of Marketing, marketing is 'the management process which identifies, anticipates and satisfies customer needs profitably'. The other answer options relate to specific activities carried out by a marketing department.

27.3 A Non-executive directors should provide a balancing influence and play a key role in reducing conflicts of interest between management and shareholders.

27.4 B The principal concern in a task culture is to get the job done. The higher education organisation has the flexibility required to implement this.

27.5 D A situation analysis is carried out when formulating strategic objectives.

27.6 C In decentralisation, the motivation and accountability of local managers is increased.

27.7 C The others are known as connected stakeholders.

27.8 D The answer A group need minimal effort. The answer B group need to be treated with care and the C answer group need to be kept informed.

27.9 D Their aim is to minimise breaches of legislative requirements and ensure compliance of the relevant standards.

27.10 B The aging population trend is caused by a decreasing birth rate and a decreasing mortality rate.

27.11 D Answers A and B would have the reverse effect. Increasing public expenditure should increase the level of consumer demand and therefore the level of economic activity.

27.12 A Structural unemployment occurs when there is a change in demand conditions.

27.13 B These are the external factors which impact the business.

27.14 B Data Protection legislation protects individuals about whom data is held, but not all data is regulated.

27.15 B Discrimination can arise on the basis of gender, race, lifestyle and age.

27.16 C Consumption is consumer spending. Investment means investment by enterprises.

27.17 A Lobbyists put their case to individual ministers or civil servants.

27.18 C The scientific management aim is for increased efficiency in production, that is, increased productivity.

27.19 B The original role was that of recording financial information. The role today is much wider.

27.20 A Tax avoidance involves making decisions which will minimise the tax liability. Tax evasion is deliberating not paying tax which is lawfully due.

27.21 A A system used to record sales and purchases is a transaction processing system.

27.22 B The internal auditor's role is to monitor the effectiveness of the controls in place. It is not their responsibility to implement systems.

27.23 C Some privatised firms are monopolies, in that they have no competitors. To ensure that they do not abuse their position, there are regulatory bodies (eg OFWAT for water) which control their policies.

27.24 B The interest rate is the price of money. A rise in interest rates will raise the price of borrowing, and increase the interest that can be made on surplus funds.

27.25 B The IASB forms financial reporting standards which businesses must implement. This ensures consistency in corporate reporting.

27.26 A The payroll, purchase ledger and sales invoicing would normally be the responsibility of the financial accountant. Gordon works in the management accounts function. Helene works in the internal audit department. Ian might work in the treasury department or the management accounts department.

27.27 A Where price inflation is high the value of money reduces steadily over time.

27.28 A The internal auditor is accountable to the highest executive level in the organisation.

27.29 C The computerised system is more costly to implement in the beginning. This is only a short-term disadvantage and the advantages outweigh the disadvantage.

27.30 D A systems audit is based on a testing and evaluation of the internal controls.

27.31 B The external auditor expresses an opinion on the financial statements.

27.32 A Substantive tests are used to discover errors and omissions.

27.33 A Teeming and lading is the theft of cash or cheque receipts. It is done by setting subsequent receipts against the outstanding debt to conceal the theft.

27.34 B One of the prerequisites for fraud is opportunity. Identifying areas of potential risk should reduce the opportunities to commit fraud.

27.35 B The Ashridge model states that an autocratic style acknowledges the least contribution from subordinates.

27.36 B Blake and Mouton designed the management grid. It is based on two fundamental ingredients of behaviour, namely concern for production (or the task) and concern for people.

27.37 B Forming the stage where the team is just coming together and may still be seen as a collection of individuals.

27.38 C A resource-investigator is popular, sociable, extrovert, relaxed; source of new contacts, but not an originator.

27.39 B Pay is a hygiene factor. According to Herzberg, hygiene factors, no matter how advanced and favourable could never motivate; however dissatisfaction with them could demotivate.

27.40 C   A consensus is the majority of opinion so the input of all team members is considered.

27.41 B   Valence is the strength of the individual preference for a given outcome or reward.

27.42 A   Pressure to reduce personnel costs and to adapt to new market imperatives has increased the use of part-time and temporary contracts of employments.

27.43 D   The wheel is the fastest followed by the Y, then the chain, and finally the circle.

27.44 B   Lateral communication may be used to co-ordinate the work of several people and perhaps departments who have to co-operate to carry out a certain operation.

27.45 A   Role playing exercises are most useful for developing and practising skills.

27.46 C   'Product' can also be replaced with the word 'service'.

27.47 C   A tests memory and problem solving skills. B tests a variety of characteristics such as ambition and motivation. D tests psychological factors such as aptitude, intelligence and personality.

27.48 B   On average men are taller than women so this is an indirect discrimination on the grounds of gender.

27.49 C   Answers A, B and D are shorter term roles than a mentor so 'medium to long-term' was the clue.

27.50 B   The tell and listen approach is where the manager tells the subordinate how (s)he has been assessed and then invites the appraisee to respond.

Mock Exams

FIA

Paper FAB

Accountant in Business

Mock Examination 1

Pilot paper

Question Paper	
Time allowed	**2 hours**
ALL 50 questions are compulsory and MUST be attempted	

DO NOT OPEN THIS PAPER UNTIL YOU ARE READY TO START UNDER EXAMINATION CONDITIONS

If you are sitting your exam on the computer, you can attempt the Pilot Paper as a computer-based exam on ACCA's website:

http://62.254.188.145/main.html

ALL FIFTY questions are compulsory and MUST be attempted

1   Which of the following are substantive tests used in the context of external audit of financial accounts?

    A   To establish whether a figure is correct
    B   To investigate why a figure is incorrect
    C   To assess whether a figure should be included
    D   To determine why a figure is excluded   **(2 marks)**

---

2   The following are four styles of management identified by Blake and Mouton:

    1   Team
    2   Middle of the road
    3   Country club
    4   Authoritarian

Which of the following are the most task efficient managerial styles as suggested by Blake and Mouton?

    A   1 and 3
    B   2 and 4
    C   1 and 4
    D   2 and 3   **(2 marks)**

---

3   In relation to the management of conflict, which of the following approaches will maximise the prospect of consensus?

    A   Acceptance
    B   Negotiation
    C   Avoidance
    D   Assertiveness   **(2 marks)**

---

4   Darragh has been appointed to the management team of a professional football club. His role includes coaching, mentoring and counselling young players who have just signed contracts with the club for the first time.

The following are his main activities:

    1   Helping the young players to settle in during their first week
    2   Identifying each player's key skills and encouraging them to develop new skills
    3   Advising the players on addressing personal issues, such as managing their finances
    4   Helping the players to anticipate opponents' reactions

Which of the following matches the correct role to carry out in each of the four activities?

    A   1. Mentor 2. Counsellor 3. Coach 4. Counsellor
    B   1. Mentor 2. Coach 3. Counsellor 4. Coach
    C   1. Mentor 2. Coach 3. Counsellor 4. Mentor
    D   1. Counsellor 2. Mentor 3. Coach 4. Counsellor   **(2 marks)**

---

5   According to Mendelow which group of stakeholders must companies keep satisfied?

    A   Those with little power and little interest in the company
    B   Those with a high level of power but little interest in the company
    C   Those with little power but a high level of interest in the company
    D   Those with a high level of power and a high level of interest in the company   **(2 marks)**

6   Martin is an experienced and fully trained shipbuilder, based in a western European city. Due to significant economic change in supply and demand conditions for shipbuilding in Martin's own country, the shipyard he worked for has closed and he was made redundant. There was no other local demand for his skills within his own region and he would have to move to another country to obtain a similar employment, and could only find similar work locally through undertaking at least a year's retraining in a related engineering field.

Which of the following describes the type of unemployment that Martin has been affected by?

A   Structural unemployment
B   Cyclical unemployment
C   Frictional unemployment
D   Marginal unemployment   **(2 marks)**

7   Which of the following is the MAIN function of marketing?

A   To maximise sales volume
B   To identify and anticipate customer needs
C   To persuade potential consumers to convert latent demand into expenditure
D   To identify suitable outlets for goods and services supplied   **(2 marks)**

8   The following are sanctions used against companies for potentially unlawful actions:

1   Investigation of its financial affairs by a government department or agency
2   Imposition of a fine by the government's company registration body
3   Refusal of the external auditor to sign the financial accounts
4   Suspension of dealings in securities by the stock exchange

Which of the above are the consequences of a listed company failing to file its accounts?

A   1 and 2
B   1 and 3
C   2 and 4
D   3 and 4   **(2 marks)**

9   The overall average age of a population in a country is directly dependent on two demographic factors: Birth rate and death rate.

Assuming equal rates of change, which of the following must lead to an overall ageing of the population?

	Birth rate	Death rate
A	Rising	Rising
B	Falling	Rising
C	Rising	Falling
D	Falling	Falling

                                                                            (2 marks)

10 Gils is conducting an appraisal interview with his assistant Jill. He initially feeds back to Jill areas of strengths and weaknesses of performance but then invites Jill to talk about the job, her aspirations, expectations and problems. He adopts a non-judgemental approach and offers suggestions and guidance.

This is an example of which approach to performance appraisal?

A   Tell and sell approach
B   Tell and listen approach
C   Problem solving approach
D   360 degree approach   **(2 mark)**

11   What is the primary responsibility of the external auditor?

    A   To verify all the financial transactions and supporting documentation of the client
    B   To ensure that the client's financial statements are reasonably accurate and free from bias
    C   To report all financial irregularities to the shareholders of the client
    D   To ensure that all the client's financial statements are prepared and submitted to the relevant authorities on time   **(2 marks)**

12   Marcus is charged with the leadership of a multi-disciplinary work team to oversee the development of a new accounting system. He determines that he must ensure that he has representatives from each of the sections in the finance directorate. He finds that the team starts to work well but gradually fails to deliver viable options. The meetings deteriorate into arguments as to who is responsible for what. There is no clear sense of direction. No one seems to take responsibility for the investigation of new options. No one seems to be assessing progress at each meeting.

Marcus may or may not be responsible for the following failures:

1   Failure to ensure effective team management

2   Failure to allow the team enough time to develop

Which failures is Marcus responsible for?

    A   1 only
    B   2 only
    C   Neither failure
    D   Both failures   **(2 marks)**

13   Wasim is the Customer Services Manager in a large leisure park. The forthcoming weekend is going to be the busiest of the year, as it is a public holiday. Wasim has to cope with several absentees, leaving him short-staffed in public areas of the park. His manager has told him that he expects him to catch up with some administrative reports that were due last week. Wasim also has to arrange for six new staff to be trained, who will be arriving imminently.

In order to manage his workload most effectively, what should Wasim do?

    A   Prioritise the tasks in relation to the most important business outcomes
    B   Deal with the reports that the manager insists be prepared
    C   Train the new recruits
    D   Carry out some of the work that the absentees would normally do   **(2 marks)**

14   In order to discharge their duties ethically, finance directors must ensure that the information published by their organisations provides a complete and precise view of the position of the business, without concealing negative aspects that may distort the reader's perception of its position.

This duty describes which of the following ethical principles?

    A   Probity
    B   Honesty
    C   Independence
    D   Objectivity   **(2 marks)**

15   Which of the following is a purpose of the International Federation of Accountants?

    A   Agreement of legally binding financial reporting standards across all member accountancy organisations
    B   Prevention of international financial crimes, such as money laundering and insider dealing
    C   Promotion of ethical standards in all member organisations
    D   Development of universally applicable detailed rules to deter inappropriate behaviours   **(2 marks)**

16   The following government policies can be used to expand or slow down the level of economic activity.

1   Taxation
2   Public expenditure

Which of the following combinations of policy would maximise expansion of the economy?

A   Increase 1 and increase 2
B   Increase 1 and reduce 2
C   Reduce 1 and increase 2
D   Reduce 1 and reduce 2   **(2 marks)**

17   Neill works as the procurement manager of JL Company, a large services company.

Information provided by Neill is most relevant to which of the following elements of the marketing mix?

A   Physical evidence
B   Distribution (or place)
C   Price
D   Processes   **(2 marks)**

18   Which of the following are features of informal networks?

1   They undermine formal structures
2   They directly support management objectives
3   They develop spontaneously
4   They reflect patterns of power and influence

A   1 and 4
B   2 and 3
C   1 and 2
D   3 and 4   **(2 marks)**

19   Malachi has been asked by his manager to obtain information about ABC Company, which is bidding for a contract offered by Malachi's company in the near future. The two statements which he will be using as his sources are the statement of financial position (SOFP) and the income statement (IS). The information he is required to obtain is as follows:

1   The equity of the company
2   Operating costs as a percentage of turnover
3   Long-term borrowings
4   Liquidity

Which of the following correctly matches the above items of information with the financial statements in which they would be found?

	1.	2.	3.	4.
A	SOFP	IS	IS	SOFP
B	IS	SOFP	SOFP	IS
C	IS	SOFP	IS	SOFP
D	SOFP	IS	SOFP	IS

(2 marks)

20   Linh owns a busy restaurant. She has had complaints from regular customers about diners failing to control their noisy and unruly children, which is spoiling their dining experiences.

Which of the following courses of action would be regarded as a pluralist solution to this problem?

A   Setting aside a separate section of the restaurant for families with children
B   Not accepting bookings from families with children
C   Advising customers that the restaurant is a family restaurant before they book
D   Taking no action, assuming that those who complain will always be a minority   **(2 mark)**

21 M Co has decided to outsource its IT support to N Co.

   Which of the following are DISADVANTAGES to M Co as a result of this decision?

   1   M Co becomes a more complex organisation
   2   Urgent IT issues at M Co may not be resolved as quickly
   3   Ongoing IT costs of M Co will increase
   4   Longer term contracts with N Co are prone to disruption

   A   1 and 3
   B   2 and 3
   C   1 and 4
   D   2 and 4   (2 marks)

22 The system used by a company to summarise sales and purchases is an example of which of the
   following?

   A   A transaction processing system
   B   A management information system
   C   An office automation system
   D   A decision support system   (2 marks)

23 The following are stakeholders of a business organisation:

   1   Manager
   2   Customer
   3   Executive Director
   4   Supplier

   Which of the above are CONNECTED stakeholders?

   A   1, 2 and 3
   B   2 and 4
   C   2 and 3 only
   D   3 and 4   (2 marks)

24 ABC Co has a system which records details of orders received and goods despatched, invoices
   customers and allocates remittances to customers.

   What type of system is this?

   A   Management information system
   B   Decision support system
   C   Knowledge management system
   D   Transaction processing system   (2 marks)

25 Role playing exercises using video recording and playback would be most effective for which type of
   training?

   A   Development of selling skills
   B   Regulation and compliance
   C   Dissemination of technical knowledge
   D   Introduction of new processes or procedures   (2 marks)

26   Renata has attended a leadership development course in which she experienced a self-analysis exercise using the Blake and Mouton managerial grid. The course leader informed her that the results suggested that Renata demonstrated a 9·1 leadership style.

What other conclusions may be drawn in relation to Renata's leadership style?

1   She maximises the involvement of her team
2   She demonstrates little concern for people in the team
3   She balances the needs of the team with the need to complete the task
4   She is highly focused on achieving the objectives of the team

A   1 and 2
B   2 and 4
C   1 and 4
D   2 and 3   **(2 marks)**

27   ABC sells mobile telephones. Each phone sold is supplied with a charger, earpiece, car charger and other accessories which can only be used with ABC Co phones. Its predictive text style is also very different to that of other manufacturers.

To which of Porter's five forces is this strategy intended to respond?

A   Bargaining power of suppliers
B   Bargaining power of customers
C   Threat of new entrants
D   Intensity of competitive rivalry   **(2 marks)**

28   DEF Co supplies a patented bottled sauce through supermarkets and independent food shops throughout the world.

Which of the following represents the main barriers to entry in DEF Co's industry?

1   Supplier concentration
2   Access to distribution channels
3   Economies of scale
4   Industry growth rate

A   1, 2 3, and 4
B   1 and 3 only
C   2 and 4 only
D   2 and 3 only   **(2 marks)**

29   Poor quality lateral communication will result in which of the following?

A   Lack of direction
B   Lack of coordination
C   Lack of delegation
D   Lack of control   **(2 marks)**

30   The following are either characteristics of a co-operative or of a public limited company:

1   Maximising the excess of income over expenditure not a primary objective

2   Members can vote according to the number of shares owned

3   Shares can be bought and sold through personal transactions of the members

4   All members are invited to attend the annual general meeting and participate in decisions at the meeting

Which of the above are the characteristics of public limited companies?

A   2, 3 and 4
B   2 and 3 only
C   2 and 4 only
D   3 and 4 only   **(2 marks)**

31   A company has advertised for staff who must be at least 1·88 metres tall and have been in continuous full-time employment for at least five years.

Which of the following is the legal term for this practice?

A   Direct discrimination
B   Indirect discrimination
C   Victimisation
D   Implied discrimination   **(2 marks)**

32   Which one of the following statements is correct in relation to monetary rewards in accordance with Herzberg's two-factor theory?

A   Pay increases are a powerful long-term motivator
B   Inadequate monetary rewards are a powerful dissatisfier
C   Monetary rewards are more important than non-monetary rewards
D   Pay can never be used as a motivator   **(2 marks)**

33   In a higher education teaching organisation an academic faculty is organised into courses and departments, where teaching staff report both to course programme managers and to subject specialists, depending on which course they teach and upon their particular subject specialism.

According to Charles Handy's four cultural stereotypes, which of the following describes the above typeof organisational structure?

A   Role
B   Task
C   Power
D   Person   **(2 marks)**

34   Which pattern of communication is the quickest way to send a message?

A   The circle
B   The chain
C   The Y
D   The wheel   **(2 marks)**

35   Which of the following measures will help an organisation to limit its environmental impact?

1   Recycling waste
2   Using energy efficient electrical appliances
3   Selecting suppliers carefully
4   Buying raw materials locally

A   1 and 2 only
B   2 and 4 only
C   1 and 3 only
D   1, 2, 3 and 4   **(2 marks)**

36   Which of the following types of new legislation would provide greater employment opportunities in large companies?

A   New laws on health and safety
B   New laws to prevent discrimination in the workplace
C   New laws making it more difficult to dismiss employees unfairly
D   New laws on higher compensation for employer breaches of employment contracts
                                                                         (2 marks)

37   What is the responsibility of a Public Oversight Board?

A   The establishment of detailed rules on internal audit procedures
B   The commissioning of financial reporting standards
C   The creation of legislation relating to accounting standards
D   The monitoring and enforcement of legal and compliance standards   **(2 marks)**

38   Richard is a highly enthusiastic member of his team. An extrovert by nature, he is curious and communicative. He responds to new challenges positively and has a capacity for contacting people, xploring anything new. However, his attention span is short and he tends to become less involved in a task once his initial interest has passed.

According to Belbin's team roles theory, Richard displays the characteristics of which of the following?

A   Monitor-evaluator
B   Plant
C   Resource-investigator
D   Company worker   (2 marks)

39   The aggregate level of demand in the economy is made up of government expenditure, _____, _____ and net gains from international trade.

Which of the following correctly completes the sentence above?

1   Savings
2   Taxation
3   Investment
4   Consumption

A   1 and 3
B   2 and 3
C   3 and 4
D   1 and 4   (2 marks)

40   James conducts a systematic review of suppliers' delivery notes.

Which of the following does the above control relate to?

A   Distribution
B   Credit limits
C   Quality management
D   Goods inwards   (2 marks)

41   Which of the following statements about price elasticity are correct?

1   It is defined as the percentage change in price divided by percentage change in demand
2   An item which has an elasticity greater than one is price insensitive
3   An item which has an elasticity of less than one is said to be inelastic
4   If demand for an item is inelastic and its price falls, total revenue will decrease

A   1 and 2
B   2 and 4
C   1 and 3
D   3 and 4   (2 marks)

42   FKT Company is considering the introduction of a code of ethics following media criticism of its selling practices.

Which of the following is most important when deciding on the content of the proposed code of ethics?

A   The minimum acceptable standards of behaviour and conduct of employees (KEY)
B   The legal requirements affecting the sales of core products and services
C   The main issues of concern to customers who have made complaints
D   The generally accepted standards by other companies operating in the same sector
                                                                                (2 marks)

43   Ilya is the union representative at Acorn College. He is also head of studies responsible for the recruitment and appraisal of lecturing and administrative staff. The union is in dispute with the government over teaching salaries and staffing levels.

What phenomenon is Ilya experiencing?

A   Role ambiguity
B   Role conflict
C   Role overlap
D   Role duplication   (2 marks)

44   Jackie leads an established team of six workers. In the last month, two have left to pursue alternative jobs and one has commenced maternity leave. Three new staff members have joined Jackie's team.

Which one of Tuckman's group stages will now occur?

A   Norming
B   Forming
C   Performing
D   Storming   (2 marks)

45   In the context of fraud, 'teeming and lading' is most likely to occur in which area of operation?

A   Sales
B   Quality control
C   Advertising and promotion
D   Despatch   (2 marks)

46   Which of the following should be considered first in order to establish an effective internal control system that will minimise the prospect of fraud?

A   Recruitment policy and checks on new personnel
B   Identification of areas of potential risk
C   Devising appropriate sanctions for inappropriate behaviour
D   Segregation of duties in critical areas   (2 marks)

47   Which of the following is a DISADVANTAGE of using a committee rather than an individual to make a decision?

A   Slower decisions
B   Unsupported decisions
C   Autocratic decisions
D   Unworkable decisions   (2 marks)

48   Which of the following would be acting in the public interest?

1   An auditor publicly disclosing the identity of a whistleblower at a client organisation
2   An employee at an airline company reporting unsafe practices
3   An auditor of a charity reporting a material fraud
4   An accountant at a listed company reporting illegal accounting to a stock exchange regulator

A   2 and 4 only
B   1 and 3 only
C   2, 3 and 4
D   1, 2 and 3   (2 marks)

49   The following activities are either legal or illegal.

1   Tax avoidance
2   Tax evasion

Which of the above are legal?

A   1 only
B   2 only
C   Both 1 and 2
D   Neither activity   **(2 marks)**

50   According to Vroom:

Force (or motivation) = _____ x _____

Which of the following words complete Vroom's equation?

A   Valence and Opportunity
B   Expectancy and Needs
C   Valence and Expectancy
D   Needs and Opportunity   **(2 marks)**

Answers to Mock Exam 1

DO NOT TURN THIS PAGE UNTIL YOU HAVE
COMPLETED THE MOCK EXAM

ACCA Examiner's answers. The Examiner's answers to all the questions in Mock Exam 1 are included at the back of this kit.

1   A   Substantive tests are tests for accuracy and they are used to establish facts. The other tests are less specific and arguably more subjective.

2   C   Only the Task and Authoritarian styles have the value of the task rated at 9 on the Blake and Mouton grid, so these are the most task efficient styles.

3   B   Negotiation gives the best opportunity for the two sides in a conflict to converge their positions. The other options either involve backing down, forcing a position, potentially increasing conflict, or leaving the issue unresolved.

4   B   Mentors usually help staff on broader work related development, including orientation and induction. Coaches work on developing specific skills of the job itself, while counsellors work with people on a personal level, perhaps if they are having non-work related or emotional problems.

5   B   Companies need to keep satisfied only those stakeholders who have high power, but little interest. The others can either be largely ignored, merely kept informed or treated as key players.

6   A   Because of the particular circumstances of the scenario where someone is made redundant from an industry in decline where skills cannot be easily transferred, where re-training might take a long time or where work is not available in the short term within a reasonable geographic proximity, this is classed as structural unemployment.

7   B   The basic principle that underlies marketing is that it is a management process that identifies and anticipates customer needs. The other distracters in the question refer to specific activities undertaken by a sales or promotion function.

8   C   The normal sanctions in such a case is that fines are imposed on companies by the registration body of the company and, where listed, the company may be delisted by the stock exchange authorities. Although the option wasn't included, sanctions against responsible directors may also be imposed.

9   D   The ageing population trend is caused by a decreasing birth rate and a decreasing mortality rate.

10   B   The 'tell and listen' approach encourages input from the individual, promoting participation in the process by the appraisee.

11   B   The external auditor has to ensure that the financial statements of the organisation truly reflect the activities of the business in the relevant accounting period. This assessment should be independent and therefore free from subjectivity on the part of the management of the client organisation.

12   A   The team leader has allowed the team to develop as they were performing well initially, but because of the later failures, has clearly failed to manage the team effectively overall.

13   A   An employee with a range of tasks or objectives to achieve and pressures to achieve them to set deadlines, should always prioritise tasks in accordance to business importance. Deciding on other criteria such as pressure applied by colleagues, whether someone is absent or not or simply because a task is urgent may damage wider business objectives.

14   D   A professional accountant acting in accordance with fundamental ethical principles is demonstrating objectivity when they give a complete and precise view, which by implication means that negative aspects should not be concealed or positive aspects accentuated.

15   C   IFAC has no legal powers against businesses, nor does it set financial reporting standards. It is an accounting association member body which promotes educational and ethical standards of behaviour amongst its member bodies, through a code of ethics and behaviour, but does not prescribe detailed rules on this.

16   C   Increasing taxation leaves individuals with less disposable income for expenditure within the economy thereby slowing economic activity. The same effect is caused by a reduction in government expenditure. Therefore economic activity can be stimulated by reducing taxation and increasing government expenditure.

17   C   Information on purchase costs of finished goods or raw materials is important in establishing the price of a product. In terms of the marketing mix, this information is most relevant to the price element as prices should be set at least to cover cost and give an acceptable level of profit.

18   D   Informal networks neither directly support nor undermine formal authority or management objectives, but they do emerge spontaneously and are often influenced by the patterns of unofficial power and influence within organisations.

19   D   The key correctly matches the information required to the particular financial statement in which they are to be found.

20   A   The pluralist solution is to cater for the needs of more than one stakeholder group without seriously compromising the interests of any individual group. Therefore setting aside a special area for families with children while having an adults only section would achieve this. The other options involve adversely affecting the rights of one or other group of stakeholders in some way.

21   D   Outsourcing functions like IT simplifies the structure of an organisation and reduces ongoing operational costs, but because support is external to the organisation, there may be a greater lead time required for resolving IT issues. Because there is less direct control over subcontractor's employees, long term projects, in particular, may be prone to disruption.

22   B   Providing a summary of sales and purchases is normally a function of a management information system. A transaction processing or office automation system would mainly concern the *recording* of transactional data, and a decision-support system would *analyse* information.

23   B   is correct because customers and suppliers deal closely on a transactional basis with the organisation, but are not internal stakeholders like managers and executive directors.

24   D   At the operational level, systems connected to individual and batches of input and output processes are known as transactional. Management information, knowledge management and decision support systems are more relevant to the tactical and strategic levels.

25   A   Role playing exercises are most effectively used for skills development, including sales training. Other common business applications include effective selection interviewing and performance appraisal interviewing.

26   B   The Blake and Mouton managerial grid enables leadership styles to be categorised on a nine point scale with reference to concern for production and concern for people. Renata is therefore highly concerned with the task and much less interested in her team as individuals.

27   C   The marketing tactic of making key accessories unique to a particular product discourages competitors from offering substitute products because the costs of so doing will be greater and entry into the market made more difficult. It does not alter the balance of power of suppliers or customers nor affect the intensity of competitive rivalry.

28   D   The main barriers to entry for a sauce manufacturer are ensuring access to a sufficient range and quantity of distribution outlets and producing enough units to benefit from economies of scale that other mass manufacturers of more generic substitute products would achieve. There is no evidence that supplier concentration or industry growth rate in such a market would be considered as significant barriers.

29   B   Poor lateral communication leads to lack of coordination. The other common business problems are connected with upward or downward channels of communication or lines of authority.

30   B   Only shareholders have voting power related to the number of shares that they own. Members of a co-operative organisation can vote but will only have one vote. Co-operatives may be owned by members, but ownership stakes cannot be exchanged between members unless the members belong to limited companies.

31 B To discriminate against someone on the grounds of characteristics which are predominately associated with their sex, gender, nationality or religion is illegal. As women are generally shorter than men, to restrict admission on the basis of height, indirectly discriminates against women. The other options are either direct discrimination, or other illegal and undesirable employment practices.

32 B According to Herzberg, money is a hygiene factor (or dissatisfier). Although it is a powerful short-term motivator, it is questionable whether each individual increase in monetary reward will have a major long-term effect. According to Herzberg, 'A reward once given becomes a right'.

33 B The task culture is appropriate where organisations can accommodate the flexibility required to adjust management and team structures to address the tasks that must be fulfilled. This is very common in large consultancy firms.

34 D The wheel facilitates transmission of the message directly to all receivers and therefore transmits most quickly.

35 D All the options describe measures that will limit environmental impact or potentially reduce the carbon footprint.

36 B Equal opportunity policies widen opportunity and enlarge the potential pool of employees to recruit from. The other options either indirectly or directly reduce the potential for staff turnover and therefore limit the number of job vacancies available at any point in time.

37 D The primary aim of a public oversight board is to eliminate or minimise any actual or potential breaches of legislative requirements and to ensure compliance with regulations applicable to organisations within their terms of reference.

38 C The scenario accurately describes the resource-investigator.

39 C The components of effective demand in the economy are consumer spending, investment by enterprises, central and local government expenditure and the net gains from international trade.

40 D Reviewing suppliers' signatures on delivery notes would be a goods inwards control relating to verifying the authenticity and origin of supplies. The other controls are either more general such as quality or to do with other specific functions such as despatch to customers and credit control.

41 D Only statements 3 and 4 are true.

42 A Compliance with legal requirements may not eliminate unethical behaviour. The issues of concern to those who complain may not be fully representative of issues of concern to customers in general. Other companies in the sector may not be concerned about ethical behaviour.

43 B Ilya as a union representative is experiencing role conflict. This is because he has a responsibility to ensure the efficient management of salary costs as head of studies, but as representative of the union would support better pay and conditions for the union members in his department which he represents.

44 B As new members are about to join the group, essentially the group is reforming which is the start of a new group development process. The other options are all later stages in group development as identified by Tuckman.

45 A Teeming and lading involves the theft of cash and is a type of fraud that is carried out by manipulating transactions. There would be most potential for this fraud within the sales department where cash may be received and remitted.

46 B Before fraud can be prevented it is first necessary to identify areas where fraud is likely to occur before preventative measures can be taken.

47 A Committees are appointed to make democratic, well considered and workable decisions, using the broader expertise of a representative group of people. However, decisions arrived at by committee can take longer to arrive at.

48 C All the actions help to protect the public interest except the first one, which may serve to prejudice further investigations or prevent effective prosecution and may dissuade other whistleblowers from acting in the public interest themselves in future cases.

49   A   Tax avoidance is a way of managing tax affairs to mitigate tax liability legally. Tax evasion is illegal.

50   C   Vroom's formula is calculated through multiplying valence with expectancy. This means a person will be motivated if the reward is both sufficiently attractive and attainable.

FIA

Paper FAB

Accountant in Business

Mock Examination 2

Question Paper	
Time allowed	**2 hours**
All FIFTY questions are compulsory and MUST be attempted	

Please note that it is not possible to predict question topics in an examination of this nature. We have based the content of this Mock Exam on our long experience of the ACCA exams. We do not claim to have any endorsement of the question types or topics from either the examiner or the ACCA and we do not guarantee that either the specific questions or the general areas that are featured here will necessarily be included in the exams, in part or in whole.

We do not accept any liability or responsibility to any person who takes, or does not take, any action based (either in whole or in part and either directly or indirectly) upon any statement or omission made in this book. We encourage students to study all topics in the ACCA syllabus and this Mock Exam is intended as an aid to revision only.

DO NOT OPEN THIS PAPER UNTIL YOU ARE READY TO START UNDER EXAMINATION CONDITIONS

ALL FIFTY questions are compulsory and MUST be attempted

1
1   Private companies can raise share capital by advertising to the general public.
2   Private companies can raise share capital from venture capitalists

Are these statements true or false?

A   Statement 1 is true and statement 2 is false
B   Statement 1 is false and statement 2 is true
C   Both statements are true
D   Both statements are false   **(2 marks)**

2   Nysslit Lerner plc, an organisation of some 400 employees, has an average span of control of three, throughout its structure. From this, which of the following inferences might one make?

A   The work is systematic and routine
B   Job satisfaction is high
C   The level of complexity in the work is high
D   The organisation is flat   **(2 marks)**

3   Which of the following is part of the research and development function of a business?

A   The analysis of survey data on consumer behaviour, produced under contract by an independent market research company
B   Organising exhibitions and sales promotions
C   Creating new products and improving existing ones
D   Contracting independent advertising agencies to promote the products being sold by the company
(2 marks)

4   What does the acronym MIS stand for?

A   Management Improvement Strategy
B   Manufacturing Innovation Strategy
C   Marketing Information System
D   Management Information System   **(2 marks)**

5   Mrs Grey likes swimming and playing badminton as part of her exercise routine. She has a budget of up to $25 to spend each week on getting fit. Each trip to the swimming pool costs $3, and each badminton session costs $4.

Her marginal utility schedule is given below:

Number of trips	Marginal utility of swimming	Marginal utility of badminton
1	90	100
2	80	90
3	70	80
4	60	70
5	50	60

Which combination of activities gives Mrs Grey the highest utility?

	Swimming	*Badminton*
A	1	5
B	3	4
C	4	3
D	2	4

(2 marks)

177

6   You have received a letter from an estate agent, requesting financial information about one of your clients, who is applying to rent a property. The information is needed as soon as possible, by fax or e-mail, or the client will lose approval.

Which of the following ethical principles, identified in the ACCA code of ethics, is raised by the decision of whether, when and how to respond to this request?

A   Objectivity
B   Technical competence
C   Confidentiality
D   Professional behaviour   **(2 marks)**

7   A large, well-established construction company organises itself on a project basis, using temporary matrix and project team structures.

What cultural type is most likely to fit this organisation?

A   Role culture
B   Power culture
C   Task culture
D   Person culture   **(2 marks)**

8   Which one of the following options sets out the required procedures for all of the various functions of a business?

A   An accounting manual
B   A function policy
C   A management information manual
D   A policy manual   **(2 marks)**

9   Which of the following is a purpose of a job evaluation?

A   Identifying individuals' training and development needs
B   Evaluating the organisation's recruitment and selection procedures
C   Improving upward communication
D   Demonstrating compliance with equal pay legislation   **(2 marks)**

10   In the short run, firms will continue to supply customers provided that they cover

A   Fixed costs
B   Marginal costs
C   Variable costs
D   Interest costs   **(2 marks)**

11   Helen, Jack, Sue and Joe work in the finance department of Y Co which has separate financial accounting and management accounting functions. Helen works on inventory valuation, budgetary control and variance analysis. Jack deals with sales invoicing and debt collection. Sue deals with quarterly sales tax returns and corporation tax and Joe carries out risk assessments and assists in project planning. Which member of the department would report to the management accountant?

A   Helen
B   Jack
C   Sue
D   Joe   **(2 marks)**

12   A company has placed a job advertisement for a full time employee and a part time employee. The part time employee's terms are less favourable than the full-time employee's terms. What type of discrimination is this?

A   Direct discrimination
B   Indirect discrimination
C   Victimisation
D   Implied discrimination   **(2 marks)**

13   Individuals may conform with the norms and customs of a group without real commitment. Which of the following terms describes such behaviour?

    A   Compliance
    B   Counter-conformity
    C   Internalisation
    D   Identification   **(2 marks)**

14   Which of the following is a negative contribution of the audit committee, in a corporate governance framework?

    A   Increasing public confidence in the credibility and objectivity of financial statements
    B   Acting as a barrier between the main (executive) board and the external auditors
    C   Giving the finance director a forum to raise issues of concern
    D   Strengthening the position of the internal audit function   **(2 marks)**

15   Which of the following is a feature of ineffective delegation by a manager?

    A   Specifying performance levels and the results expected of the subordinate
    B   Obtaining the subordinate's agreement with the task and expected results
    C   Ensuring that all the subordinate's decisions are confirmed or authorised by the superior
    D   Ensuring that the subordinate reports the results of her decisions to the superior   **(2 marks)**

16   In the context of fraud, which of the following statements is *false*?

    A   Deliberate manipulation of depreciation figures is difficult because of its cash flow effects.

    B   Failure to record expenses accurately will inflate the reported profit figure.

    C   Selling goods to friends (with a promise of buying them back at a later date) is potentially fraudulent.

    D   Employees within or outside the payroll department can perpetrate payroll fraud.   **(2 marks)**

17   If you are a team leader, seeking to evaluate the effectiveness of your team, which of the following criteria should you use?

    Criteria:
    (i)   Contribution to organisational objectives
    (ii)   Fulfilment of group task objectives
    (iii)   Satisfaction of the development needs of members

    A   Criterion (ii) only
    B   Criteria (i) and (ii) only
    C   Criteria (ii) and (iii) only
    D   Criteria (i), (ii) and (iii)   **(2 marks)**

18   In the context of motivation theory, what are Douglas McGregor's Theory X and Theory Y?

    A   Extreme types of managers
    B   Extreme sets of assumptions that managers may have about workers
    C   Extreme types of employees
    D   Extreme sets of attitudes workers may have about their work   **(2 marks)**

19   In the context of interpersonal skills for counselling, ... is the skill of seeing an issue from the other person's point of view and reflecting your understanding back to the other person.

    Which of the following terms correctly completes this sentence?

    A   Rapport-building
    B   Empathy
    C   Active listening
    D   Non-verbal communication   **(2 marks)**

20   Which one of the following is **not** an offence relating to money laundering?

A   Concealing the proceeds of criminal activity
B   Tipping off
C   Dealing in price affected securities
D   Failing to report suspicion of money laundering   **(2 marks)**

21   Of the following patterns of group communication, which was found to be the fastest for problem-solving?

A   Wheel
B   Chain
C   Circle
D   Y   **(2 marks)**

22   Lockett suggested a number of barriers to effective performance appraisal, including 'appraisal as unfinished business'. What is meant by this phrase?

A   Appraisal interviews are subject to interruption or left incomplete
B   The manager is embarrassed by the need to give feedback and set challenging targets, and leaves the interview with unresolved issues.
C   Appraisal is used as a wrapping up of the unresolved performance issues of the past year, rather than focusing on future improvement and problem-solving
D   Appraisal is seen as a sort of show-down, in which unresolved conflicts can be brought into the open   **(2 marks)**

23   In the context of work planning, a .... is an undertaking that has a defined beginning and end and is carried out to meet established goals within cost, schedule and quality objectives.

Which word or phrase correctly completes this definition?

A   Contingency plan
B   Schedule
C   Project
D   Strategy   **(2 marks)**

24   Which of the following is a potential consequence of an organisation, fraudulently understating its results?

A   Excessive distribution of profits to shareholders
B   Restricted access to loan finance
C   Unrealistic expectations in the financial markets
D   Potential shortfalls in working capital   **(2 marks)**

25   The price elasticity of demand (PED) of good A is negative, its income elasticity of demand (IED) is positive and its cross elasticity of demand (XED) with respect to good X is negative. What is the nature of good A?

A   A good bought for purposes of ostentation, complementary to X
B   An inferior good, substitute for X
C   A normal good, complementary to X
D   A Giffen good, substitute for X   **(2 marks)**

26   In the context of Tuckman's model of team development, which of the following sequences of stages is correct?

A   Norming, storming, forming, performing
B   Forming, storming, norming, performing
C   Storming, forming, norming, performing
D   Forming, performing, storming, norming   **(2 marks)**

27   In the regulatory system surrounding financial accounting, which body has as a key objective the development of a single set of enforceable global accounting standards?

    A   The Accounting Standards Board
    B   The International Accounting Standards Board
    C   The European Union
    D   GAAP
    (2 marks)

28   In the context of human resource planning, which *two* of the following documents are the outputs of a process of job analysis?

    (i)   Human resource plan
    (ii)   Job description
    (iii)   Person specification
    (iv)   Performance appraisal

    A   (i) and (ii)
    B   (i) and (iii)
    C   (ii) and (iv)
    D   (ii) and (iii)
    (2 marks)

29   Which of the following would Herzberg class among 'hygiene factors'?

    (i)   Salary
    (ii)   Job security
    (iii)   Gaining recognition
    (iv)   Challenging work

    A   (ii) and (iv) only
    B   (i) only
    C   (i), (ii), (iii) and (iv)
    D   (i) and (ii)
    (2 marks)

30   According to the Ashridge studies on leadership style, what is most important to subordinates about the style of their leader?

    A   Consultation
    B   Direction
    C   Consistency
    D   Authoritarian
    (2 marks)

31   If a government increased its expenditure and reduced levels of taxation, the effect would be to (i) .... demand in the economy and to (ii).............. the size of the Public Sector Net Cash Requirement.

    Which words correctly complete this statement?

    A   (i) stimulate, (ii) reduce
    B   (i) reduce, (ii) reduce
    C   (i) stimulate, (ii) raise
    D   (i) reduce, (ii) raise
    (2 marks)

32   Which of the following employee selection methods has the highest 'predictive validity': that is, which is best at predicting a candidate's performance in the job?

    A   Interviews
    B   Personality testing
    C   Assessment centres
    D   Work sampling
    (2 marks)

33   The following, with one exception, are 'building blocks' for team building. Which *one* is the 'blockage'?

    A   Diverse mix of personalities
    B   Members do not challenge or criticise
    C   Regular reviews of performance
    D   Clear objectives   **(2 marks)**

34   .... learning is a method in which managers are brought together as a problem-solving group to discuss a real work issue, and a facilitator helps them to identify how their interpersonal and problem-solving skills are affecting the process.

What word correctly completes this definition?

    A   Experiential
    B   Action
    C   Off-the-job
    D   Behavioural   **(2 marks)**

35   Which view of ethics states that right and wrong are culturally determined?

    A   Ethical relativism
    B   Cognitivism
    C   Teleological
    D   Deontological   **(2 marks)**

36   Which of the following is a feature of an ineffective job advertisement?

    A   It narrows the pool of people who might go on to apply for the job
    B   It provides all information necessary to make an application
    C   It maximises the attractiveness of the job and organisation to potential applicants
    D   It is relevant and appropriate to the nature of the job and the desired applicants   **(2 marks)**

37   The concept of .... is based on the belief that the types of individual difference which are protected by anti-discrimination legislation are crude and irrelevant to successful performance, and that an organisation can benefit from embracing all kinds of difference.

Which words correctly complete this sentence?

    A   Equal opportunity
    B   Person culture
    C   Managing diversity
    D   Diversification   **(2 marks)**

38   Emma, John, Pratish and Rekha all work for W Co. Emma ensures that goods are only purchased when they are required. John ensures that goods that are purchased are purchased from authorised suppliers. Pratish pays the suppliers' invoices and Rekha evaluates the financial stability of potential suppliers. Three of the members of Q Co work in the purchasing department and one works in the accounting department. Which member works in the accounting department?

    A   Emma
    B   John
    C   Pratish
    D   Rekha   **(2 marks)**

39   In the context of employee development, who developed the well-known classification of learning styles: 'Activist', 'Pragmatist', 'Theorist', 'Reflector'?

    A   Kolb
    B   Honey and Mumford
    C   Tuckman
    D   Ashridge Management College   **(2 marks)**

40   Fish and chips are considered complementary products. If the price of fish rises, what will the impact be in demand for chips?

    A   Rises
    B   Stays the same
    C   Falls
    D   Doubles   **(2 marks)**

41   A female employee is frequently subjected to rude remarks about her dress and weight by male colleagues, as well as jokes of a sexual nature. The woman finds this offensive and hurtful – even though her colleagues say it is 'just a bit of fun'.

What type of discrimination (if any) would this represent?

    A   Indirect discrimination
    B   Victimisation
    C   Harassment
    D   No discrimination is involved   **(2 marks)**

42   In the context of internal control systems which of the following would be included in the 'control procedures'?

    A   Strategies for dealing with significant identified risks
    B   Clear definition of authority, responsibility and accountability
    C   Detailed policies and procedures for administrative and accounting control
    D   Senior management commitment to competence and integrity   **(2 marks)**

43   Which of the following statements about training and development is false?

    A   A gap between current performance and required performance is a learning gap which requires training

    B   Training and development activities can have measurable benefits for organisations

    C   Education may form part of training, which in turn may form part of employee development.

    D   A 'learning organisation' is one which facilitates the learning of all its members.   **(2 marks)**

44   Stephanie works in the internal audit department of M Co. Her duties involve using substantive tests in order to detect fraud. She produces reports to senior management detailing her findings. For which type of audit is Stephanie responsible?

    A   Operational audit
    B   Transactions audit
    C   Efficiency audit
    D   Management audit   **(2 marks)**

45   Julie and Nick are both on the same salary and grade at P Co. Julie is the finance director and Nick is the operations director. A new project team has been created to consider an alternative office location for P Co. Julie and Nick are part of this team. When Julie and Nick communicate with each other, what type of communication is this?

    A   Downward
    B   Diagonal
    C   Lateral
    D   Upward   **(2 marks)**

46   External audit differs fundamentally from internal audit in all the following areas, except one. Which is the only area in which they are partially similar?

    A   Relationship with the client company
    B   Body to which it reports
    C   Purpose of the appraisal activity
    D   Procedures used   **(2 marks)**

47   .... is the study of the aggregated effects of the decisions of individual economic units (such as households or businesses).

Which word correctly completes this sentence?

A   Ergonomics
B   Demographics
C   Globalisation
D   Macro-economics   **(2 marks)**

48   An IT support firm assesses the performance of its staff in four key categories: knowledge currency, technical ability, interpersonal skills and relationships with clients. On each of these criteria staff are marked by ticking a position on a line as follows.

Excellent ____Average_____Poor

What method of appraisal is described by this system?

A   Overall assessment
B   Guided assessment
C   Graphic scale
D   Graphic curve   **(2 marks)**

49   What is the primary purpose of a performance appraisal system?

A   To ensure that employees get adequate feedback on their performance

B   To ensure that there is a fair basis for pay review

C   To ensure that there is a fair basis for promotion and succession planning

D   To improve organisational performance by ensuring that every member develops towards their best contribution.   **(2 marks)**

50   Which of the following is not an advantage of a principles-based ethical code?

A   It prevents narrow, legalistic interpretations
B   It can accommodate a rapidly-changing environment
C   The illustrative examples provided can be followed in all similar situations
D   It prescribes minimum expected standards of behaviour   **(2 marks)**

Answers to Mock Exam 2

1   B   **Rationale:** The key difference between private and public companies is that only public companies can advertise their shares to the general public. Both private and public companies can raise share capital from venture capitalists.

Pitfalls: You had to get your 'private and 'public' companies the right way round.

2   C   **Rationale:** The organisation has a narrow span of control: this would typically be the case if the work is complex, as it requires closer supervision.

Pitfalls: Remember: narrow span typically means tall organisation; wide span typically means flat organisation.

Ways in: Work through each option. Systematic/routine work would not need such a narrow span of control. Nothing can be inferred about job satisfaction from the information given. With a control span of three in a fairly large organisation, the organisation must be tall...

3   C   **Rationale:** Options A, B and D would all be part of the marketing function.

4   D   **Rationale:** Options A and B were simple distractors. The usual acronym for a Marketing Information System is MkIS.

Pitfalls: Read all the options carefully: fine differences are often used to test your focus.

5   B   **Rationale:** Utility is greatest at the point where:

$$\frac{\text{Marginal utility of swimming}}{\text{Price of swimming trip}} = \frac{\text{Marginal utility of badminton}}{\text{Price of badminton session}}$$

$$= \frac{60}{3} = \frac{80}{4} = 20$$

= 4 swimming trips and 3 badminton sessions

Note: 4 swimming trips and 3 badminton sessions cost a total of $24 and so are within the $25 budget. Mrs Grey's overall total utility is restricted by her budget, so the total cost of any combination she might wish to choose must be less than $25.

6   C   **Rationale:** Confidentiality is the immediate ethical issue. You need the client's authority to disclose the information: you may also need to confirm the identity of the person making the request, and take steps to protect the confidentiality of the information if you send it (ie not using fax or e-mail). The other ethical principles do not apply here.

7   C   **Rationale:** A task culture (in Harrison's classification) suits project management structures, with their focus on deliverables (project completion) rather than processes. Role culture suits bureaucratic cultures; power culture, simple/entrepreneurial structures; and person culture, professional partnerships.

Pitfalls: Just because the organisation is large and well-established, don't immediately jump to the conclusion that it is a bureaucracy (role culture)!

8   D   **Rationale:** Every employee will be expected to have read the areas relevant to their functions and the policy manual should always be readily available for easy reference.

9   D   **Rationale:** Equal pay legislation requires that women be paid equal pay to men for work 'of equal value' (to the organisation): this is established by job evaluation. The others are potential purposes of a performance appraisal. Equal pay is about the value of the job, not the value of the job holder. If you hesitated over option B, think of performance appraisal as a way of monitoring whether people really do as well in the job as the selection system predicted they would when they were hired!

10   C   **Rationale:** In the short run, firms will continue to supply customers provided that they cover variable costs. They will incur fixed costs whether they produce any output or not. Therefore provided revenues cover variable costs and therefore make a contribution towards fixed costs, it is beneficial for the firm to continue producing.

11   A   **Rationale:** The Financial Accountant is responsible for activities such as payroll, receivables and payables ledger, credit control, financial accounts and taxation. Jack and Sue would report to the financial accountant. The Treasurer (if there is one) would be responsible for project (investment) appraisal, and his or her priority would be funds management. Joe would report to the treasurer.

Pitfalls: These are essential distinctions: any combination of the tasks and titles could be tested.

12   B   **Rationale:** This is indirect discrimination because most part time employees are women. If it were direct discrimination then the advert would actually state that women had less favourable terms.

13   A   **Rationale:** Compliance is behaving in such a way as to conform, regardless of underlying commitment or attitude: it applies to organisations as well as individuals! Counter-conformity is rejection of group norms. Internalisation is 'inner' acceptance and ownership of the norms. Identification is a separate idea: it is one of the processes through which norms are reinforced in a group.

14   B   **Rationale:** This may sound like an 'independence' benefit, but the key word is 'barrier': the main board needs to take responsibility for the financial statements and be open to question by auditors.

15   C   **Rationale:** There is a fine distinction between option D (making the subordinate accountable) and option C (interfering!) If the superior doesn't trust the subordinate to make decisions, she shouldn't have delegated at all. Options A and B should clearly be effective practice.

16   A   **Rationale:** Depreciation is an expense that doesn't have any cash flow effect, so the figures are easily tampered with: eg understating depreciation to give a healthier net book value. Option B is clearly true. Option C is true because this can be used to create fictitious sales values or manipulate year end results. Option D is true because, for example, any employee can falsify time-sheets, and payroll staff can channel payments to bogus staff accounts.

17   D   **Rationale:** The criteria for team effectiveness are *both* fulfilment of task objectives (which should contribute to organisational objectives) *and* member satisfaction, where that contributes to the ability of the group to fulfil its task (eg in the development of members' skills and abilities).

18   B   **Rationale:** Theory X and Y are only managerial assumptions – which then *influence* the kinds of motivational approaches and leadership styles the manager will adopt. They do not describe actual types of people (managers or employees), nor actual attitudes held by workers.

Pitfalls: You are often asked to show critical awareness and understanding of theories, so it is worth getting this distinction clear.

19   B   **Rationale:** The closest distractor is active listening, as reflecting understanding is one of the ways a listener can be 'active'. (Other ways include questioning, summarising, showing attentive body language, giving feedback and so on.) Rapport-building is the skill of making another person feel at ease with you, and willing to communicate with you. Non-verbal communication is, broadly, 'body language'.

20   C   **Rationale:** This could be insider dealing, if the person dealing was an insider and was using inside information.

21   A   **Rationale:** The wheel is fastest, because the leader acts as a communication hub and focuses the group.

Pitfalls: This may seem like very detailed learning, but communication patterns were the subject of a question in the Pilot Paper...

22   C   **Rationale:** This is what Lockett meant by the phrase. Option A is a simple distractor. Options B and D describe other barriers: 'Appraisal as chat' and 'Appraisal as confrontation'.

23   C   **Rationale:** A project is distinguished from routine work because of these characteristics. A contingency plan is a plan for what should be done if changes or problems occur. A schedule is a method of timetabling tasks and allocating them to people with appropriate time scales. A strategy is a long-term plan relating to the direction of the firm or business unit.

24   B   **Rationale:** Finance may be hard to come by because the financial health of the firm (ability to maintain and pay off loans) is understated. The other options are impacts of fraudulently *over-*stating results.

                Pitfalls: Ensure that you read the question carefully and address understated, not overstated, results.

                Ways in: This should have been clear if you worked through each of the options. Once you identified that some of the distractors were overstatement impacts, you would have a good idea what to look for.

25   C   **Rationale:** Goods of ostentation and Giffen goods have positive PED. Inferior goods have negative IED. Substitutes have positive XED.

26   B   **Rationale:** Forming is the tentative 'getting to know each other' stage; storming, the conflict that results as people begin to assert themselves; norming, the 'settling down' stage, as roles, behaviours and working methods are agreed; and performing, 'getting down to work'.

                Pitfalls: This can be confusing: make sure you get the terminology right, because it is solid territory for exam questions.

27   B   **Rationale:** The IASB has this as a key objective. The ASB issues Financial Reporting Standards in the UK. The EU is interested in harmonisation of standards, but does not have global jurisdiction. GAAP is a distractor: it refers to 'Generally Accepted Accounting Practice', a set of all the rules which govern accounting, gathered from the full range of applicable sources.

                Ways in: You should have been tipped off to the international element by the word 'global'. Combine that with 'accounting standards' and you could take an educated guess at the correct answer, if you had to.

28   D   **Rationale:** Job analysis involves finding out what are the task, skill and knowledge requirements of a job. This information is then output in the form of a job description (tasks, duties, objectives and standards of a job) and a person specification (reworking of the job description in terms of the kind of person needed to perform the job). A human resource plan (option (i)) is a much broader statement of the future skill requirements of the organisation as a whole, and how they will be met (by recruitment, training, retention and so on). A performance appraisal (option (iv)) analyses how a job holder *does* the job – not the nature of the job itself.

                Pitfalls: there is a whole cluster of related and unrelated terminology relating to the analysis and description of jobs, 'ideal' (prospective) job holders, and the performance of actual current job holders. You need to sort out in your mind which is which...

29   D   **Rationale:** Hygiene factors are extrinsic or environmental factors (salary and job security), while motivator factors are to do with the satisfactions of the work: challenging work is clear in this category – and recognition could be in either.

                Pitfalls: Examiners keep testing Herzberg because students keep confusing hygiene and motivator factors! Don't make this mistake!

                Ways in: You could have been confident about 'salary' as a hygiene factor, and confident about challenging work as *not* a hygiene factor – which narrows your options to two, while you decide about job security...

30   C   **Rationale:** Consistency was found to be more important to subordinates than any particular style.

31   C   **Rationale:** Demand would be raised because firms and households would have more money (after tax) for consumption or saving/investment. The increased expenditure would not be covered by revenue from taxation, so the change would be financed by a higher PSNCR (borrowing mount).

                Pitfalls: You have to be able to think through all the permutations of fiscal and monetary policies and their impacts on the economy and (where relevant) business decision-making.

32 D **Rationale:** Work sampling (via portfolios of work or trial periods, say) have the highest reliability (followed closely by cognitive selection tests). Personality testing and assessment centres (group selection exercises) are slightly less reliable. Interviews, ironically, have a very low predictive power – at about the same level as reference checking.

Pitfalls: It is worth getting the limitations of interviewing, in particular, firmly in your mind.

33 B **Rationale:** Failure to challenge or criticise is *not* a positive thing, in this context, but a symptom of poor communications: the 'building block' would be developing a climate in which people can speak their minds, constructively. The other options describe positive building blocks in the areas of membership, review and control and objectives. (The terminology of 'building blocks' and 'blockages' is drawn from a model by Woodcock, but it is not essential to know this.)

34 B **Rationale:** Experiential learning is 'learning by doing', usually involving self-managed learning by reflection, planning and adjustment. Action learning is classed as on-the-job learning, because it involves real work problems and groups. Option D is just a distractor.

35 A Ethical relativism

36 C **Rationale:** Job advertisements must be positive, but they should also be honest, in order to manage applicants' (and future employees') expectations. Options B and D should be obvious. You may have hesitated over option A, but advertisements should encourage unsuitable applicants to rule themselves out before applying (and wasting the organisation's time).

37 C **Rationale:** Equal opportunity is a narrower concept, based on securing non-discrimination on the basis of those 'crude' dimensions of individual difference (sex, age, disability and so on). Person culture is a distractor drawn from a common model of organisation culture types, and diversification from an organisational strategy involving widening its range of products/markets.

Pitfalls: If you are in a hurry, you may see the words 'non-discrimination legislation' and jump to 'equal opportunities'. Remember to read question stems carefully.

38 C **Rationale:** Paying suppliers' invoices would be a function of the accounts department, once the purchasing department has authorised the invoices for payment. You may have hesitated over option D, but evaluating potential suppliers is a key element in supplier appraisal and selection, not a finance matter. (However, in some companies the finance department would do the supplier appraisal because of their technical skills or knowledge but this is not the norm.)

39 B **Rationale:** Learning styles is Honey & Mumford. Kolb devised the experiential learning cycle (Act, Analyse, Abstract, Plan). Tuckman, in a completely unrelated area, developed a group development model (Forming, Storming, Norming, Performing). Ashridge developed the 'Tells, Sells, Consults, Joins' leadership style model.

Pitfalls: The syllabus mentions specific writers, so you should be able to attribute well-known theories and models to their authors correctly.

Ways in: The more of the options you could recognise and attach to their respective models, the closer you are to the right answer!

40 C **Rationale:** Because chips are a complementary product to fish, a rise in the price of fish will lead to a fall in the demand for chips.

41 C **Rationale:** Sexual harassment is unwanted conduct of a sexual nature, and it includes the examples given (as well as more overt sexual conduct such as inappropriate body contact). This may also sound like victimisation, but victimisation is a separate form of discrimination, involving penalising someone because they are involved in a claim of discrimination against an employer.

42 C **Rationale:** Options A, B and D relate to the 'control environment' which embraces the overall organisational and cultural context of control. Options A, B and D were highlighted as aspects of a strong control environment in the Turnbull report.

43   A   **Rationale:** A gap between current 'competence' and required 'competence' may be amenable to learning or training. A gap between current 'performance' and required 'performance', however, may be caused by other problems to do with supervision, systems, resources, motivation and other factors. The other options are true.

Pitfalls: There is no reason why you should not face a 'broad brush' question like this, rather than a detailed topic. You need to be mentally flexible in such a case: highlight the topic keywords of each option, to focus on the right area for each.

Ways in: You should have found options B and D easy to tick off – which narrows your choices – and if you think through option C, it should make good sense.

44   B   **Rationale:** A transactions audit aims to detect fraud and uses only substantive tests. Operational, efficiency, management or value-for-money audits basically monitor management's performance throughout all the activities of the organisation.

45   C   **Rationale:** Lateral (or horizontal) communication flows between people of the same rank, in the same section or department or in different sections or departments.

Ways in: Hopefully you would have been able to disregard option A as 'downward' suggests communication from superior to subordinate. Similarly option D.

46   D   **Rationale:** Some of the procedures and techniques used are very similar – but the differences in relationship and scope are significant. Internal auditors are employees or contractors of the company: external auditors are members of independent accounting firms. Internal auditors report to the board of directors or others charged with governance (eg an audit committee): external auditors report to the shareholders. Internal auditors appraise operations: external auditors appraise financial records and statements in order to consider whether the accounts give a true and fair view of the organisation's position.

47   D   **Rationale:** Macro-economics looks at a complete national economy or economic system: factors such as economic activity and growth, inflation, unemployment and the balance of payments. The other options are pure distractors, drawn from other disciplines.

48   C   **Rationale:** This is a graphic scale because it is shown in diagrammatic form. It is related to a rating scale (or grading) system, which might assign the value A to excellent, C to average and E to poor, for example. Overall and guided assessment use narrative comments on the appraisee.

49   D   **Rationale:** This may seem like a basic point, but it has been inadequately recognised over the years – hence the poor reputation of performance appraisal in most organisations. The primary purpose is problem-solving and improvement and development planning. Option A suggests a one-way view of appraisal: modern approaches stress collaborative dialogue. Option B and C are problematic, because employees should not be led to expect an inevitable link between performance and bonuses or promotions.

50   C   **Rationale:** Although the examples may be good guides for conduct in many instances, circumstances will vary, so they should not be seen as totally prescriptive.

ACCA examiner's answers

1   A   Substantive tests are tests for accuracy and they are used to establish facts. The other tests are less specific and arguably more subjective.

2   C   Only the Task and Authoritarian styles have the value of the task rated at 9 on the Blake and Mouton grid, so these are the most task efficient styles.

3   B   Negotiation gives the best opportunity for the two sides in a conflict to converge their positions. The other options either involve backing down, forcing a position, potentially increasing conflict, or leaving the issue unresolved.

4   B   Mentors usually help staff on broader work related development, including orientation and induction. Coaches work on developing specific skills of the job itself, while counsellors work with people on a personal level, perhaps if they are having non-work related or emotional problems.

5   B   Companies need to keep satisfied only those stakeholders who have high power, but little interest. The others can either be largely ignored, merely kept informed or treated as key players.

6   A   Because of the particular circumstances of the scenario where someone is made redundant from an industry in decline where skills cannot be easily transferred, where re-training might take a long time or where work is not available in the short term within a reasonable geographic proximity, this is classed as structural unemployment.

7   B   The basic principle that underlies marketing is that it is a management process that identifies and anticipates customer needs. The other distracters in the question refer to specific activities undertaken by a sales or promotion function.

8   C   The normal sanctions in such a case is that fines are imposed on companies by the registration body of the company and, where listed, the company may be delisted by the stock exchange authorities. Although the option wasn't included, sanctions against responsible directors may also be imposed.

9   D   The ageing population trend is caused by a decreasing birth rate and a decreasing mortality rate.

10 B   The 'tell and listen' approach encourages input from the individual, promoting participation in the process by the appraisee.

11 B   The external auditor has to ensure that the financial statements of the organisation truly reflect the activities of the business in the relevant accounting period. This assessment should be independent and therefore free from subjectivity on the part of the management of the client organisation.

12 A   The team leader has allowed the team to develop as they were performing well initially, but because of the later failures, has clearly failed to manage the team effectively overall.

13 A   An employee with a range of tasks or objectives to achieve and pressures to achieve them to set deadlines, should always prioritise tasks in accordance to business importance. Deciding on other criteria such as pressure applied by colleagues, whether someone is absent or not or simply because a task is urgent may damage wider business objectives.

14 D   A professional accountant acting in accordance with fundamental ethical principles is demonstrating objectivity when they give a complete and precise view, which by implication means that negative aspects should not be concealed or positive aspects accentuated.

15 C   IFAC has no legal powers against businesses, nor does it set financial reporting standards. It is an accounting association member body which promotes educational and ethical standards of behaviour amongst its member bodies, through a code of ethics and behaviour, but does not prescribe detailed rules on this.

16 C   Increasing taxation leaves individuals with less disposable income for expenditure within the economy thereby slowing economic activity. The same effect is caused by a reduction in government expenditure. Therefore economic activity can be stimulated by reducing taxation and increasing government expenditure.

17 C   Information on purchase costs of finished goods or raw materials is important in establishing the price of a product. In terms of the marketing mix, this information is most relevant to the price element as prices should be set at least to cover cost and give an acceptable level of profit.

18	D	Informal networks neither directly support nor undermine formal authority or management objectives, but they do emerge spontaneously and are often influenced by the patterns of unofficial power and influence within organisations.
19	D	The key correctly matches the information required to the particular financial statement in which they are to be found.
20	A	The pluralist solution is to cater for the needs of more than one stakeholder group without seriously compromising the interests of any individual group. Therefore setting aside a special area for families with children while having an adults only section would achieve this. The other options involve adversely affecting the rights of one or other group of stakeholders in some way.
21	D	Outsourcing functions like IT simplifies the structure of an organisation and reduces ongoing operational costs, but because support is external to the organisation, there may be a greater lead time required for resolving IT issues. Because there is less direct control over subcontractor's employees, long term projects, in particular, may be prone to disruption.
22	B	Providing a summary of sales and purchases is normally a function of a management information system. A transaction processing or office automation system would mainly concern the *recording* of transactional data, and a decision-support system would *analyse* information.
23	B	is correct because customers and suppliers deal closely on a transactional basis with the organisation, but are not internal stakeholders like managers and executive directors.
24	D	At the operational level, systems connected to individual and batches of input and output processes are known as transactional. Management information, knowledge management and decision support systems are more relevant to the tactical and strategic levels.
25	A	Role playing exercises are most effectively used for skills development, including sales training. Other common business applications include effective selection interviewing and performance appraisal interviewing.
26	B	The Blake and Mouton managerial grid enables leadership styles to be categorised on a nine point scale with reference to concern for production and concern for people. Renata is therefore highly concerned with the task and much less interested in her team as individuals.
27	C	The marketing tactic of making key accessories unique to a particular product discourages competitors from offering substitute products because the costs of so doing will be greater and entry into the market made more difficult. It does not alter the balance of power of suppliers or customers nor affect the intensity of competitive rivalry.
28	D	The main barriers to entry for a sauce manufacturer are ensuring access to a sufficient range and quantity of distribution outlets and producing enough units to benefit from economies of scale that other mass manufacturers of more generic substitute products would achieve. There is no evidence that supplier concentration or industry growth rate in such a market would be considered as significant barriers.
29	B	Poor lateral communication leads to lack of coordination. The other common business problems are connected with upward or downward channels of communication or lines of authority.
30	B	Only shareholders have voting power related to the number of shares that they own. Members of a co-operative organisation can vote but will only have one vote. Co-operatives may be owned by members, but ownership stakes cannot be exchanged between members unless the members belong to limited companies.
31	B	To discriminate against someone on the grounds of characteristics which are predominately associated with their sex, gender, nationality or religion is illegal. As women are generally shorter than men, to restrict admission on the basis of height, indirectly discriminates against women. The other options are either direct discrimination, or other illegal and undesirable employment practices.
32	B	According to Herzberg, money is a hygiene factor (or dissatisfier). Although it is a powerful short-term motivator, it is questionable whether each individual increase in monetary reward will have a major long-term effect. According to Herzberg, 'A reward once given becomes a right'.

33	B	The task culture is appropriate where organisations can accommodate the flexibility required to adjust management and team structures to address the tasks that must be fulfilled. This is very common in large consultancy firms.
34	D	The wheel facilitates transmission of the message directly to all receivers and therefore transmits most quickly.
35	D	All the options describe measures that will limit environmental impact or potentially reduce the carbon footprint.
36	B	Equal opportunity policies widen opportunity and enlarge the potential pool of employees to recruit from. The other options either indirectly or directly reduce the potential for staff turnover and therefore limit the number of job vacancies available at any point in time.
37	D	The primary aim of a public oversight board is to eliminate or minimise any actual or potential breaches of legislative requirements and to ensure compliance with regulations applicable to organisations within their terms of reference.
38	C	The scenario accurately describes the resource-investigator.
39	C	The components of effective demand in the economy are consumer spending, investment by enterprises, central and local government expenditure and the net gains from international trade.
40	D	Reviewing suppliers' signatures on delivery notes would be a goods inwards control relating to verifying the authenticity and origin of supplies. The other controls are either more general such as quality or to do with other specific functions such as despatch to customers and credit control.
41	D	Only statements 3 and 4 are true.
42	A	Compliance with legal requirements may not eliminate unethical behaviour. The issues of concern to those who complain may not be fully representative of issues of concern to customers in general. Other companies in the sector may not be concerned about ethical behaviour.
43	B	Ilya as a union representative is experiencing role conflict. This is because he has a responsibility to ensure the efficient management of salary costs as head of studies, but as representative of the union would support better pay and conditions for the union members in his department which he represents.
44	B	As new members are about to join the group, essentially the group is reforming which is the start of a new group development process. The other options are all later stages in group development as identified by Tuckman.
45	A	Teeming and lading involves the theft of cash and is a type of fraud that is carried out by manipulating transactions. There would be most potential for this fraud within the sales department where cash may be received and remitted.
46	B	Before fraud can be prevented it is first necessary to identify areas where fraud is likely to occur before preventative measures can be taken.
47	A	Committees are appointed to make democratic, well considered and workable decisions, using the broader expertise of a representative group of people. However, decisions arrived at by committee can take longer to arrive at.
48	C	All the actions help to protect the public interest except the first one, which may serve to prejudice further investigations or prevent effective prosecution and may dissuade other whistleblowers from acting in the public interest themselves in future cases.
49	A	Tax avoidance is a way of managing tax affairs to mitigate tax liability legally. Tax evasion is illegal.
50	C	Vroom's formula is calculated through multiplying valence with expectancy. This means a person will be motivated if the reward is both sufficiently attractive and attainable.

REVIEW FORM

Name: _____   Address: _____

_____

Date:_____   _____

How have you used this Practice & Revision Kit?
(Tick one box only)

☐ Distance learning (book only)

☐ On a course: college _____

☐ As a tutor

☐ With 'correspondence' package

☐ Other _____

Why did you decide to purchase this Practice & Revision Kit? *(Tick one box only)*

☐ Have used complementary Interactive Text

☐ Have used BPP Texts in the past

☐ Recommendation by friend/colleague

☐ Recommendation by a lecturer at college

☐ Saw advertising

☐ Other _____

During the past six months do you recall seeing/receiving any of the following?
(Tick as many boxes as are relevant)

☐ Our advertisement in *ACCA Student Accountant*

☐ Our advertisement in *Teach Accounting*

☐ Other advertisement _____

☐ Our brochure with a letter through the post

☐ ACCA E-Gain email

☐ BPP email

☐ Our website www.bpp.com

Which (if any) aspects of our advertising do you find useful?
(Tick as many boxes as are relevant)

☐ Prices and publication dates of new editions

☐ Information on Practice & Revision Kit content

☐ Facility to order books off-the-page

☐ None of the above

Have you used the companion Interactive Text for this subject?   ☐ Yes   ☐ No

Your ratings, comments and suggestions would be appreciated on the following areas

	Very useful	Useful	Not useful
Introductory section (How to use this Practice & Revision Kit)	☐	☐	☐
'Do You Know' checklists	☐	☐	☐
'Did You Know' checklists	☐	☐	☐
Possible pitfalls	☐	☐	☐
Questions	☐	☐	☐
Answers	☐	☐	☐
Mock exams	☐	☐	☐
Structure & presentation	☐	☐	☐
Icons	☐	☐	☐

	Excellent	Good	Adequate	Poor
Overall opinion of this Kit	☐	☐	☐	☐

Do you intend to continue using BPP Interactive Texts/Kits?   ☐ Yes   ☐ No

Please note any further comments and suggestions/errors on the reverse of this page.

Please return to: Ian Blackmore, BPP Learning Media Ltd, FREEPOST, London, W12 8BR

REVIEW FORM (continued)

Please note any further comments and suggestions/errors below